Some Men

Recent Titles in
OXFORD STUDIES IN CULTURE AND POLITICS
Clifford Bob and James M. Jasper, General Editors

Fire in the Heart
How White Activists Embrace Racial Justice
Mark R. Warren

Nonviolent Revolutions
Civil Resistance in the Late 20th Century
Sharon Erickson Nepstad

Democracy in the Making
How Activist Groups Form
Kathleen M. Blee

Ethnic Boundary Making
Institutions, Power, Networks
Andreas Wimmer

Women in War
The Micro-processes of Mobilization in El Salvador
Jocelyn Viterna

SOME MEN

Feminist Allies and the Movement to End Violence Against Women

Michael A. Messner, Max A. Greenberg, *and* Tal Peretz

OXFORD
UNIVERSITY PRESS

OXFORD
UNIVERSITY PRESS

Oxford University Press is a department of the University of
Oxford. It furthers the University's objective of excellence in research,
scholarship, and education by publishing worldwide.

Oxford   New York
Auckland   Cape Town   Dar es Salaam   Hong Kong   Karachi
Kuala Lumpur   Madrid   Melbourne   Mexico City   Nairobi
New Delhi   Shanghai   Taipei   Toronto

With offices in
Argentina   Austria   Brazil   Chile   Czech Republic   France   Greece
Guatemala   Hungary   Italy   Japan   Poland   Portugal   Singapore
South Korea   Switzerland   Thailand   Turkey   Ukraine   Vietnam

Oxford is a registered trademark of Oxford University Press
in the UK and certain other countries.

Published in the United States of America by
Oxford University Press
198 Madison Avenue, New York, NY 10016

Library of Congress Cataloging-in-Publication Data
Messner, Michael A.
Some men : feminist allies and the movement to end violence against women / Michael A.
Messner, Max A. Greenberg, and Tal Peretz.
    pages cm. — (Oxford studies in culture and politics)
Includes bibliographical references and index.
ISBN 978-0-19-933876-4 (hardcover: alk. paper) — ISBN 978-0-19-933877-1
(pbk.: alk. paper)   1. Women—Violence against—Prevention.   2. Men—Political
activity.   3. Feminism.   I. Greenberg, Max A.   II. Peretz, Tal.   III. Title.
HV6250.4.W65M4785 2015
362.88082—dc23
2014022452

9 8 7 6 5 4 3 2 1
Printed in the United States of America
on acid-free paper

To the memory of
Chris Norton (1950–2012)
and
Allan Creighton (1946–2013)
Pioneering antiviolence activists and lifelong advocates for social justice

CONTENTS

List of Illustrations   ix
Preface: Men Upstream   xi
Acknowledgments   xiii

1. "This is men's work"   1

2. Diving In: The Movement Cohort, 1970s to 1980s   26

3. Digging In: The Bridge Cohort, Mid-1980s to 1990s   62

4. Plugging In: The Professional Cohort, Mid-1990s to the Present   95

5. Earning Your Ally Badge: Men, Feminism, and Accountability   135

6. Conclusion: Men, Feminism, and Social Justice   170

Appendix 1: List of Interviewees with Demographic Descriptors   191
Appendix 2: The Authors' Moments of Engagement   201
Notes   211
References   235
Index   247

LIST OF ILLUSTRATIONS

FIGURES

1.1   Feminist engagements with violence against women   *12*

1.2   Birth years of interviewees   *20*

2.1   *Brother*, a male liberation newspaper, summer 1971   *35*

2.2   California Anti-Sexist Men's Political Caucus at a political march, circa 1980   *40*

2.3   Don Conway-Long, Craig Norberg-Bohm, Mick Addison-Lamb, and Mark Benson-Robinson, core members of Rape And Violence Ends Now (RAVEN), St. Louis, Missouri, circa 1980   *57*

3.1   *Changing Men* magazine, "Men Confront Pornography" cover, fall 1985   *74*

4.1   "MY STRENGTH IS NOT FOR HURTING" poster   *124*

4.2   "MY STRENGTH IS NOT FOR HURTING" poster   *125*

4.3   Men at Walk a Mile in Her Shoes, 2013   *129*

4.4   Man at a Slutwalk, 2012   *130*

6.1   "MY STRENGTH IS FOR DEFENDING" poster   *171*

6.2   "MY STRENGTH IS FOR DEFENDING" poster   *172*

TABLE

6.1   Paradigmatic shifts in views on gender and violence   *178*

PREFACE: MEN UPSTREAM

Women cluster at the edge of a river, washing clothes. Suddenly, one of them spots a basket floating down the river toward them. She wades in to see what it is, discovers to her horror a crying baby in the basket, and pulls it to shore. A few minutes later, another basket floats toward them and a second woman wades out to rescue the baby. When a third basket appears, one of the women proceeds to hike upstream. "Wait," one of the group exhorts, "you must stay here to help us rescue the babies." "You rescue the babies," the hiking woman replies, "I'm heading upstream to find out who's putting the babies in the water, and I'm going to stop them."

We don't know the origins of this story—it has the feel of an Old Testament parable—but we have heard several versions of it in recent years, especially as a metaphoric fable that captures the approach and goals of activists who work to prevent gender-based violence. This "upstream-downstream" story has recently become a central metaphor in various health prevention campaigns, especially among those who work to prevent gender-based violence. For instance, since 2005, the Virginia Department of Health Division of Injury and Violence Prevention has published *Moving Upstream: Newsletter for the Primary Prevention of Sexual and Intimate Partner Violence*. More recently, the California Coalition Against Sexual Assault (CALCASA) in 2012 also deployed this metaphor in its continued efforts to build its "PreventConnect" national network of gender-based violence prevention workers, dubbing the current effort "Moving Upstream 2.0."[1]

The violence prevention community's adaptation of the upstream-downstream fable often reflects a gendered division of labor: for several decades, it has been almost exclusively women who have labored downstream, carrying out vital and exhausting "rescue work" with a depressingly steady stream of survivors of rape, domestic violence, stalking, and sexual harassment. In the 1970s, when a small number of men became appalled by men's violence against women and asked how they might support the women's rescue efforts, they were given a reply similar to that delivered to white liberals during the Civil Rights Movement: we don't need your help here; if you want to make a contribution, head upstream, talk with boys and men, teach them to stop raping and hitting women.

This is a book about men who took seriously this charge to become active feminist allies. Some men: a small number of pioneers starting in the late 1970s, followed by growing numbers today—men who marched upstream to work with boys and men to prevent sexual assault, domestic violence, and other forms of gender-based violence. It is also a book about social movements and social change. The men who first tackled antirape and anti–domestic violence work in the late 1970s and early 1980s did so in the midst of a welter of feminist movement activism and with hopes that their work would contribute to a wide range of rapid and radical social change. The men who do such work today are equally passionate about stopping gender-based violence, but they labor within a social context that is very different from that of their predecessors.

Today's activists are volunteer service workers, paid employees, or even independent contractors—not grassroots movement activists. They fan out of campus-based offices, community nonprofits and publicly funded organizations into schools, workplaces, sports teams, and the U.S. military, educating boys and men, deploying professionally developed antiviolence curricula. In this book, we ask what is lost and what is gained when efforts previously seen as attempts to radically change the structure of society are now viewed more pragmatically, as organizational strategies to change specific attitudes and behaviors that underlie, for instance, campus-based sexual assault or family violence among military veterans. Are some rapes prevented? Is domestic violence stopped, or at least mitigated? Do those who continue to do the hard and often thankless downstream work—still today, mostly women—feel that the men working upstream are truly their allies, helping them transform the world in ways that might one day render such downstream rescue work no longer necessary? And to what extent is the gendered partnership of upstream and downstream work helping to move us toward a world that more closely resembles a feminist vision of equality, justice, and peace?

ACKNOWLEDGMENTS

The research for this book was initially launched with a grant from the University of Southern California's Advancing Scholarship in Humanities and Social Sciences program. The study was also supported in its early stages with funds from the USC Dornsife Center for Feminist Research's New Directions in Feminist Research seminar. We thank Raquel Gutierrez, Jeanne Weiss, and Rebecca Zobeck for the administrative support services they provided for the CFR seminar. Dean Dani Byrd, Sociology Department Chair Rhacel Parrenas, and Gender Studies Chair Alice Echols facilitated the final stage of writing by supporting a flexible teaching load for coauthor Michael Messner. We appreciate the many supportive conversations we had during the course of this work with faculty and graduate student colleagues at USC.

A number of individuals helped us along the way as research informants or assisted us in locating interviewees or securing permissions, including Kristen Barber, Martin Button, Rick Cote, Bob Dunn, David Lee, Kaya Masler, Craig Norberg-Bohm, Rob Okun, Monica Ramsey, Rich Snowdon, Jeff Spoden, John Stoltenberg, and Christine Williams. Others generously helped us to broaden our ideas and build our scholarly bibliography for this study, notably Bob Blauner, Jess Butler, Raewyn Connell, Shari Dworkin, Bob Feinglass, Allan Johnson, Michael Kimmel, Paul Lichterman, Patricia Yancey Martin, Jo Reger, and Verta Taylor. Elizabeth Cooper, Heather Derby, Michela Musto, and Kyra Norsigian ably transcribed the life history interviews.

We are grateful to colleagues who read and commented on chapter drafts, helping us sharpen the writing and the organization of the book. Among those generous readers are Kristen Barber, Nathaniel Burke, Alice Echols, Pierrette Hondagneu-Sotelo, April Hovav, Chelsea Johnson, Jim Messerschmidt, Caitlin Myers, and the anonymous readers at Oxford

University Press. James Cook, our editor, and James Jasper, the series editor, at OUP have been supportive from day one.

We appreciate the love and support of our families and loved ones during the several years of research and writing that went into this project. Mike is grateful for the ongoing support from his ever-hyphenated family, Pierrette Hondagneu-Sotelo, Miles Hondagneu-Messner, Sasha Hondagneu-Messner, Melinda Messner-Rios, and Anita Messner-Voth. Max is thankful for the bottomless support of Kyra Zola Norsigian. He is also indebted to his friends at Peace Over Violence, who showed him the everyday challenges and triumphs of antiviolence work. Tal thanks Becky, Israel, Shani, and Roni Peretz, and the late Dr. Aronette White, who first asked him to interview feminist-identified men.

This book would not have been possible without the brave pioneering work, determined effort, and creative activism of the feminist antiviolence movement of the past near half-century. It is to this movement that we feel most accountable, and to whom we hope this book makes a useful contribution. More specifically, we want to express our deep gratitude to the sixty-four antiviolence activists who generously gave their time to share their thoughts with us. We learned a great deal from these individuals and were both humbled and inspired by the depth of their commitment to progressive social change. We dedicate the book to the memory of two of those we interviewed, Allan Creighton and Chris Norton, both of whom died before this book was published. Allan and Chris helped to pioneer feminist antiviolence work in the late 1970s, and they continued through their lives to work for peace and social justice. Their voices appear prominently in this book, and we trust that their wisdom, feminist commitment, and political savvy will continue to inspire readers, as they have inspired us.

Some Men

CHAPTER 1

"This is men's work"

Allan Creighton sits at his desk in his UC Berkeley office, his back to the second-floor window through which are visible some of the university's athletics facilities. His office is stuffed with books, piles of papers, and posters about multiculturalism, stopping violence, and ending Islamophobia. Creighton exudes a gentle demeanor; his lined face, thinning hair, and slender, bending frame betray his sixty-six years, but neither age nor four decades of violence prevention work have dampened his passion. Instead, he radiates a steady optimism and a determined love for his job as the social justice and violence prevention health educator at the university.

Creighton has just returned from leading a workshop with resident advisors in the campus dorms, "training the new RAs on dealing with residents who might have had to deal with sexual violence or stalking or dating violence." Creighton is heartened with these young people's smarts and sensitivities. But he is not satisfied; his work is far from done. He knows that acquaintance rape, battery, stalking, and other forms of interpersonal violence are still rampant on most college campuses. A national study by the Department of Justice revealed that on a college campus of 10,000 students, roughly 350 women annually are victims of attempted or completed rape, and the vast majority of rapes are perpetrated by acquaintances, not strangers.[1] Creighton knows, too, that victims of sexual assault routinely suffer chronic physical and emotional problems and are thirteen times more likely to attempt suicide than those who are not victims of this crime.[2] And he knows that transforming his campus and the surrounding community into a rape-free environment will entail men's stepping up and taking responsibility for making this change.

Allan Creighton is in this for the long haul. Inspired by feminism in the 1970s, he poured many years of unpaid labor into grassroots social movement organizations—including as a founding member of the 1978–1981 activist group Men Against Sexist Violence (MASV), the first men's pro-feminist, antiviolence group in the San Francisco Bay Area. In the 1980s and 1990s, he volunteered for a battered-women's shelter in Oakland and pieced together low-paying work with the Oakland Men's Project, a multiracial community effort to work with boys and men around violence prevention, and Men Overcoming Violence (MOVE), a men's antibattering program that was part of a rapidly developing national network. In those years, he says,

> the women's rape crisis centers and domestic violence shelters . . . were getting a lot of pressure to do stuff about men, [but] to do stuff about men, you have to turn all the resources that are really only available for women in crisis. You have to change everything to try to hire men and do men's programming, so there [was] a very strong push and pull, and we were trying—those of us at OMP and MOVE were trying to take the position, "This is men's work. Men need to do this; don't be putting it up to the shelters and their funding."

Creighton's determination that his men's groups not compete with women's crisis centers and shelters for money meant that their own work continued to be funded by small donations and eventually from an unsteady trickle of money from foundation grants. Following several decades of tenuous employment with grassroots groups and community nonprofits—earning in his early years ten dollars, sometimes fifty dollars a week—Creighton appreciates having finally landed in 2003, in his mid-fifties, a regular professional job at the university. "I'd worked on the outside of systems so long, [I wondered] what would it be like to work on the inside of a system? But I think behind that was also getting older; I need to work and have some position that is gonna be able to fund me until old age."

Allan Creighton's story is a chronicle of a full life of commitment to social change. His work against rape and domestic violence arcs across four decades, from grassroots activism, through building independent nonprofits, to finally taking a job with a university health center in a position that undoubtedly exists thanks to the successes of social movements in institutionalizing the progressive values of feminism and multiculturalism. In his lifetime, Creighton witnessed—and helped to usher in—a transformation of antiviolence work from unpaid grassroots political activism to institutionalized programs with built-in career paths for professionals, supported by steady (though modest) funding streams.

Jackson Katz is vibrating with energy. The work he does is similar to Allan Creighton's, but Katz's physical display of masculinity couldn't be more different from Creighton's quiet and gentle manner. The muscular former college football player has a youthful, amped-up demeanor, channeling his passionate sense of urgency that men must take responsibility to stop violence against women. He speaks to us in his home office—a modest structure stuffed floor to ceiling with books and papers, nestled behind his home in Long Beach, California. We are fortunate to connect for this interview, as Katz is a man continually on the move—zipping from this airport to that city and then on to the next, delivering keynote addresses and conducting antiviolence trainings.

For more than two decades, Jackson Katz has labored within the belly of the beast, engaging men in antiviolence work by the thousands, from college football teams to the U.S. Marine Corps. Katz understands that men's violence against women can take place in the home, on the street, or in the workplace, but antiviolence activists often point to high-status homosocial male organizations and groups—such as fraternities, organized sports, and the military—as particularly important (and difficult to penetrate) loci of male privilege, sexism, and violence. It is precisely these organizations that Katz seeks to transform. Indeed, following this interview, he will be jetting to Norfolk, Virginia, to conduct an antiviolence training with U.S. Navy personnel.

It's not just his personal style that's different from Allan Creighton's. Jackson Katz is fifteen years younger—fifty-one when we interviewed him—which means that when he first engaged with antiviolence work as a young man, the social context was very different. The Most Valuable Player of his high school football team—a self-described "traditionally masculine super jock kind of guy"—Katz went on in 1978 to play football at the University of Massachusetts. There he discovered that his discomfort with some of what he found in jock culture began to make sense when he "started taking courses with the word *gender* in the name . . . [snaps his fingers] it was instantaneous, like, 'Oh, my god, this is making so much sense!'" As a sophomore he became the first man at UMass to minor in women's studies. In 1980, he joined the campus health center's Men's Awareness Sexual Health program and started providing campus peer education to engage men in preventing violence against women. His experience and his public position as a jock gave him both confidence and public legitimation for doing this work:

> I started realizing, "Wow this is really a big problem," and I knew that as a man, I was in a position to do something about it. *And* as a man who had been

successful in sport, I was very empowered, if you will . . . [I was] completely unintimidated by the male sports culture and the jock culture, and while I'm Jewish—so I wasn't in the center of it and I felt the exclusion—in certain ways it empowered me, my success in that field empowered me. And I think that some of my big thinking and ambitious thinking, that's in some cases way more far-reaching than [with] the other men who do this work, comes probably from that experience.

Katz's work has been ambitious indeed. By 1988, he had helped start Real Men, an antiviolence men's organization in Boston that worked in a coalition with women's antiviolence organizations. In 1991–92, funded by the U.S. Department of Education, Katz created a pilot program to "train male college student athletes to use their status on campus within male peer cultures to speak out about rape, sexual assault, sexual harassment, domestic violence." This curriculum provided the foundation for the now-common "bystander" approach to antiviolence work.[3] And the idea of deploying athletes as campus leaders in the effort to stop violence against women was itself a counterintuitive innovation, as by then men's organized sports had been identified by researchers as a major site for the production—even celebration—of sexist attitudes and assaultive behaviors.[4] By the time Northeastern University hired Katz in 1993 to run the Mentors in Violence Prevention (MVP) program, he had already become a fixture on the national college lecture circuit.

In 1997, an assistant to the undersecretary of the Navy heard Katz speak and thought that the MVP model could work well in the Marine Corps' Family Advocacy Program, then being developed to prevent domestic violence. The military had good reason to want to develop programs to prevent gender-based violence. Several incidents of sexual violence blew up very publicly in the early 1990s, including the 1991 Tailhook scandal, in which more than a hundred Naval and Marine Corps officers sexually assaulted scores of women, as well as a few men; and the 1995 rape of an Okinawan schoolgirl by four U.S. military servicemen. Following these and other incidents, the military began paying closer attention to the issue of sexual assault and harassment within the military—most of it perpetrated by men against servicewomen—as well as the persistent problem with U.S. military personnel's sexual assaults of women in and surrounding overseas bases.[5]

Jackson Katz has now worked with the Marine Corps for fifteen years, and his violence prevention work has since spread to every branch of the U.S. military. With discernible pride, Katz says, "By the summer of 2012, all U.S. Air Force personnel are required to go through what they're calling 'bystander intervention training'—*all* personnel, that's four hundred thousand plus. And the main constituent part of bystander intervention training is MVP."

Today, Katz is widely known as a "rock star" in the national violence prevention community.[6] He defines his work as feminist, but, unlike Creighton, Katz's initial engagement with antiviolence work began when feminism was in decline as a grassroots movement and when organizations—schools, universities, workplaces, sports teams, and even the U.S. military—were beginning to see a need and had started to budget funds to engage men in discussions of how they can prevent rape and domestic violence. For several years, Katz has been an independent contractor—really, a successful antiviolence entrepreneur heading up MVP Strategies—who sees himself as an agent of social change. Jackson Katz is a man of action. His strategy focuses on engaging leaders to change institutions from the top down. In this regard, it helps that he's a man who carries the masculine habitus of the football player; he can talk with coaches, athletic directors, athletes, soldiers, even generals and admirals—men of power who respect him, relate to him, and listen to him.

Twenty-nine-year-old Gilbert Salazar speaks to us at a coffee shop in Salinas, California, walking distance from his office at the Monterey County Rape Crisis Center, where he has served for the past two years as the rape prevention education manager. He sips tea as he reflects on his work, what it means to him, and what brought him there. In a few hours, he will be back in action at a local high school, where he organizes "My Strength" violence prevention groups with young men barely a decade younger than him. Salazar is the lone man working in the Salinas branch of the county Rape Crisis Center. While his colleagues devote most of their time to serving women survivors of men's violence, Salazar's job is to work with boys to prevent future rapes, sexual harassment, and intimate-partner violence.

Salazar's pathway to gender-based violence prevention was not through the feminist movement, as was the case with Creighton; nor was it stimulated by feminist-inspired campus men's groups, as with Katz. Born and raised in a working-class Latino community in southern California, Salazar came to this work in a more roundabout manner. During college, he coupled his classroom education about social justice with community service-learning that focused on gang violence prevention with Latino boys. After college in 2008, he took a job facilitating the Youth Alternatives to Violence program with Sunrise House, a community nonprofit that focused on drug and gang rehabilitation, and the job was a neat fit for Salazar's hope to work with Latino boys. This sort of work made perfect sense in Salinas, an agricultural town of 153,000 people in central California that in recent decades had experienced a steady demographic shift toward a majority Latino/a and foreign-born population that is increasingly young and poor.[7] In the past decade, Salinas had gained national media attention for having one of the highest rates of gang-related violence in the nation— higher than Los Angeles, Oakland, or other urban areas often viewed as hotbeds of assault and murder.[8]

After working in drug and gang rehab for two years, in 2010 Gilbert Salazar saw that the Monterey County Rape Crisis Center was searching for someone to fill the position of rape prevention education manager. He applied and got the job. And although his previous focus had been more on preventing the boy-on-boy, man-on-man violence that was prevalent in the community, he began to learn about the gender dimensions of violence: "Sexual violence was not my initial focus. . . . I wanted to focus on boys with low socioeconomic status, boys of color . . . but I think sort of slowly, I saw: I went to a conference last year about the link between sexual violence and domestic violence . . . and that made the link more clear, especially when it comes to men in gangs."

Gilbert Salazar's career pathway reflects a broadening base to antiviolence work—a growing number of paid jobs in community nonprofits, supported by money from foundations and the federal government—that has enabled a new generation of young men to plug in to antiviolence jobs. And unlike the men of Creighton's pioneering generation, today's antiviolence activists include a growing number of men of color. These young men like Gilbert Salazar tend to bring a different set of concerns and priorities to the work; their life experience and values often bring into central focus race and class inequalities, boys' violence against other boys, and boys as victims of violence in families and on the street.

Salazar and other younger men of color bring a broader, more intersectional approach to working against gender-based violence. This has the advantage of moving beyond the white, professional-class assumptions that may have been implicit in earlier formations of antiviolence work, thus making the work more relevant to boys of color, poor and working-class boys, immigrant boys. However, this trajectory and approach may also reflect a generational shift away from direct engagements with feminism, thus potentially depoliticizing antiviolence work, shifting it toward a social services, rather than a social change, orientation. When asked if he felt that in doing sexual violence prevention he was part of a social movement, Salazar replied, "It is sort of a movement that I didn't quite give consent to be involved in. I love working with boys but I just think, how could someone be part of a movement if they haven't studied it? . . . It's a job, nine-to-five—I feel part of a movement when I'm with the boys, and we're talking."

Allan Creighton, Jackson Katz, and Gilbert Salazar are part of a growing network of men whose paid occupation is to engage boys and men to stop gender-based violence. Though their passions and goals are congruent, the groups they work with are very different: Creighton works with university students, Katz with men in the U.S. military and on college sports teams, Salazar with poor Latino boys in high school settings. And it's not only their work contexts and clients that differ. They represent three generations of men who engaged with feminism and with anti-violence work at different historical moments: Creighton, starting in the 1970s, during the mass eruptions of grassroots feminist activism; Katz in the late 1980s and 1990s, a time of feminist movement decline and the first bubblings of organized antiviolence work in campus centers and community nonprofits, when modest monetary support for violence prevention began to flow from the federal government; and Salazar in the current moment, when feminism as a grassroots movement is largely in abeyance but some feminist values have been institutionalized in schools, community organizations, and, to a certain extent, the state.

Today, a growing number of men are involved in antiviolence work, but their numbers pale in comparison with the tens of thousands of women who in recent decades have launched rape crisis centers, staffed hotlines and domestic violence shelters, run campus and community women's centers, and mobilized on the local and national levels to change laws, reform institutions, and challenge sexist beliefs and practices that fuel violence against women. There is no question that today's women activists and professional leaders who work against gender-based violence welcome men's involvement and see it as crucially important. Phyllis Frank is the assistant executive director of VCS Incorporated, a family service agency in Rockland County, New York. A four-decade veteran of feminist antidomestic violence and antirape activism, Frank was instrumental in launching some of the first women's shelters in the 1970s. Although "the shelter movement began as women only," Frank began to see the importance of men's involvement: "It's crucial. It's crucial [or] we're never going to change—we're never going to change the culture without participation from the dominant group." Janeen McGee, currently the executive director of RAVEN, in St. Louis, Missouri, one of the first men's organizations to work against domestic violence, agrees: "We like men being visible . . . and where we really need them is in community education, violence prevention." Patti Giggans, executive director of Los Angeles–based Peace Over Violence, put it simply: "I think it's very important. Men need to be allies . . . We need to make room for men." Shelley Serdahely has a similar view. Following a long history of working mostly with all-women antiviolence organizations, eight years ago she joined Men Stopping Violence in Decatur, Georgia, where she is now director of development. When asked if it is important for men to be working in this field, she responded enthusiastically:

> Oh, absolutely. Absolutely. Because the only way we're going to end violence against women, the only way it's going to end is when men decide that they're going to take responsibility and end it. And that's not going off on their own, but working with women in this movement, in partnership. And I believe that men will respond to other men, in a way that they will not respond to women. And that's been my history as a white person working in the civil rights movement, that it was like my job to reach out to white people—so I started Whites Against Racism, which wasn't hugely successful, but it was somewhat successful. That's our job, if we're part of an oppressor group; our job is to educate that group. So men have a responsibility to take that on, and I think they're the only ones who can really do it and be successful.

Nina Alcaraz, the deputy director of the Monterey County Rape Crisis Center, and the supervisor of Gilbert Salazar, echoes Serdahely's statement. When we asked her how best to influence poor boys of color, she said, "I think that it's incredibly important for men to be doing this. . . . When young men get to see adult males, their role models doing this work, I think that not only does the message kind of have a deeper resonance with them when they hear it from a male, but it also gives them a different perspective of what their future can be."

But women who have been working in the antiviolence field for years—some even for several decades—are also cautious in their optimism and enthusiasm, pointing to strains and tensions that inhere in men's violence prevention work. Janeen McGee echoes a concern we heard from several women, and even from a few of the men, that while women's work often goes unappreciated, the few men who enter the field get unearned praise just for showing up: "When a man has done something or has spoken up, there's a lot of credit given very easily . . . you don't have to do a whole lot; the bar's pretty low in terms of being able to impress folks." And it's not just disproportionate applause and praise that men receive. Because their presence is so rare and because the women hope that men's voices will be "heard" where women's voices might be ignored, men who enter the antiviolence field can quickly escalate into positions of leadership and prominence. "If you're a man," says Shelley Serdahely, "you don't have to earn your stripes as much." In fact, you may even earn substantially more money. Several women worried, for instance, about the rock-star earnings that prominent antiviolence men can command as speakers for campus or community events. Leiana Kinnicutt, senior program specialist with Futures Without Violence in Boston, Massachusetts, summarizes the importance of men's involvements in antiviolence work, as well as the tensions and dangers of men's receiving unearned privileges when they do get involved.

> Men need not only to be a part of this, as an essential ingredient, but their involvement should be welcomed and celebrated, . . . [but] it's kind of swung the other way: any man in the room, everyone like gets up and starts clapping for him and it's just ridiculous, so just 'cause you show up doesn't mean that we're going to throw you a party. So I think that there's some suspicion around, you know, true partnership with women, between women and men working on this issue, and whether men go off rogue on their own and claim this movement as theirs without remaining grounded, or connecting and taking direction from the women that they're trying to help.

This is a book that explores the importance and promise of men's engagements with violence prevention, feminism, and gender politics, with all of its passionate commitments to personal and social change, cross-cut with its fraught tensions and contradictions. And it is also a book that will make clear that gender-based violence prevention, like all progressive activism, is always fundamentally historical—that is, activism, including the work of allies from privileged groups (like whites doing antiracist work, heterosexually identified people joining "gay-straight alliances," and men supporting feminism), is always variously enabled and constrained by social and historical contexts.[9] Activists ride the waves and harness the tides that enable progressive actions in any historical moment, while also navigating institutional barriers and limits on this activism. Our examination of men's experiences in gender-based violence prevention, starting with the late 1970s and stretching through to the present, sheds light on male feminist allies as historical actors.

HISTORIC SHIFTS IN VIEWS OF VIOLENCE AGAINST WOMEN

Recent decades have seen fundamental shifts in how violence against women is viewed. The first shift came about in the late 1960s and 1970s, when the women's movement jolted the nation from its somnolent post–World War II reassertion of "natural" patriarchal privilege in workplaces, professions, families, and politics. The second shift began in the mid-1980s, as a radical grassroots feminist movement fragmented and declined, and liberal feminists simultaneously began to succeed in reforming institutions like the state, law, academia, and social work to prevent violence against women under a largely depoliticized public health approach. Each of these paradigmatic shifts differently inspired and enabled men's violence prevention work, while creating distinct challenges for those who engaged in the work.

In the pre-feminist 1950s and early 1960s, violence against women was barely even on the map as a social problem. Domestic violence and spousal rape were largely invisible, and when they were visible they were viewed largely as individual, private matters—or worse, as a joke. It was not uncommon to hear a male comedian of this era draw guffaws from his audience by throwing the punch line: "So I went home and beat the wife!" It was a running gag, for instance, when Jackie Gleason, on the popular 1950s television comedy *The Honeymooners*, would shake his fist at his wife, Alice, and issue an angry threat, "One of these days, Alice, POW! Right in the kisser! . . . Straight to the moon!"[10]

Stranger rape was sometimes seen as an issue before the 1970s, but it was mostly viewed through the lens of individual pathology, with the rapist imagined to be a crazed deviant who attacks a lone woman from the bushes on a dark night. Frequently, this collective fear of the lone rapist was projected onto black men. The "myth of the black rapist," as Angela Davis called it, stretched back to the post–Civil War reconstruction era, where it performed two functions: first, the myth justified lynching and other racist terror that impeded black males' ability to participate as full citizens in public life; second, casting lynching as a "defense of white womanhood" deflected critical scrutiny away from acts of domination and violence perpetrated by white males.[11]

For a century, the myth of the black rapist linked race and gender in a way that obscured and therefore supported the continuation of vast social inequalities. As late as the 1960s, it was widely assumed that good men, normal men, especially white middle-class men, would not rape a woman. And again, it was not unusual to hear people in this era talk about stranger rape with a humorous note: "I figure if you're getting raped, you may as well just lie back and enjoy it" was a common refrain, told with a wink and a chuckle.

The Rise of a Grassroots Feminist Movement

By the start of the 1970s, a reawakened feminist movement asserted a radical paradigm shift in views of sexual assault, domestic violence, sexual harassment, and related forms of public and domestic terror inflicted against women. Women in small consciousness-raising groups shared with each other their own stories of violence in families and relationships and started to understand that sexual and domestic violence, rather than being a shameful individual experience with an unusually deviant father, husband, or boss, was a shared experience, a pattern woven into unequal power relations between women and men.[12] Institutions like police, courts, and workplaces were, at best, slow to respond to these feminist claims. So feminists took matters into their own hands, pouring tremendous resources—initially through informally organized groups and networks with few or no financial resources—into working with survivors of sexual assault. Volunteer-staffed rape crisis hotlines and drop-in counseling centers, women's self-defense workshops, and shelters for women and children who had been the target of domestic violence emerged in scores of communities and on college campuses.[13] Rape was no longer a laughing matter—or, at least rape jokes were now increasingly contested.[14]

The feminist naming of violence against women as a social issue was nothing short of a radical paradigm shift. Susan Brownmiller's powerful 1975 book *Against Our Will: Men, Women and Rape* and other feminist texts on violence against women were widely read, reshaping public views on sexual assault.[15] Foundational to this emergent feminist paradigm was the assertion that men who rape or hit women are not isolated individuals, deviating from some normal form of masculinity. Rather, men's violence against women was now understood as *overconformity* with a culturally honored definition of masculinity that rewarded the successful use of violence to achieve domination over others. This paradigm shift implied that successfully ending violence against women would involve not simply removing a few bad apples from an otherwise fine basket of fruit. Rather, working to stop violence against women meant overturning the entire basket: challenging the institutional inequalities between women and men, raising boys differently, and transforming the normative definition of manhood in more peaceful and egalitarian directions. Stopping men's violence against women, in other words, was now seen as part of a larger effort at revolutionizing gender relations.

In Figure 1.1, we introduce a framework that conceptualizes feminist engagements with violence against women along two intersecting axes: first, a vertical axis of time, from "after violence" on the top to "before violence" on the bottom; and second, an actor axis between recipients (or survivors) of violence on the left and perpetrators of violence on the right, running perpendicular to the time axis.[16] These two axes delineate four realms of feminist engagement with violence against women.

	Recipient of Violence	Perpetrator of Violence
After Violence	*Realm A* *Responses to Survivors* • Shelters • Support groups	*Realm B* *Responses to Perpetrators* • Legal reform (law, police, courts) • Therapy
Before Violence	*Realm C* *Safety for Potential Targets* • Self-defense • Risk reduction	*Realm D* *Prevention with Potential Perpetrators* • Prevention with boys and men

Figure 1.1
Feminist engagements with violence against women.

Feminist activists built realms A, B, and C concurrently, starting in the late 1960s and 1970s.

In the 1970s, this multilevel feminist antiviolence challenge drew mostly derision from men. As a result, women contributed nearly all of the incipient antiviolence work. By the end of the decade, feminist women had created rape crisis centers, domestic violence hotlines and shelters, and women's self-defense classes[17] and had begun to challenge how police, the courts, workplaces, social work, and other institutions viewed and responded to sexual assault, sexual harassment, and domestic violence. Some feminist women strategized how to prevent future acts of violence, but the vast majority of their efforts were directed to working with women survivors of violence and advocating for change in how the police and courts responded to sexual and domestic violence (Fig. 1.1, realms A and B). These women's work was akin to that of military medics on a battlefield: exhausting all their energies to alleviate the damage done, while remaining mostly powerless to stop the continued carnage.

This 1970s era of feminist activism thus forced the "upstream question," which was also simultaneously "the man question" (realm D, Fig. 1.1): What role can and should men play in preventing future acts of violence against women? And indeed, nearing the end of the decade, a few men had begun to pay attention, asking how they might take responsibility, as men, to stop future violence against women.[18] Chapter 2 of this book chronicles the experiences of men in the late 1970s and early 1980s, the first wave of activist feminist allies inspired during what we call a historical moment of "movement feminism." These men, whom we call the Movement Cohort, formed small local organizations, often in dialogue with feminist women's domestic violence shelters and antirape organizations, and eventually started connecting with regional and national networks of other men who shared the goal of doing violence prevention work with boys and men.

Movement Abeyance and Feminist Institutionalization

The feminist paradigm shift of the 1970s occurred with the force and speed of a powerful earthquake, jarring the foundations of how people thought about violence against women. In the 1980s and into the 1990s, the radical power of feminism fractured under a broadside of antifeminist backlash[19] and fragmented internally from a bevy of corrosive disputes among feminists around issues of race and class inequalities, and especially from the "feminist sex wars"—divisive debates over sex work, sadomasochism, and especially pornography.[20]

Some key feminist political efforts such as the Equal Rights Amendment (ERA) had failed, and feminism was no longer as visible as a mass movement "in the streets"; in 1989 sociologist Verta Taylor described the moment not as a time when the feminist movement had disappeared so much as a time of "movement abeyance." Taylor argued that the popular view of historical feminist movement "waves"—first, second, third—falsely implied that between these "waves" feminism died out, only to await rebirth decades later. Instead, Taylor argued, during periods of movement abeyance (i.e., after the winning of women's suffrage in 1920, and again after the gains of the late 1960s through the early 1980s), activists in submerged networks continued to fight for equality, sustaining below-the-radar efforts that created the possibility for future political mobilizations.[21] Taylor is clearly correct that feminist activists of the 1980s and 1990s continued in submerged networks to agitate for social change, but this transitional period was also a time of successful and highly visible feminist institutional reform, including, as we will see in Chapter 3, the building of myriad community-based and campus-based rape crisis and domestic violence centers.

As feminists institutionalized local bases for antiviolence work, the state became an important site of contestation for scarce resources. Feminists in the United States have rarely been as successful in wresting concessions from the state as those in nations with stronger welfare state traditions. In the Nordic nations, much of Western Europe, and Australia,

feminists have had more direct input into forming social policies beneficial to women on, for instance, family leave policies and workplace equality. As early as 1989, sociologists Franzway, Court, and Connell analyzed
the challenges faced in Australia by what they called the "femocrats,"
elected feminist officials who pressed for feminist reform while trying to
remain true to their roots in the women's movement.[22] Especially at the
federal level of policy making, U.S. feminists of the 1980s and 1990s faced
few such contradictions, locked out as they were (with very few excep-
tions) from direct policy making in Congress, the Senate, and the White
House. However, one key piece of national legislation, the Violence Against
Women Act (VAWA), was passed in 1994, spearheaded by then-senator
Joe Biden with the support of feminist advocacy organizations. The VAWA
beefed up law enforcement around violence against women and initiated
a crucial flow of funding for community organizations that support survivors of gender-based violence. And, important for our purposes here,
a trickle of VAWA funds have helped to fund violence prevention efforts
through states, counties, schools, and community organizations, thus
helping to create and sustain opportunities for men to engage in paid violence prevention work with boys and young men.

We will show in Chapter 3 how male antiviolence activists straddled
a perilously thin line in navigating how to be accountable allies during
this transitional time of feminist movement abeyance and professional
institutionalization. By the mid-1980s, some of the pioneers of men's antiviolence activism had moved on to new kinds of work. Others, including
a younger group of activists whom we call the Bridge Cohort, began to
reshape antiviolence work in more pragmatic directions during this period
of transition, when movement feminism was in decline and mainstream
institutions were starting to respond to feminist claims that violence was
a social issue.

Professionally Institutionalized Feminism

The feminist movement fell short of its more revolutionary goals of radical social transformation, but it ultimately succeeded in ushering in substantial liberal reforms of institutions, including law, politics, academia,
workplaces, and families. These very successes set in motion a second
paradigm shift that proceeded more gradually and with less fanfare than
the first. This shift resulted in the current historical moment that we call
"professionally institutionalized feminism," characterized by the rise of
the public health model as a dominant paradigmatic frame for violence

prevention work. During this current historical moment, antiviolence work is done less by unpaid grassroots movement feminists and increasingly by community and campus organizations with institutionalized budgets (albeit still fairly minimal and vulnerable) and standardized violence prevention curricula. These organized antiviolence efforts are led by paid professionals who are frequently part of statewide and national professional networks and buttressed by the assistance of volunteers, often college students doing service work or graduate students doing unpaid internships that might feed in to careers in social work, academia, law, or community nongovernment organizations that focus on reducing gender-based violence.

The emergent paradigm of professionally institutionalized feminism recasts "violence against women" as "gender-based violence," opening space for thinking about the connections between violence against women and violence against gay, lesbian, queer, and transgender people; sexual assaults of boys and men; and gender-based bullying in schools. Even though this expansion of the antiviolence field is important, the language of this new paradigm risks decentering *women*, who are still the major victims of gender-based violence, and the major source of activist response to it. Now absorbed within a larger public health promotion agenda, the antiviolence paradigm also tends to re-individualize and largely depoliticize the understanding of the causes and thus the interventions to stop gender-based violence. In particular, today's commonly used antiviolence curriculum departs from the previous strategy of viewing core definitions of masculinity as causing violence against women. The current standard curriculum, we will show, strategically sidesteps the off-putting guilt of previous curricula—so often experienced as "anti-male"—by instead appealing to boys' and men's sense of masculine honor. In effect, today's antiviolence pedagogy *deploys* dominant forms of masculinity, rather than arguing for masculinity's eradication or radical transformation. Put another way, late 1970s and early 1980s antiviolence activists like antipornography activist John Stoltenberg argued that stopping violence against women must entail "refusing to be a man," but today's pedagogies, such as the national "My Strength" curriculum (designed by Stoltenberg), implore their charges to step up and *be a good man*.[23]

This current shift creates a broader field for action—including an impressive expansion of what we call "plug-in" opportunities for younger men to do violence prevention work as volunteers or service workers and even for a growing number of paid professional positions in violence prevention with boys and young men in schools, communities, workplaces, and the military and via social media. Chapter 4 of this book will examine the experience of a younger group of men we call the Professional Cohort, who conduct violence prevention work today within this context of professionally institutionalized feminism. We will argue that this new context has enabled a broader field of action for men's participation in antiviolence work but this work nevertheless has shallower political roots. Just as with their predecessors, men doing violence prevention today must navigate the challenges of what it means to be a man doing this work. And, we will show, in varying degrees they are aware of and develop creative strategies to circumvent the limits of the relatively depoliticized institutional context that shapes their work.

PRIVILEGED ALLIES

Men who engage in violence prevention work are making history but under conditions created largely by women. We describe these men as "allies" to foreground two aspects of their relationships and work with feminist women. First, however passionate these men's commitments and efforts, it is arguable that the idea of working with boys and men to stop gender-based violence would never have occurred to any of them if feminist women had not first put the issue on the map with their own courageous downstream activism. Second, from the first stirrings in the early 1970s, men's feminist activism has always existed in a state of tension and contradiction with men's access to male privilege.

Connecting these two points, we can see that feminist activism arose from women because it was women who had been systematically devalued, exploited, and often brutalized within an unequal system of gender relations. Put simply, it was clearly and directly in women's interests to see, and to act to change, patriarchal social arrangements. If we define male privilege—domination of public life, feeling no obligation to do housework or child care, assuming the right to sexual access to women's bodies—as a set of gendered interests shared by men, then it follows that it was not in men's interests to "see" women's subordination, much less to act to change it. During the past few decades, the men who began to see and challenge women's subordination have learned to view the world, at least in part, through women's points of view and have begun to empathize with women and to accept and value women's leadership in the politics of gender. For these men, this has entailed grappling with their own socialization as men, including their access to taken-for-granted, unearned privileges given to men simply because they were men.

The men of the 1970s were not the first feminist allies. Michael Kimmel and Thomas Mosmiller collected an exhaustive documentary history of men in the United States from the eighteenth through the mid-twentieth centuries who supported equal rights for women, suffrage, education, and the right to birth control. To be sure, these men were few in number and were often despised or ridiculed by other men, but their work as allies was crucial, for instance, in helping to build the first women's colleges and in women's eventually winning the vote in 1920.[24] In the 1970s, 1980s, and 1990s, men consciously entered the fray of gender politics, their actions dispersed along an array of positions, ranging from overtly antifeminist to profeminist.[25] Men who allied themselves with feminists in the 1970s and 1980s struggled at times to define themselves. They were often uncomfortable calling themselves "feminists," owing to the then-common understanding that feminist consciousness and identity emerged directly from women's experiences of subordination—experiences that men could not share or fully understand. And many feminist women were saying this directly to men, in effect fortifying a boundary around feminism as a women's identity category.[26]

Most male allies at that time settled on the term "profeminist," a label that emphasized both their political commitments and their positions as movement outsiders (or at times, with tongue in cheek, as a "men's auxiliary" to the women's movement). Today's men who are engaged in antiviolence work spend less time agonizing over labels—in fact, the younger of these men are often disinclined to label themselves at all—preferring instead to talk about the work they do, rather than engage in theoretical debates about men's relationship to feminism.[27] This, as we will show, is in part because of major shifts in feminism itself in recent years, including a younger generation's openness to seeing feminism not so much as a personal identity that places one inside a category but rather as a perspective or a moral position on gender equality, a perspective that can be taken by a person of any gender.

Research Questions About Allies

We find the term *ally* to be accurate in describing how most of the men in our research define their antiviolence work. We also find it useful in connecting our research questions on men, feminism, and violence prevention with writings by and about people from other privileged groups who have allied with those who press for social justice,[28] like white people working against racism,[29] heterosexually identified people opposing homophobia and heterosexism,[30] and U.S. citizens supporting the safety and rights of undocumented Mexican immigrants.[31]

Who are these men, and what were their pathways to becoming feminist allies?[32] Did childhood experiences like growing up seeing their mothers beaten up by their fathers or being themselves victims of sexual violence predispose them to their later opposition to violence? Were these men motivated by values of social justice and peace, grounded perhaps in religious or political commitments, or developed through previous participation in antiwar, civil rights, or other progressive movements? Did they perhaps identify and empathize with women, from their having experienced oppression, marginalization, or violence as gay men or as men of color?

What are the experiences and challenges that men activists have faced in doing violence prevention work? What does it mean to them to ally themselves with efforts that, at least at first glance, aim to undermine their own privileges as men? How does a person from a privileged group relate as an *accountable ally* to the people of color; to gay, lesbian, or queer people; and, in the case of our study, to the women who started and have such a personal stake in the movement?[33]

Sociologist James Jasper has shown that social movement groups routinely face a range of common dilemmas.[34] In this book, we will explore how various historical moments, including shifting moments of social movement formation, make possible, constrain, and create dilemmas for ally activism. What sorts of strategies do male allies create to navigate the strains and tensions of their publicly visible roles of working with boys and men to stop gender-based violence, and how do these strategies change in response to shifting historical conditions in feminism and in social institutions? How do women who work with these men view the men's commitments, contributions, and limits as allies? These are the questions we sought to address with our research.

LIFE HISTORIES OF ANTIVIOLENCE ACTIVISTS

We began the research for this book intending to conduct life history interviews with two generations of men: older men, most of them now in their late fifties and sixties, who were feminist-inspired pioneers of violence prevention starting in the late 1970s, and younger men who are doing violence prevention work today. As we began to conduct interviews, we realized that our initial idea of a two-generation comparison was flawed, for two reasons. First, our early interviews hinted at the importance of a gradual transition period, stretching roughly from the mid-1980s through the mid-1990s. During this period, with movement feminism in decline and professionally institutionalized feminism in the making, men's anti-violence work was also undergoing transformation. We needed to understand what was going on during this transitional time period.

A second reason we found our proposed two-generation comparison to be inadequate is because of the very limits of thinking of activists as belonging to distinct "generations." As Figure 1.2 shows, we conducted life history interviews with fifty-two men, ranging in age from twenty to seventy. Roughly, the older men engaged with feminist violence prevention work during the period of grassroots movement feminism, the middle-aged men during the transitional period, and the younger men during the present moment of professionally institutionalized feminism. But it's really not so simple as to conclude that, for instance, all of the older men shared the same experiences. We found, for example, that the older men in our study who became engaged with violence prevention work around 1990, during the transitional period, had very different experiences than did the same-aged men who began the work in the late 1970s. The key point of comparison, we realized, was not "generation" but rather men's historical "moments of engagement" with feminism and violence prevention work. "Moments of engagement," a concept adapted from the work of sociologist Raewyn Connell, helps us think about how life histories unfold contextually, through interaction with the social world. Seen this way, Connell explains, life histories become coherent not simply as individual stories but rather as individual and collective accounts of history making: "The project that is documented in a life-history story is itself the relation between the social conditions that determine practice and the future social world that practice brings into being. That is to say, life-history method always concerns the making of social life through time. It is literally history."[35]

Life history interviews, in short, can capture the dynamic relationship described in 1959 by sociologist C. Wright Mills between the individual and society, between biography and history.[36] Connell observes, however, that life-history research is unusually time-consuming, so it is difficult to yield large samples. Thus, she suggests collecting life histories from a sample of people strategically chosen for their ability to yield data that illuminate the dynamic processes of social change. We have done just that, particularly in our selecting an array of interviewees across a large age span. And in the interview itself, rather than attempting to capture the totality of one's full life history (probably impossible anyway, even if the goal is to write a complete biography), we targeted our questions to the interviewees' life trajectories as they engaged with particular themes: family gender

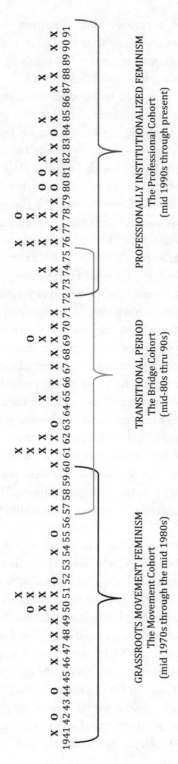

Figure 1.2
Birth years of interviewees.

relations, masculinities, feminist politics, antiviolence organizations, and gender-based violence. In this sense, our interviews are *theorized life histories,* more akin to a memoir—targeted as they are to particular themes of interest—than to a full-on biography.

Figure 1.2 shows graphically the age range of our individual interviewees and our groupings of individuals into three cohorts whose historical moments of engagement correspond with the three overlapping time frames that emerged as salient in the research. We emphasize the fuzzy (but not entirely arbitrary) overlap between our labeling of these three time periods and three cohorts. In fact, any such attempt at historical periodization inevitably runs up against the reality that although there may be key marker events we can read as road signs signaling major historical transitions, in real life most such shifts are gradual and messy transitions that can most clearly be read *as* transitions in retrospect.

A key theme that emerged from our interviews with men was their engagements—passionate, committed, sometimes confused, or even conflicted—with feminist women. Older men spoke of deep conflicts over how to be accountable allies with feminist women—and in the context of a fragmenting movement, with *which* feminist women. Younger men spoke of sometimes feeling that they were walking on thin ice in their work and of the critical scrutiny they were subjected to as perhaps the only man working in an organization made up otherwise entirely of women. Men of all ages also told us of instances of unearned credit and privileges they sometimes received, simply because they were "rare men," doing work that many more women have found was relatively thankless. It made sense to us, therefore, to supplement our research with targeted interviews with twelve women (depicted also on Fig. 1.2), spanning roughly the same age span, who work with men in antiviolence organizations. Women initiated the work against gender-based violence, and they continue to do the vast majority of it. So, although this is a book that focuses on men's experiences in gender-based violence prevention, we also consider how women activists view the importance, contribution, limits, and perils of men's work as allies.

We sought purposely to interview a wide age range of men and women, and we also sought a sample that reflects the sexual, geographic, and racial/ethnic diversity that exists in men's antiviolence work. Of the fifty-two men we interviewed, five identified as bisexual, six as gay, one as queer, two as "straight-bisexual," and the rest as heterosexual. It is our impression that of the first group of men to engage in profeminist ally work in the 1970s, a disproportionate number were gay or bisexual. It is a sad twist of history that we were unable to properly sample in our study the gay and bisexual men who were part of the backbone of the 1970s surge of profeminist activism, as many of these gay profeminist activists died during the first tragic sweep of the HIV/AIDS epidemic.

Thirty-six of the fifty-two men we interviewed identified as white (nine of these also as Jewish), seven as African American, five as Latino, and one each as Native American, Jamaican, South Asian, and multiracial. The men of color in our sample are weighted more toward the younger half of the age spectrum, reflecting a shift away from what was a mostly white movement in the 1970s and early 1980s. A large proportion of profeminist and antiviolence men in the 1970s were Jewish men. Scholars such as Harry Brod and Michael Kimmel have written personally and analytically about the reasons for Jewish men's centrality in profeminist activism, including having experienced a sense of marginalization as boys and young men, a focus on intellectualism in defining Jewish masculinity (often disparaged as feminine in the United States), and the instilling of a powerful moral obligation to stand up for the oppressed and to work for social justice in the post-Holocaust generation of Jewish American youth.[37] Though clearly not all Jewish American men are profeminists, much less committed to peace,[38] it is still true today that a disproportionate number of men who work against gender-based violence are Jewish.

Of the women we interviewed, seven of twelve identified as white, three as African American, one as multiracial African American, and one as Pacific Islander/Filipina. In the book, when we discuss or give quotes from individual men or women, we will note the person's age when it seems important to underline or contextualize the individual's experience as a member of a historical cohort. Similarly, we will note the individual's racial/ethnic identification, sexual orientation, geographic region, political or religious affiliation, or other demographic descriptors only when it seems salient for the particular point we are making (e.g., if we are describing how a man's violence prevention work with boys engages the intersections of race and gender, we may note that the man identifies as white or as Latino). Otherwise, a reader who wants to know more about an individual interviewee can turn to Appendix 1 for a full list of demographic descriptors of interviewees.[39]

As researchers, our understandings of the issues we analyze in this book are also shaped by our own "moments of engagement" with feminism and with antiviolence work. Mike Messner first engaged with feminism as a college student in the early 1970s and witnessed men's first stirrings of violence prevention work as a graduate student in the late 1970s. Max Greenberg and Tal Peretz are younger men, for whom feminism was part of the cultural ether when they were growing up in the

1980s and 1990s, and they first engaged with feminist antiviolence work as undergraduates in the 2000s. Appendix 2 is a short self-reflexive essay that outlines our own moments of feminist and antiviolence engagement and suggests how these engagements shaped, enhanced, and perhaps limit our perspectives.

OUTLINE OF THE BOOK

The middle chapters of this book examine the three overlapping historical moments discussed above. In Chapter 2 we focus on the Movement Cohort, the first group of men who engaged with feminist antiviolence activism in the mid-1970s through the mid-1980s, riding the tide of a mass grassroots feminist movement. These were mostly younger men—college students and men in their twenties. With a close-up focus on the experiences of a grassroots group of men in the San Francisco Bay Area, and supplemented with interviews from individuals in other geographic regions, we will show how these men routed to feminism largely through previous engagements with other social movements of the day. Feminist ideals of equality, peace, and nonviolence resonated with these men's already existing progressive passions and commitments, and they came to view antiviolence work with boys and men as part of a larger collective movement of radical social transformation. But feminism also created new and difficult challenges, including to their very identities as men. Grassroots collectives of men struggled to come to grips with what might be called "inner work" versus "outreach"—between their own therapeutic struggles with the emotional "costs of masculinity" and their commitments to public political action. And by the start of the 1980s, the divisive debates among feminist women about pornography—and especially the extent to which antiviolence feminists came to view pornography as the primary target for radical activism—placed these men in confusing situations in terms of, on the one hand, how to be accountable to feminist women, while on the other hand how most effectively to appeal to boys and men in their public outreach work. These conflicts, we will show, led in some cases to the breakup of men's antiviolence organizations, and to some men leaving and moving on to other kinds of political activism. But the strategies and networks created by the men of the Movement Cohort began to lay the groundwork for the more systematic violence prevention work of subsequent decades.

In Chapter 3, we focus on the experiences of two sorts of men: veterans of the Movement Cohort who continued with antiviolence work, and new recruits, younger men of a Bridge Cohort who engaged during a mid-1980s through late 1990s period of transition. During this time, movement feminism was fading into abeyance, in part from having absorbed a virulent multifront backlash and from the destructive schisms among various feminist groups. At the same time, liberal feminists were beginning to see success in building mass national organizations and in wresting reforms from various institutions. Men's antiviolence activism during this time also hit a period of relative abeyance. But a few individuals began to carve out more entrepreneurial paths in developing antiviolence consulting agencies and businesses. Others took professional degrees, developed careers, and carved out violence prevention specialties in the helping professions. Still others helped to develop community nonprofits and began to build regional and national organizations and coalitions.

By the mid-1990s, as we will show in Chapter 4, these organization-building efforts had begun to usher in the current period of professionally institutionalized feminism. In the United States, the most public historical benchmark of this institutionalization was the passage of the Violence Against Women Act in 1994. Of equal importance in this time period is the relative stabilization of antiviolence organizations and funding sources, coupled with a growing network of antiviolence professionals connecting across numerous institutions—academia, law, social work, community nonprofits, and foundations. This institutionalization of violence prevention work created a wider field of opportunities for men. We show how some veterans of the Movement and Bridge cohorts, now men in their forties, fifties, and sixties, came to hold paid leadership positions in antiviolence work, while younger men of the emergent Professional Cohort volunteer or hold entry-level paid positions, conducting educational outreach with boys in schools. These men, younger and older, work within a field that has been substantially broadened, and they are hopeful and even optimistic (as are the women they work with) that their work is having an impact. However, they also face a set of challenges, not the least of which is the extent to which the very institutionalization that makes their violence prevention work possible takes a professionalized form (including its health-oriented curriculum) that threatens to sever violence prevention work from its political roots and its vision of feminist social transformation. We will show how the men who are doing the work today are aware—some more, some less—of this challenge, and we will discuss the strategies that some deploy to retain a feminist (and sometimes also an antiracist) impulse in their work.

Men who do antiviolence work today are also, like their predecessors, struggling with questions of accountability but today in professional contexts that are still defined primarily as "women's work." We show in

Chapter 5 how this creates a dual set of challenges for men—intense critical scrutiny, as well as moments of unearned praise and privilege—both resulting from the fact that they are still among the very few men doing this work. We will outline how women in the antiviolence field see both the promise and the challenges of men's entry into the field, especially how male privilege in feminist and antiviolence contexts threatens to silence women's voices. The ways that men navigate the interactional twins of critical scrutiny and unearned praise is a bellwether, we will argue, for how sophisticated and effective their work as allies is.

In the final chapter, we pull back from the experiences of the men we interviewed and reflect more generally—in part by bringing in more centrally the voices of the women we interviewed—on men's actual and potential contributions to feminism and to antiviolence activism. We reflect on the current historical moment to ask what has been lost and what has been gained, what are the limits, and what are the possibilities in this moment of professionally institutionalized feminism. We point to emergent social formations—including expanding definitions of what constitutes a social movement—that create new challenges and possibilities for forms of activism against gender-based violence that are reinfused with politics and reconnected to broad visions of social change. In particular, we point to how some of today's professionals and activists are deploying intersectional strategies that connect work on gender-based violence to concerns around racism, class inequality, poverty, and war. And we reflect on the promise of emergent transnational networks of activists against gender-based violence, bridging the Global North and the Global South. We suggest that these two developments—intersectional activism within the United States and transnational feminist networks—hold the potential of reinfusing politics into antiviolence work and, more broadly, of recentering questions of social justice and social transformation in activist work against gender-based violence.

CHAPTER 2

Diving In: The Movement Cohort, 1970s to 1980s

The auditorium of San Francisco's Galileo High School thundered with the cheers and stomps of hundreds of women, gathered in a freshly united fervor to stop men's violence against women. Radical feminist leader and provocateur Andrea Dworkin lit up the room with what historian Carolyn Bronstein called "a powerful, apocalyptic speech."[1] "Sex and murder are fused in the male consciousness," Dworkin proclaimed. "Erotic pleasure for men is derived from and predicated on the savage destruction of women."[2] It was November 4, 1978, and as the crowd poured from the auditorium the group's numbers swelled to several thousand and streamed into San Francisco's streets. Carrying candles and banners and chanting, "No more profit off women's bodies!" the marchers formed what many say was the first-ever "Take Back the Night" march.[3] Activist and writer Susan Brownmiller described the historic moment in her memoir: "[Andrea Dworkin's] call to action accomplished, three thousand demonstrators took to the streets, snaking past Broadway's neon peeps, 'adult' book stores, and garish massage parlors while Holly Near sang from an amplified truck and local artists weaved through the line bobbing surreal effigies of madonnas and whores."[4]

Not mentioned in any of the written accounts of that singular moment in the history of feminist activism is that the auditorium was packed *mostly* with women, but not exclusively.[5] In the last row of the balcony sat a half-dozen young men who had come to show their support in the effort to stop men's violence against women. As Dworkin's speech ended, and the crowd stood to surge into the streets, a contingent of women began a rhythmic chant, *"NO PRICKS IN THE PARADE! NO PRICKS IN THE PARADE!"* As the chant grew louder, the men slunk down in their seats and shot sideways glances at each other. They exited to the lobby and caucused amidst the welter of noise and fervor. Chris Norton, then twenty-eight years old, recalls, "'No Pricks in the Parade' left us all very confused. *What should we do?"*

The men in the balcony weren't exactly political neophytes. Most were veterans of the anti-Vietnam war and other radical movements of the time. And over the past few years, they had become passionately engaged with feminism, at a deeply personal level, and at the level of community politics. They were core members of Men Against Sexist Violence, a grass-roots activist group in the Oakland-Berkeley area that had formed during the previous year.[6] MASV was sparked when several men met at a confer-ence at Laney College in Oakland in April 1977 to discuss men, feminism, and violence. Inspired, a core group of about ten men began to meet regu-larly and eventually developed relationships with local feminist women's organizations. By January 1978, MASV was a thriving grassroots group, ranging from twenty to forty members. Many of the men had previously been members of men's consciousness-raising or counseling groups and were practiced in talking with other men about homophobia, sexism, and the emotional limits of masculinity. But many of them saw MASV as a place to shift gears—to move from feminist-inspired personal growth to public, political activism.

In early 1978, a committee of MASV men began their outreach work, engaging boys and men in discussions about masculinity and violence with the goal of stopping rape and other forms of violence against women. They had little idea where to start, so they requested a train-ing on sexual violence from the then-vibrant group Women Against Violence in Pornography and Media.[7] Though there was as yet no curricu-lum for working with boys and men around sexual violence issues, the WAVPM training, along with readings of key feminist texts of the time—particularly Brownmiller's groundbreaking 1975 book on rape, *Against Our Will*—provided a foundational theory on which to build their activ-ism. Central to this theory was the idea that violence against women—and especially sexualized violence as depicted in pornography—was a lynchpin of patriarchy. Men who wanted to be allies in building a gender-egalitarian world—and that's precisely how the MASV men saw themselves—were politically and morally obligated to work with boys and men around this central issue. "We were sort of the men's auxiliary of WAVPM," Chris Norton explained, "the men's auxiliary of the antipor-nography movement."

By late 1978, MASV men had begun to fan out into the community with a slide show on pornography and violence, which they would eventually present to more than fifty high school groups, and to numerous college and community groups. A MASV subgroup started a biweekly public radio show on men. A few of them visited Atascadero State Prison, to speak with sex offenders and prison officials. And the group showed up for public events, like the WAVPM action at a movie theater to protest what feminists saw as an exploitative depiction of teen prostitution in the 1978 film *Pretty Baby*.[8] One of the men we interviewed told us that he and other MASV men had also wielded spray-paint cans in late night "commando raids" to deface sexist billboards. In short, by the end of 1978, MASV was a group of young men publicly engaged on several fronts as feminist allies.

Some of the WAVPM organizers of the 1978 Take Back the Night rally had invited the MASV men to participate, as had some women from BAWAR (Bay Area Women Against Rape), and the men's feminist women friends. So here sat the MASV men, in the back row of the balcony listening to Andrea Dworkin, whose writings had been a major source of inspiration for core MASV members. When a contingent of the women started their angry chant for the pricks to get out of their parade, loudly claiming this as a women-only space, the MASV men, in the words of Chris Norton, "felt very confused about exactly what we were supposed to do." But as they caucused, other women approached them and urged them to remain: " 'You'd better not leave', they told us. 'It's important for men to be in the march.' So we got that encouragement to go, but we felt like we had to kind of be, you know, at the very end of the march."

Indeed, the men did decide to march, but at the tail end of the parade, allowing a bit of space between themselves and the thousands of women who preceded them. Greg Ross, then thirty-one years old and a Vietnam veteran, laughs as he recalls the moment: "We walked at the very end of the whole thing and three steps behind the last possible group. So we went in supplication. I'm surprised they didn't make us wear burkas or something, you know what I mean?—'cause we were going, but in supplication." And Chris Anderegg, then a twenty-seven-year-old activist, recalls the march as indicative of the fine line that profeminist men were walking at the time, trying to be allies with a feminist movement that itself did not agree about what role, if any, men should play: "That was always an interesting contradiction of 'We want you, we don't want you blah-blah-blah.' But you know, we were just trying to be allies and I didn't take it personally—to be there to march and then having women in the march chanting against us. You know, 'cause it was in a time also when the women's movement was very politicized and there were a lot of political divisions there as well."

As an activist group, MASV was alive for only three years—from early 1978 through the end of 1980. Their story illustrates several of this chapter's central themes. First, we explore how the historical context of movement feminism had, by the late 1970s, inspired groups of men across the nation to engage positively with feminism, and to take seriously the feminist call for men to work with boys and men to stop rape and domestic violence. Next, we describe pathways to ally work: Who were these men? Compared with the many men who responded to feminism with confusion or even hostility, what led this small number of young men to align themselves, very publicly, with feminism, and commit themselves to antiviolence work with boys and men?

We then explore how the context of movement feminism that had inspired men's profeminist consciousness and action simultaneously generated several strains and tensions that male feminist allies sought to navigate. First, profeminist men of the 1970s and early 1980s struggled to strike a balance between two seemingly contradictory positions: a therapeutic orientation toward helping themselves and other men overcome the emotionally crippling "costs of masculinity," while also fighting against men's institutionalized privileges, including how violence against women was thought to buttress this privilege. Second, like feminist women of this time, the men struggled with social class and racial/ethnic differences within their groups, and also in their outreach with diverse groups of boys and men. And third, male allies grappled with how to be accountable allies with feminist women, while avoiding descending into (or projecting on to boys) a crippling guilt. The men were torn, as were feminist women of the time, by what came to be known as "the feminist sex wars": debates generated from within the feminist movement concerning how best to stop violence against women while also liberating women's sexuality.[9] As the movement to stop violence against women narrowed to a focus on antipornography activism, feminist debates about sexuality, power and violence became more divisive.[10] Was there room for men's voices in this debate? Could men rightly join the feminist parade as equals, or should they be relegated to silent support? If they were to be accountable allies with feminist women, then to *which* feminist women should they be accountable?

THE WOMEN'S MOVEMENT AND THE MEN

The late 1970s were watershed years, not only for MASV in the Bay Area but also for similar groups springing up across the nation. For young men, especially those in college or university communities, feminism had now been in the air for nearly a decade. Feminist protests and marches for equal rights, reproductive freedom, and stopping violence against women had become commonplace. A few women's studies courses had made their way into college curricula. Grassroots women's groups on campuses and in communities had launched rape and domestic violence hotlines, women's shelters, and women's self-defense classes. And tens of thousands of young men were being confronted, baffled, challenged, and even inspired by the feminist transformations of their sisters, lovers, women friends, and political allies.

By mid-decade, some men had formed their own men's consciousness-raising groups, and within a few years they had begun to move to public action. "There was a lot of urgency," MASV member Santiago Casal explained. "People felt it just because, you know, the context of feminism, and guys were being challenged in their relationships." Other men across the continent were experiencing that same sense of urgency. As MASV was forming on the West Coast in 1977 and 1978, a group of men in Boston formed a pioneering anti–domestic violence group called Emerge, and men in St. Louis launched their own such group, Rape and Violence Ends Now (RAVEN). The work of these men's groups was mostly local, but national networking began almost simultaneously, mostly through annual national conferences on men and masculinity that had begun in 1975, eventually coalescing into the profeminist National Organization for Changing Men (NOCM) in 1983.[11]

In this chapter we focus on the stories of a dozen men—today ranging in age from fifty-five to seventy—who engaged with feminism during this explosive historical moment. Five of these men were core members of MASV; two others were San Francisco Bay Area antirape activists peripherally affiliated with MASV members; two men were founding members of RAVEN in St. Louis; and three others were engaging with grassroots feminist groups and antiviolence work in New York, Ohio, Toronto, Los Angeles, and elsewhere. Certainly these profeminist men were not typical men of their generation. Who were they? What were their pathways into antiviolence work? Why and how were they so positively inspired by feminism, while so many other men at the time were dismissive or overtly hostile to feminist women? We will show that these men's positive engagements are explicable as a collective outcome of two factors: personal experiences that created egalitarian and antiviolence predispositions, coupled with conducive social contexts—politically radical, peace-oriented, and feminist interpersonal relationships, communities and social movements—that enabled these predispositions to play out in the form of progressive and feminist action.

SOFT MEN, FEMINIST CONTEXTS

Growing up in the 1950s and 1960s in Urbana, Illinois, Craig Norberg-Bohm was "always a soft boy, always more sensitive. I was always on the victim side of the equation, afraid of the guys who were harder." Both he and his sister had been sexually assaulted, he by an older man during his childhood, "So I knew men were dangerous, and I was afraid of dangerous men." In 1974, a freshly minted college graduate who had "managed to avoid going into the military" during the Vietnam war, he moved into a household in St. Louis with a group of friends, three of whom were "women who were involved with the women's movement" and were "very gung-ho" about starting the city's first women's center, which included a hotline for rape and domestic violence crisis calls.

One day on the street in 1975, Norberg-Bohm spied a poster advertising a conference on men and masculinity. He recalls the poster's title to this day: "'Straight white men wrestling with the master culture'—and it showed a guy shivering in a cold wind. I was like, *'that's me!'* I related intensely to the idea." He attended the conference, in Knoxville, Tennessee,[12] and was inspired by young men from Illinois who had started a campus group against rape. When he returned to St. Louis, Norberg-Bohm organized his own conference, out of which was formed the St. Louis Men's Project. Nicknamed SLUMP (undoubtedly with Midwestern tongue-in-cheek), the group launched two community projects: a men's childcare service that supported feminist women's meetings and public events, and, in collaboration with women's centers, "an ending men's violence project [that] turned into an ongoing project called RAVEN, Rape and Violence Ends Now." For the next ten years, along with co-founder Don Conway-Long and a handful of others, Norberg-Bohm contributed countless hours of work to RAVEN— much of it unpaid, some of it eventually for a small stipend that was supplemented by his work as a lab scientist. "I was an idealist," he said, and through feminism he had "found a purpose" and a community that enabled him to develop his "soft" and "sensitive" proclivities and his personal antipathy toward violence into a source of pride and action.

Craig Norberg-Bohm's story is typical in many ways of this early wave of men who started the first men's antirape and anti–domestic violence groups. Most of them were boys in the 1950s and early 1960s, during a time when narrow conceptions of masculinity—John Wayne films of war or the Wild West, Superman comic books, and burly football players in their schools and on television—idealized muscular toughness, emotional stoicism, the successful use of violence, and sexual conquests of women. This ascendant postwar "hegemonic masculinity," to borrow sociologist

Raewyn Connell's term, was created partly in opposition to marginalized and subordinated masculinities—a "real man" was *not* peaceful, nurturing, or indecisive; he was not a sissy, a crybaby, or a loser.[13]

Experiences with Violence

Several of the men we interviewed who eventually became profeminist allies grew up like Craig Norberg-Bohm as "soft" not-so-athletic boys who were frequently traumatized and disparaged as effeminate by other boys. Most were not the muscular and heterosexy boys that the popular girls desired. Some of them, too, like Norberg-Bohm, experienced male violence firsthand as boys and young men. A handful of them had violent fathers who were also in some way affiliated with the military and warfare. Don Conway-Long, who eventually would cofound RAVEN with Norberg-Bohm, says he grew up as "a military kid, Navy background, rather violent father in a lot of ways—particularly emotionally, but some physical violence against me as a kid." Similarly, Tim Beneke, one of the first antirape activists (peripherally affiliated with MASV in the Bay Area), grew up as an "Army brat" who, by the time he was thirteen years old, "had lived in twelve houses in nine cities, and constant fractured change." During this time, he said, "I experienced regular fear of my father, who was severely violent starting when I was ten, and beat up my mother and broke almost all the furniture in the house. Terrified me. I think I experienced an unspoken, an unspeakable fear of being killed by him." MASV member Chris Anderegg's father worked for the state department, and Chris recalls growing up in various African nations in a context of danger, especially in the Congo during the 1959 Civil War: "We were around war a lot, and—and my father was also violent sometimes."

Some of these men's early experiences with violence took place not in families but at the hands of other boys in schoolyards on playgrounds, or in the street. Michael Kaufman, who as a Canadian adult would become a world leader in gender-based violence prevention, was born in Cleveland, Ohio, and spent much of his youth in racially segregated Durham, North Carolina, during the height of the Civil Rights Movement. His first experiences of violence were not in his family: "I had the most wonderful dad on the planet, and parents who had a very respectful relationship and . . . so for me, experiences of violence as a child were completely boy-on-boy violence." Kaufman's parents were not activists, but they took an ethical stand with respect to racism: if a restaurant or theater was not integrated, then the Kaufman family would not go there. This stance eventually drew some fire on young Michael, who was physically assaulted and humiliated by a group of boys. In the sixth grade, he recalls "getting attacked and literally beaten up, and being taunted with three words: 'Yankee' ('cause I was from the North), 'Nigger-lover,' and 'Jew'. . . . It was awful. I mean, you know, it was frightening, it was, you know, it made me feel—like dirt." Though at the time he felt powerless to fight back, eventually he began to learn more about social oppression, and this childhood experience "reverberated, because it taught me in my guts, literally, that I was part of—that I wasn't separate from those that are oppressed. Whatever my parents hadn't already taught me, in terms of identifying with the under-dog, that—that cemented it for me."

Unlike most of these other men, Mark Stevens, who would eventually become a national leader in gender-based violence prevention on college campuses, was an athletic boy who, for the most part, "fit in" with other kids. But a recurrent motif in his male peer group seemed to be "you got to get in a fight to get a notch in your belt. You gotta hit someone in the face." Despite his immersion in sports, Stevens had a gut-level aversion to violence: "I didn't like being hurt. I didn't see the heroism in being hurt in that sort of way. It didn't make sense to me." He attributed part of his antipathy to violence to growing up in a "liberal family" in the 1950s, where he saw his father and his grandfather as "nonviolent people," and also to "growing up with Judaism," hearing in temple a message of "peace-fulness about how to treat people fairly and respectfully."

These men's experiences with violence in families and in their peer groups created deep emotional predispositions—embodied proclivi-ties or aversions to later engagements with violence. Sociologist James Messerschmidt's poignant study of nine adolescent boys' use or rejection of interpersonal violence is helpful in thinking about predispositions, not as inborn natural drives but as deeply rooted psychological and emotional inclinations, grounded in salient previous experiences.[14] Messerschmidt identifies a constellation of childhood and adolescent experiences and contexts that help to explain how some boys become violent, while oth-ers don't. Families, of course, are important. Boys who grow up in violent family environments[15] and who have experiences with fathers and other older males who teach them to value male violence are more likely later to assault others. Boys who do not observe violence in their families, who are taught by parents that violence is wrong and that it is honorable to walk away from fights, are more likely to eschew violent behavior. Peer groups also matter. Boys who are immersed in adolescent male pecking orders that are constituted by fighting and bullying, that deploy homophobic insults to group members and outsiders, and that celebrate sexual domination tend to embody predispositions toward assaultive behaviors. Boys immersed in nonviolent peer groups are less likely to assault other people.

Some of the men we have introduced thus far in our study fit Messerschmidt's model; Stevens and Kaufman, for instance, were predisposed to shun violence by their nonviolent families and their progressive Jewish upbringings. However, several others of these men experienced just the sort of family and peer violence that might predict their developing predispositions to using violence in their own relationships. Yet they became antiviolence activists. To be sure, boys who experience violence in their youth too often do replicate these violent behaviors as adults. However, under different social conditions, these same preconditions can incline toward antiviolence consciousness and action. Put another way, context matters.

Social Movement and Feminist Contexts

There are four interrelated, historically specific experiences that were central to shaping these men's pathways into antiviolence action. First, all of them were part of a generation of young people who were immersed in a welter of radical social movement activism during the 1960s and early 1970s. Second, by the early 1970s, these men had close-up connections with feminist women—in universities, in collective households or food co-ops, and in relationships with sisters, girlfriends, and lovers—that resulted in a growing respect for women and an extension of their existing progressive social justice commitments (on race, social class, and war) into the field of gender relations. Third, in the early to mid-1970s, many of these men formed small men's consciousness-raising groups, modeled after feminist women's groups, and before long the groups began to form loose local and eventually national networks of profeminist men. As they listened to women, read feminist literature, and discussed sexism with each other in their groups, these young men learned to see the impact of men's violence on women's lives—sometimes firsthand, as when a woman they were close to was raped, beaten, or sexually harassed. As a result, the men developed a deeper empathy for women. Fourth, as the feminist women in their lives challenged their incipient men's groups, a sense of responsibility and urgency to stop the violence erupted, thus leading to the first organized attempts by men to work with boys and men to prevent violence against women.

All of these men spoke of the 1960s "New Left," the student movement, and especially the movement against the Vietnam war as bedrock to their formation as young adults.[16] Several also noted the importance of the Civil Rights Movement. Their involvement in these movements shifted their conventionally moderate or liberal political orientation to radical. Though he had come from a family that was "conservative politically," Paul Kivel was radicalized in the 1960s as a college student in Portland, Oregon, and became a grassroots political activist "involved with work and antiracism work." During his stint in the Navy, Greg Ross became one of thousands in the U.S. military who turned against the war. On his return from Vietnam, Ross became an active member of Vietnam Veterans Against the War, first in Buffalo, New York, and later in the Bay Area. As part of these social movements, these men came to view injustices to blacks, to the poor, and to Vietnamese peasants as logically interconnected results of "the system." If peace and justice were eventually to prevail, a radical social movement was needed to fundamentally transform the institutions of society.

These men's experiences in the antiwar movement and the New Left created a template for their openness to feminist articulations of social justice. Indeed, the earliest bubblings of men's profeminist activism— for instance, the 1971 "male liberation" newspaper cover shown in Figure 2.1—depicted a moment of public agitation against the sexism of *Playboy* magazine that reiterated the language and styles of antiwar protests of the day: "Nixie Agnie Hoovie Heffie All Pigs," a protestor's sign

Figure 2.1
Brother, a male liberation newspaper, summer 1971.

claimed about the president and vice president of the United States, the head of the FBI, and the owner and publisher of *Playboy*.

But clearly, immersion in the antiwar movement was not fully sufficient to bring about feminist awakenings in activist men. After all, by the start of the 1970s many feminist women had become disillusioned and disgusted with the unapologetic sexism that permeated the New Left. Feminist pioneer Robin Morgan's angry 1970 essay "Goodbye to All That" resonated with a growing separatist tendency among radical women who experienced New Left organizations not as liberating, but "as a microcosm of capitalist economy, with men competing for power and status at the top, and women doing all the work at the bottom (and functioning as objectified prizes or 'coin' as well)." The men we interviewed tended to agree with Morgan's challenge that a truly progressive man must "divest himself of cock privilege . . . It's up to the 'brothers'—after all, sexism is their concern, not ours; we are too busy getting ourselves together to have to deal with their bigotry."[17]

The men we interviewed took this challenge to heart and attempted to put it into practice. In fact, some of them spoke of their own disenchantment with the male-dominated left. Greg Ross had "gotten burned out" with the revolutionary posturing and political infighting in Vietnam Veterans Against the War.[18] Chris Norton said that he and some other male members of the socialist left and the antiwar movement also were "rejecting militarism and the traditional terms of being masculine or man, and were looking for some new way." In feminism, Norton saw the possibility of "humanizing socialism, or getting rid of some of the hard-edged, more Stalinistic tendencies that some socialist movements could have." But just precisely what feminism might mean for these men was an open question, and it took various forms of interaction with feminist women before the men's feminist awakenings coalesced into group action.

Feminist Engagements

By the early 1970s, Paul Kivel had moved to the Bay Area, where he "got involved with the People's Food System, which was a quite extensive network of alternative food co-ops and supply and distribution centers." Several of the founding MASV members were also part of this grassroots "food conspiracy." This and other social activism put Kivel and the others in direct contact with feminist women: "The women's movement was alive and well and thriving and challenging all of us who were men to look at our practices—not just our personal behavior, but our collective practices, and to think about the implications of not just gender roles but male power in institutional settings."

Kivel's immersion in progressive groups and contact with feminist women in the 1970s shifted his views and his commitments. "I was hearing from women," he said, "[about] the tremendously devastating impact [violence] had not just on them individually but as they set up shelters and rape-prevention centers. . . . I was learning about the extensiveness, the depth of it, the complexity of it." Kivel had already connected with other like-minded men who were resonating with women's antiviolence work: "A lot of us as men were responding to the women's movement . . . we'd say, 'What can we do?' And they'd say, 'Well our hands are full working with the women. It's men who are violent. Talk to the men'."

"Talk to the men." Several of the men we interviewed were hearing the same words from feminist women in their political circles. Men's friendships and intimate relationships with women were changing, too. Chris Norton said, "[Women] were wanting to change the balance of power in relationships or change what they were shooting for, or what they wanted." Feminist women friends and partners were, Norton said, "pulling back" from men, becoming "kind of unreachable" and less inclined now to do the traditional emotional labor of caring for men's feelings.

> Some of the women were telling some of the men, you know, 'You need to get your shit together. And you need to figure out a little—some of this stuff on your own, and not expect us to figure it out for you.' I mean, all these big changes were going on, and I think the guys had kinda' learned from the women that maybe it would be good to have some place where they could come and talk about things, and so that's how the men's center got set up, was they started doing counseling sessions and having drop-in counseling groups.

Two years before joining Norton and others to found MASV, Larry Mandella joined a men's consciousness-raising group. It was "a period in which a lot of women that I either knew personally or knew of, were joining women's consciousness raising groups and it seemed like a powerful experience to them and it just caught my attention and . . . I did eventually join this group of guys and what we did was we met on Monday evening [and] we were really kind of figuring out on our own, what it meant to be a bunch of men together talking." Eventually, Mandella's group started a community drop-in counseling service for men.

When Allan Creighton left graduate school in 1978 without finishing, he describes himself as having been "pretty unhappy." He "landed in the Bay Area for the first time and my younger sister was among that wave of women who were doing a lot of stuff on violence against women, the first rape crisis center got started in Oakland. And, you know, I'd go to demonstrations and there'd be a couple of guys at the end of the march and we'd talk to each other. Larry and Chris were already in a men's group, I think. That's how I found out about MASV."

For these men, it was a revelation to find a group of like-minded men with whom they could talk with mutual openness and vulnerability about relationships, violence, feelings, and sex. Mark Stevens started his first men's consciousness-raising group at San Diego State University in 1977; "The women were saying, 'We're sort of tired of taking care of you guys, it's important for you to start to take care of yourself'." His men's group really took off: "it was a big hit." Clearly, men's groups were filling a therapeutic need for many men. Still reeling from the trauma of his war experience and his subsequent disenchantment with the antiwar movement, Greg Ross found his way to the East Bay Men's Center, where "you could get like free therapy and I definitely needed all the therapy I could get at that point." There, he found a group of men like him who "feel out of place and they're trying to do something in the world." A couple of these men had just started MASV, and Ross, who always felt like a bit of an outsider, recalls laughing at the fact that he was the "number 13" man to join the group. The main draw for the still-fragile Ross was that the group was "this place where I could connect with men. As friends or something, but it was safe."

Don Conway-Long's experiences in St. Louis in many ways mirrored those of the MASV men. Conway-Long's first foray into discussing sexism and violence with men was a life-changing experience: "meeting these men that were honest, open, and trying so hard to confront these issues but not knowing answers any better than I did, you know, so we were working on it together." But talk was not enough. Soon he met Craig Norberg-Bohm, and they were challenged by women to do something: "We knew women who were in Women's Self Help Center, the first group in St. Louis working with battered women. And they were basically telling us, 'You say you're supportive of us, do something about it.' 'Uhhh what?' You know how it is: 'Work with the men.' 'Uh, what? Us? We don't know anything about that!'" Not long after, Conway-Long left a Ph.D. program and, along with Norberg-Bohm, threw himself into building RAVEN.

For some of these men, the call to action had a very personal dimension. Greg Ross had returned "traumatized" from Vietnam following "four years being off the coast of Vietnam on this ship that was capable of throwing two-thousand pound shells twenty miles, and... when we would be firing those guns twenty-four-seven for weeks, knowing how much destruction that [caused], and that I had a part in it." On his return, Ross suffered from "survivor's guilt" and serious posttraumatic stress disorder. In retrospect, he can see that finding MASV and doing antiviolence work at that time was "like a karmic payback, so to speak. It was a way of paying off my karmic debt around all that."

Don Conway-Long was dealing with his own karma. As a young man in his midtwenties, he was appalled to realize that he, now in his first marriage, was replicating some of his father's violence with his own wife: "I was doing behaviors that I would now define as violent. Breaking things, shoving, pushing, lots of arguments." The women's movement and a growing feminist-inspired empathy for women gave Conway-Long, Ross, and other men a way to reframe the meaning of violence in their lives. Feminism, and the growing network of profeminist men, supplied a moral imperative to act, and a political frame for thinking of antiviolence action as both a personal act of transformation (perhaps even redemption) and part of a larger collective effort at social change.

In 1979, an act of gender-based violence jolted MASV member Larry Mandella, when his brother was murdered while intervening to prevent a violent assault. "My brother came upon a man [with a gun] in the street who was confronting what turned out to be his own wife. . . . And my brother said something to this man, to interrupt what was going on and the man turned the gun on my brother and shot him." At that time, Mandella was already engaged with feminism and had just begun doing violence prevention work with MASV, so he viewed his own tragedy as more than some random street assault. His brother's murder "put a whole other urgency in my personal life to the very thing that we were working on. It made it very real."

It got very personal for Tim Beneke, too. As a twenty-nine-year-old in 1979, the self-described Berkeley "dropout hippie," who saw himself more as an independent "observer" than movement activist, was conducting research for what would become his groundbreaking book *Men on Rape*,[19] when a close woman friend of his was raped. Not long after that, the woman he was in a relationship with, who was "very much identifying with feminism," was subjected to a brutal form of street harassment.

> I felt outrage at the shit men did to women. I mean, conscious outrage. She was taking a bus home, across from a fraternity on Grand Avenue in Berkeley—it was like 9:30 or so at night, and there were guys in the fraternity shouting things at her, "Hey pussy hair, hey this, hey that." And one guy walked over to her and said, "Are you standing here 'cause you're waiting to be raped?" And she was trembling, frightened, and said, "No I think you're really sick." "Hey fellas she thinks I'm really sick, ha ha." That *outrage* . . . so my friend Clark and

I said, "Why don't we just go with you? And you can do the talking you know, we'll just go with you and we'll walk over to the fraternity house and tell them what happened. Tell them we're going to report all this. And you can write a letter to the editor of the *Daily Cal*." So we did that, the three of us, with Clark, he was pretty outraged too. So anyway, we did that, and there was just like stark silence when we walked in and said this to them. She said something, she wrote a letter to the editor describing what had happened . . . this fraternity had a reputation and so forth. They were put on suspension. So it was very empowering for her.

It was empowering for Beneke, too, to act so publicly as a feminist ally and to see concrete results. For other men, their initial actions were rarely so triumphant; instead, their first forays into profeminist activism were often awkward, confusing, and sometimes scary, and they felt perhaps a bit like tilting at the windmills of a powerful and intransigent patriarchy. But their collective outrage and urgency, coupled with the sense of feeling connected—directly with a group of like-minded men, and less directly with the women's movement—fueled a sense of empowered optimism. If they could change, they reasoned, other men could, too. And if they could be catalysts for other boys and men to change, then a feminist revolution was possible. Local groups connected regionally in organizations like the California Anti-Sexist Men's Political Caucus, depicted at a 1980 political march in Figure 2.2. "We were part of a movement," said MASV member Chris Anderegg. Santiago Casal echoed that thought; the work they were doing in MASV "totally related to everything" he was doing, including

Figure 2.2
California Anti-Sexist Men's Political Caucus at a political march, circa 1980.
©1981 Changing Men Magazine, reprinted by permission of Rick Cote.

progressive public radio, antiracism work, prison support, and community radical therapy.[20] When Mike Messner interviewed Chris Norton in 1980[21] during the height of his MASV activism, Norton described the group's work as part of a broader revolutionary effort, a sense that one's actions were connected with a vision of radical social transformation:

> I have a real strong vision of a collective society where there's a lot less class boundaries, where there's more of a sense of people working together, being part of one society all being connected, without the sort of oppression that we see now; where everyone is valued . . . that's inclusive [of] working people and women and racial minorities; where old people and young people are all valued; where people are raised up with a sense that they're important and they can do what they want with their life—their creativity can be cherished and maintained and can be part of the productive process too. A society that doesn't oppress people in other parts of the world, in fact, where people cooperate with each other and it's thought to be something that you naturally want to do.

These profeminist allies of the 1970s and early 1980s tended to share a version of this broad vision of social transformation, a sense that their antiviolence work with boys and men was at once "very personal," while at the same time "totally related to everything" else that they were doing. In addition, their paths to becoming feminist allies against sexual and domestic violence tended to follow a common pattern[22]: first, a passionate immersion with the New Left and the antiwar movement was followed by disenchantment with the sectarian squabbling and masculinist chest beating of the male-dominated movement; second, light bulbs of new insight about gender and sexuality burst in their imaginations, through direct contact with feminist women and feminist writings; third, following women's examples, they formed small groups of like-minded men to explore the personal meanings of feminism, and to begin to forge new ways to be men; and fourth, the incipient men's groups were challenged—often by feminist women—to move beyond the comfort of consciousness-raising and therapeutic modes, to social action. From there they forged out into their communities and started to "talk to the men." And that is where the real challenges began.

THE POLITICAL MINEFIELD OF MEN'S PROFEMINISM

The women's movement ignited in the late 1960s and early 1970s, fueled by a sense of urgency, excitement, and optimism. Young activists believed that if they dedicated themselves to the hard work of collective organizing, rapid and radical social transformation was truly possible. But this context of movement activism also set up difficult challenges quite similar to those faced by activists in other social movements. The first such challenge was a contradiction built into the project of "men and feminism": the attempt by men's groups to strike a balance between their own "internal" therapeutic work (dealing with the emotional, relational, and health "costs of masculinity" to themselves and other men), versus their commitment to being allies with women in illuminating and undermining men's institutionalized power and privilege.[23] Second, like many feminist women's organizations at the time, men's groups struggled to come to grips with differences and inequalities among men, especially along lines of social class, race, and sexual orientation.[24] And third, as the men moved into public antiviolence work with boys and men, they did so in dialogue with groups and leaders in the women's antirape and anti-domestic violence community, which by the start of the 1980s was focusing more and more on antipornography activism. As the women's movement splintered internally around the "feminist sex wars," how would profeminist men's groups—especially those engaged in antiviolence work—position themselves? If they wanted to be strong and reliable allies, accountable to feminist women's groups, then *to which women* should they be accountable? As we will see, men's groups and individual men navigated these three challenges variously. Some groups, like MASV, eventually dissolved under these strains and tensions. Others, like RAVEN, adapted and survived.

The Costs and Privileges of Masculinity

By the mid-1970s, small clusters of men had formed men's consciousness-raising groups, in which they adopted emergent feminist perspectives on masculinity to discuss deeply personal issues. They struggled to overcome their fears of emotional vulnerability with other men, discussing their own doubts and pain around family relations, sexuality, intimacy, homophobia, public success and failure, and violence. But this inward turn of men's feminist-inspired therapy was not enough for most of the men we interviewed. They had absorbed the critical feminist idea that the "costs of masculinity" (poor health, lower life expectancy, shallow relationships, fears of intimacy) could only truly be confronted when properly understood as the flip side of men's institutional power and privilege in a patriarchal society. Put another way, men could be fully human only if and when they shared power equally with women.

Larry Mandella had initially been drawn to men's groups as sources of support for self-transformation, but his counseling collective "was pretty much just inwardly directed. And the idea of doing something in the community, doing something that affected the issues on a much wider basis really appealed to me." MASV was just the ticket, and from the start the new group simultaneously formed a therapy committee and a political action committee. MASV's twin goals of ("inward directed") therapeutic support for its members, coupled with public action (outreach), were theoretically two sides of the same social change coin; after all, these men had absorbed from feminist women the dictum that "the personal is political."

When Mike Messner interviewed Chris Norton in 1980, while MASV was in full swing, Norton described MASV as "a political action group [with] a component of support. That's what makes it a good group; it has a mixture of both." In reality—especially as MASV became more publicly engaged with violence prevention work—these twin goals were increasingly a source of tension. When we interviewed him over thirty years later, Chris Norton's retrospective view reflected these strains: "Some people felt like they wanted to be politically active, other people were more interested in self-discovery. And they felt like they wanted to kind of use the group more as a support group and so I think there was . . . a little bit of a tension in the air."

Part of this tension blossomed from the sense of urgency that was built into the men's growing relationship with feminist antirape activists, especially the women of the radical antipornography movement. As MASV grew and became more publicly engaged, many of the women in their lives were challenging them to move beyond therapy, and *do something now* to stop men's violence against women. There was also a growing skepticism among feminist women, and many of their male allies like the men of MASV, that the nationally emergent "men's liberation movement" was more concerned with the harm done to men by "the limits of the male sex role" than with undermining men's patriarchal privileges and stopping men's violence against women. Amidst this urgent politicized context, Norton says, he then came to view the group's counseling collective as "too self-indulgent. But looking back in hindsight, I think it was actually just the right thing to be doing, 'cause I think that's what a lot of the guys really needed." As they increasingly "went public" with antiviolence organizing, the Bay Area group's energies tipped more to community action and outreach, and less to internal therapeutic work. In retrospect, this seems ironic: from the members' earlier consciousness-raising groups to MASV's own structure that included a strong therapeutic orientation, these men grappled directly with issues related to the emotional costs of masculinity, their own experiences with violence as boys and young men, distant relationships with fathers, their own fears, and insecurities around heterosexual relations with women. Feminist theory informed them how these costs of masculinity were linked to men's power and privilege, and the men worked to make these connections in their group work. But as the group turned outward to public work, they became less openly sympathetic toward boys' and men's pain or insecurities, instead too often projecting their own male feminist guilt onto the boys and men they were attempting to educate. Two powerful forces pushed MASV toward this less-than-effective mode of public engagement: the largely underexamined white and middle-class basis of their own group, and a narrow form of what came to be understood as "political correctness," rooted in their commitment to the antipornography strand of the women's movement.

White, College-educated, Middle-class

By the late 1970s and early 1980s, working-class women and women of color had begun to illuminate what sociologist Maxine Baca Zinn and her colleagues would eventually criticize as "the false universalization" of white middle-class women's experiences and interests in the women's movement.[25] Scholars of men and masculinities as well as activist profeminist men began to echo these concerns.[26] Like most in the growing network of profeminist men in the United States, the men of MASV were primarily white, college-educated, and of middle-class origins. The men of MASV identified as leftists, some of them even as Marxists, and so they saw themselves as pro-working class, and in their group discussions they scrutinized their own classism and racism. Moreover, despite their own middle-class origins and college educations, several like Norton and Mandella seemed to eschew professional careers, in favor of developing working-class trades, as carpenters. Norton produced a Christmas special on public radio, discussing the needs and struggles of incarcerated men, and periodically the group strategized to recruit a more diverse membership. Nevertheless, the predominantly white and middle-class foundation of the group created less-than-visible boundaries that tended to exclude or marginalize the few men of color and men of working-class origin who shared an interest in what came to be called "men's issues."

When Greg Ross joined MASV as the group's thirteenth member, he was happy to find a like-minded group of men, but he never felt that he wholly fit in. It was "disconcerting," he said, to have to compartmentalize his working-class origins and his status as a Vietnam veteran: "Generally I didn't talk about those parts of my life. I definitely didn't talk about being a Vietnam vet. I had learned that early on—that you just keep that to yourself, 'cause you just got too much shit for it." But silence, for Ross, was just not part of his personality; it especially enraged him when the group did things that he thought reflected their unexamined class privilege and anti-working-class bias, sometimes in the very act of trying to grow and diversify the membership of the group.

> I became quite disruptive in the organization 'cause I had a hard time with— they wanted to start charging dues but it was beyond what I could pay as a childcare worker [laughs], you know that's what I was doing for a living. You know, people were like, "It's not that much money," and I went, "Well, to you it's not." The dues paying came at the exact same time that people were saying, "Well we have to bring more people of color and working-class people in." And I'm like saying, "As a person of working-class origin, fees do not jive unless you're talking about $5 a month, you know?" I remember once we did an out- reach thing at the Men's Center to try and bring more working men, men of color in. And the three guys who planned it and facilitated it, it was so trun- cated and so compartmentalized and so—*middle-class*, to me, that at some point, something happened and I just, I lost it. I started screaming at them, and they were like, "Calm down *bla-bla-bla*," and the five or six working-class guys that showed up, three of them kind of like said, "Well wait, this is the most honest we've heard yet, we kind of like this guy, what he's saying, you know. If there's more like him, we might want to join," you know.

As the group's number swelled to around thirty members, a couple more working-class men, and one African American Vietnam vet, joined MASV. Ross recalls, "I never felt completely comfortable but as it started to fill up I met other working-class men that were coming in. We were a minor- ity." The class and race tensions stretched beyond money issues. The public antiviolence work itself, from Ross's perspective, was too often permeated with a white and middle-class bias, especially when the group seemed to assume that violence was perpetrated mostly by poor and working-class men, somehow rendering invisible the violence of more privileged men: "There were issues of certain levels of ignorance—you know, mid- dle and upper middle-class men molest their children too, it's not all just trailer trash that do it." Once, at a public event where Ross and another Vietnam vet were scheduled to read their antiwar poetry, an older femi- nist woman representing Bay Area Women Against Rape preceded them on the stage. Ross laughs now, as he recounts what was then a painful public scene: "She stood there and said that she was absolutely convinced that all the pornography in America was manufactured and brought in by Vietnam vets. And then we're supposed to go on and read our poetry! Ha! So Steve and I turned to BAWAR people and said, 'We're not going out there. You know, we survived Vietnam, we know when to run.'"

Ross became confrontationally vocal in MASV meetings, even disruptive about the group's unexamined class bias. Eventually, he retreated from the group's political work and focused more on his own emotional healing. Santiago Casal, the only Latino man in the group, observed many of the same issues but dealt with them differently. Casal grew up in a working-class family—his father was Spanish, his mother Cuban—in a "Chicano environment" in Southern California: "I grew up in kind of gang culture and low riding culture and so on, you know, and that's my foundation until I got out of the Army and went into college."

For Casal, MASV was never the most important thing he was doing; it was part of a larger whole, just one of several political commitments he maintained in the community. Still, being the only Latino in MASV, "was a strain, 'cause—as I recall, I don't think there were any others, no African Americans, no Latinos there that I can remember—I don't think there's any Asians in there either. That was a strain to be in that context because—you know, to me, it was guys [who] were coming from a privileged place. . . . So I, I think that's part of what kept me away from, you know, not plunging in and participating in as many things as I might have."

But it wasn't simply his own comfort level that concerned Casal. He could see that the group's white and middle-class basis affected their outreach work, especially when they conducted workshops in public schools, talking about pornography and sexual assault with boys of color and working-class kids: "The reality is to talk about these issues with a more street-level African American or Latino is not something these guys could do. You know, even when we went into schools that had classes that were mixed, where you'd have African Americans and Latinos, the strain was there, in terms of how—how people talked, you know? How you presented and so on, the language you used, the style that you used, and so on." Casal's description of the class and race limits of MASV's work with boys reveals his unique point of view, his knowledge grounded in different experiences from those of most of the other MASV men, reflecting what sociologist Patricia Hill Collins called an "outsider-within" perspective on the group's possibilities and limitations:[27]

I mean, if you walk into a Chicano barrio or a hardcore African American ghetto, their stylistic ways of interacting with each other are, you know, rooted in the realities of the code of the street, and it's a harsher way of being in lots of ways, you know, that code. So guys like—you know, I love these guys, but,

I mean Chris and Larry and so on, they're soft, you know? They're soft guys. That's a good, wonderful thing, you know? They're not guys who could survive in that environment very well, you know? And that's who you are. It comes across. And so if you're trying to talk with, you know, even a working-class white guy or a black or brown person who's, you know, more into the realities of the street, people are not going to—they're gonna tune you out for the most part, you know? And so it becomes laughable, more laughable.

Rather than pull entirely away from MASV, Casal strategized how he might stretch and educate the men in the group. He had worked in state prisons and mental institutions, had produced a radio documentary called *Child Sexual Abuse, the Crime of Ordinary Men,* and had a continuing connection with Atascadero State Prison, where many of the state's convicted sex offenders were incarcerated. In 1980, Casal decided to arrange for visits to the prison with some of the MASV men. The official reason to visit the prison was research: the group needed to learn about what motivated sexual assault, so they could more effectively prevent it. But Casal had a second surreptitious motivation: he hoped that the visits to the prison would serve as a kind of shock treatment that might in some ways toughen up the "soft men" of MASV as they listened to stories from men who had done "horrendous stuff." Casal hoped also that while looking into these men's eyes, the men of MASV would learn more about their own class- and race-biased stereotypes of rapists or child abusers, seeing and identifying with the incarcerated men's humanity:

Here you sit around in these circles of guys that did—some, more mild stuff, but other people just horrendous stuff. And they seemed pretty normal for the most part, you know? And I think I knew that before we went down there. For the group, I said "Man you're going to be surprised, who you're gonna see there." I think it was very eye opening for these guys—these more sensitive guys, who were, you know, genuinely trying to look at themselves and assess who they are and what their attitudes toward women were and so on. To see the other side of it and see guys who had really done some things, and I think people walked out of there realizing that—'cause when we would ask people, when you got down to the core, you know, what's going on there? You know, particularly when you're dealing with kids, little kids. "How did you sexually abuse a child, you know, a three-year-old, a four-year-old?" And they would consistently say that they were looking for love, I mean, really it boiled down to—they said it in different ways, but in essence that was it, you know? In a sense, they're not talking about *sexual* stuff, they were just looking for like this human contact, but they did it in this abuse way. You know?

And so it—I remember it being very impactful for everybody to go and sit there for a couple days in these circles with guys.

Allan Creighton was one of the MASV men who participated in the Atascadero Prison visits. A white man of middle-class origin who had done several years of graduate work in philosophy, Creighton certainly experienced at Atascadero the shock of recognition that Casal hoped he would.

> [We] went into the prison in the morning. The guards open up, vacuum room, the air pushes out, door closes behind you, locks, then the next door opens [laughs]. And we're going in to see—I'm not even sure what horrible names I probably had internally in mind for the, basically the *sexual predators* we were gonna see. And walked in and it was an open ward and the counselor said, "Here's a guy you want to meet." You know, "Here's a guy standing right here you want to meet," but internally I was freezing as I turned around and looked into the face of somebody who looked like my sister's boyfriend. Namely, a regular guy. Just a regular guy. And really nice guy, that's the thing—nice guys.

Sitting and talking with sex offenders, for Creighton, humanized these men in ways that would affect his prevention work for years to come. He and other MASV men became more aware that sex offenders were not "other" men—men strictly of the lower classes or of marginalized racial groups. Instead, the Atascadero visits complicated and deepened their views, partly in ways that Santiago Casal had hoped they would, although not so much that the middle-class and white basis of MASV could be fully transcended.

THE FEMINIST SEX WARS

What many dubbed "the sexual revolution" exploded in the 1960s. Operating on many levels—scientific and medical (most notably the sex research of Masters and Johnson), print media (most visibly *Playboy* magazine and its competitors), popular music (rock and roll's shift from romantic love toward overt expressions of sexual desire), and Hollywood (a dramatic relaxation of depictions of nudity and sexuality in popular film)—the culture as a whole was experiencing an opening up of sexual discourse and expression. For many young people of the era, the cultural turn against sexual repression was summed up simply in the slogan, "If it feels good, do it."

The ascendant women's liberation movement in the mid-1960s echoed this ethos of sexual liberation, with a feminist slant. Women's consciousness-raising groups focused on freeing women of sexual repression and enhancing women's sexual pleasure, many of them reading and discussing feminist writer Ann Koedt's influential 1968 essay "The Myth of the Vaginal Orgasm," and in turn celebrating the liberation of the clitoral orgasm.[28] Feminist-oriented popular literature, such as Erica Jong's top-selling novel *Fear of Flying*, celebrated women as empowered sexual subjects.[29] In short, from its outset, sexual liberation was a central tenet of women's liberation.

By the early 1970s, this view had begun to shift. As awareness of rape deepened to include an understanding of what came to be called "date rape" and "spousal rape," and as radical feminist women became increasingly disillusioned with the male-dominated New Left—in part because many male leaders tended to treat women in the movement as subordinated sex objects—feminist articulations of enhancing women's pleasure faded in favor of increased emphasis on the dangers of sexuality for women. Sexual Liberation—especially in its commercial outlets like *Playboy* magazine—was increasingly criticized as a movement that, under the guise of "liberation," enhanced men's pleasure by expanding the sexual exploitation of women. Emergent feminist theories argued that men's domination—especially sexual domination—of women's bodies was the foundation of patriarchy. Rather than seeing a rapist as a deviant, a crazy man, a stranger who jumps out of the bushes to attack a woman, the rapist was recast as everyman, a man expressing in a more extreme way the very same sexual objectification and bodily domination of women that is at the heart of "normal" patriarchal heterosexual relations. In 1971, feminist writer and activist Susan Griffin summed this up, calling rape "the All-American crime," and adding that "if the professional rapist is to be separated from the average dominant heterosexual [male], it may be mainly a quantitative difference."[30]

No feminist ever claimed that all men rape women (a false charge frequently aimed at Andrea Dworkin, for instance), but increasingly feminists asserted that all men benefit from the terror inflicted on women by a rape culture. As Brownmiller wrote in *Against Our Will*, rape "is nothing more or less than a conscious process of intimidation by which *all men* keep *all women* in a state of fear."[31] As rape, sexual harassment, and domestic violence were reframed less as acts of individual deviance and more as extreme expressions of normal patriarchal treatment of women, the work of antiviolence organizing became increasingly politicized. Simultaneously, the issue of pornography moved to the center of the antiviolence feminist agenda. Sexual objectification of women in the media, exemplified in its foundational and ugliest forms in pornography, was viewed as the lynchpin of patriarchy, and thus the central issue on which to focus political activism. Activists like Dworkin, Catherine MacKinnon, and others pressed a line of thinking that pornography, rather than merely "representing" women's violent subjugation, *is* violence against women. Feminist writer and leader Robin Morgan summed up this causal formula: "Rape is the perfected act of male sexuality in a patriarchal culture—it is the ultimate metaphor for domination, violence, subjugation and possession. . . . Pornography is the theory, and rape the practice."[32]

For the ascendant antipornography feminists, pornography was cast as the "central contradiction" of patriarchy. Activism that aimed to stop pornography, therefore, *was* activism to stop violence against women. It is no accident that San Francisco's first Take Back the Night marches in the late 1970s paraded directly into heart of the city's commercial sex district. By 1980, swelling to a membership of roughly a thousand women, WAVPM was the largest and most publicly visible organization of antiviolence activists in the Bay Area.

Contrary to current popular caricatures of 1980s feminism, not all feminists had jumped on the antipornography bandwagon, abandoning sexual liberation. By the mid-1970s, sex workers had begun to organize in groups like COYOTE,[33] not only asserting their rights as workers but also contesting feminist views of them as disempowered objects of men's control. Some lesbians joined with gay men to oppose antipornography efforts, arguing that open sexual expression, especially in gay and lesbian media, had been central to their own coming-out processes. And feminists of various stripes—high-profile scholar-activists like Kate Ellis, Jessica Benjamin, Gayle Rubin, Ellen Willis, and Deirdre English, joined by younger scholars like Alice Echols—called for debates within feminism about the "pleasure and danger" continuum of women's sexuality.[34] Fearful that, coupled with the emergent antisex Christian Right, feminist antipornography organizing would help to usher in a new era of sexual repression—especially of women, gay men, and lesbians—and observing that not all commercial pornography is violent, feminist sex radicals argued that the most liberatory move would be for women to take the lead in *expanding* forms and expressions of sexual desire.[35] Some "prosex feminists" began to produce their own "feminist erotica."

Despite these countervoices, the most visible feminist activism from the end of the 1970s through the mid-1980s was the antipornography movement, increasingly symbolized in Dworkin's passionate public oratory.

Feminist scholar Gayle Rubin lamented, "With little debate, antiporn ideas became a coercive dogma and a premature orthodoxy . . . a dangerous, costly and tragic mistake," and a "misguided crusade" with "potentially disastrous consequences."[36] But Dworkin and a growing movement of activists saw the realm of sexuality as a dangerous war zone, and they viewed the antipornography movement as a battle for the very survival of women. From this point of view, those who sought debate about sex work or pornography as complex and contradictory realms of pleasure and danger, of power and desire, were thus not true feminists. Though it is possible, as feminist cultural critic Alice Echols suggests, that leaders like Dworkin and MacKinnon saw their antipornography movement as "a calculated attempt to unify and fortify a movement seriously divided by issues of race, class, and sexual preference and badly demoralized by the antifeminist backlash,"[37] it seems in retrospect that the feminist sex wars drove the wedge that ultimately split the movement wide open. It is in the context of this fissuring of the women's movement that men's profeminist activism emerged.

Allies in a National War

Many profeminist men were inspired by Andrea Dworkin, but she was not an uncritical booster of the incipient men's movement. She was invited to deliver a keynote address to the 1983 Midwest Men's Conference, a regional gathering of profeminist men in St. Paul, Minnesota. Similar to like-minded men nationally, the five hundred men who attended the conference were trying to build a coalition of new sorts of men—gentle, nonviolent, non-homophobic, loving, and committed to peace and equality. Their meeting was punctuated by group hugs, open expressions of emotion, and collective music led by profeminist troubadour Geoff Morgan. Dworkin parachuted in and out, offering no words of celebration for the soft and gentle new man, instead laying down a blistering critique of how progressive men's therapeutic focus on their own guilt and pain kept them from taking action:

> Hiding behind the guilt, that's my favorite. I love that one. Oh, it's horrible, yes, and I'm so sorry. You have the time to feel guilty. We don't have the time to feel guilty . . . we women. We don't have forever. Some of us don't have another week or another day to take time for you to discuss whatever will enable you to go out in those streets and do something. We are very close to death. All women are. And we are very close to rape and we are very close to beating. We are inside a system of humiliation from which there is no escape for us.[38]

Dworkin ended her speech with a call to arms for the men to step up and join with women as allies in a war: "I want to see this men's movement make a commitment to ending rape. . . . I want to see you use those legendary bodies and that legendary strength and that legendary courage and the tenderness you say you have in behalf of women; and that means against the rapists, against the pimps, and against the pornographers. It means something more than a personal renunciation. It means a systematic, political, active, public attack. And there has been very little of that."[39]

Although a few men reacted negatively to Dworkin's speech, most of the men in the audience were inspired. Many, especially those in the growing antiviolence men's coalition—and including most of the men of this generation whom we interviewed—believed at the time that Dworkin's critical analysis of the men's movement was spot-on, that a therapeutic focus on men's pain was not only self-indulgent but, worse, kept the men from diving into crucially important public work, using their positions as men to stop rape.

Even though a twin focus on men's privileges and the costs of masculinity were clearly joined in feminist theory, the political context of the 1970s made it increasingly difficult to tackle both simultaneously, and Dworkin had driven a wedge that further separated these two principles. By the late 1970s, the incipient national "men's liberation movement" had already begun to polarize around the split between those who focused on personal and therapeutic work with men and those who focused more on opposing men's institutional power and privilege over women. A contingent of men who emphasized the costs of masculinity drifted toward what would eventually in the 1980s devolve into an antifeminist men's rights movement. The more politically radical end of the 1970s spectrum, which eventually would define itself as a profeminist (or antisexist) men's movement, struggled initially to fight simultaneously against both the costs of masculinity and men's power and privileges: feminism called for men to relinquish their traditional power over women, but it promised that in the process men would become healthier, happier, and more fully human.[40] The men in MASV and RAVEN identified with this politically radical approach—working to equalize power with women in their personal and public lives, while retaining a perspective that was sensitive to boys' and men's (including their own) emotional needs.

National networks of antiviolence activists continued to grow, fueled largely by a growing number of local groups of men who, like MASV in the Bay Area, Emerge in Boston, and RAVEN in St. Louis, and Men Against Pornography in New York City, were working with boys and men to stop violence against women. A central question for these men was how to be accountable allies with feminist women. Many agreed that as members of the privileged sex it was important to follow women's leadership. Don Conway-Long says that when he and Craig Norberg-Bohm started to organize locally around domestic violence prevention in St. Louis, and then nationally, they knew that it was important to learn from the women.

> When the shelters begin popping up, we stayed very closely related to them. When we did training, we brought women from all those areas to train the new men, it was very very important for us to make sure this was a fundamental part of what we did. We also knew that we needed to seek women's leadership and seek women's supervision and eventually pay women to come in and supervise the peer counselors or, you know, just looking at their work and how they went about their work and making sure that this was fine from the perspective of battered women's advocates.

This idea of being directly accountable to women was a core principle of profeminist men's organizing. When Santiago Casal produced a live call-in radio show with feminist fat liberation activist Judy Freespirit, he was nervous in advance as to whether he could conduct the show in a responsible way. "I thought to myself—Judy Freespirit was this enormous woman, right?—If we do this show and Judy Freespirit says something to me you know, that this is good, that you did a good job, that would be my criteria for success. I was trying to be responsible, you know, to that movement. So we aired the show, calls were coming in like crazy because men are really stimulated, and at the end of that, she looked over, she put her hand on my hand and she said, 'Good job'." It was this sort of validation from women that profeminist men consistently sought. And although most, in retrospect, still see this as a principled political position of accountability for male profeminist allies, some like antirape activist Tim Beneke see it also as a deeply rooted psychological need: "There's a lot of pleasing-mommy stuff, which [we] talked about in 1981. Just wanted to please women and be good boys. It was motivating people, and that's part of my motivation."

A MASV Effort

Whether following women's leadership was a principled political position, a deep psychological need, or some combination of both, in the context of the feminist sex wars the question of *to which women to be accountable* became more politicized. When it came to stopping rape, it was the feminist antipornography movement that was most vocal, was best organized, and seemed to hold the moral high ground. Unlike many men who were put off by what they saw as the "anti-male" rhetoric of radical feminists, many profeminist men across the nation were moved by the passionate moral outrage of feminist antipornography national leaders, and inspired by the brave activism of local antipornography women's groups. The men of MASV threw their lot in with the antipornography feminists. They provided support for women's protests and received training from the women as they prepared their own antiviolence curriculum—mainly, a slideshow that depicted sexist and violent portrayals of women in mass media—to take into schools and the community. "We took our lead from them," Chris Norton says of MASV's relationship to WAVPM. "We basically just took their analysis and presented it." But in retrospect, Norton says, "You know, I wonder if the guys kind of felt like—well, you know, it didn't, it didn't feel like it was coming from our core, you know, from who we were, other than maybe from our guilt."

Fellow MASV member Chris Anderegg has similar misgivings: "In retrospect, I think that focusing on pornography was a mistake." When it came to outreach into places like public high schools, it made for presentations to which most young men likely turned a deaf ear. The focus on porn, in particular, was a tough sell for talking with boys and young men. Allan Creighton recalls a slideshow discussion he led for a class at Berkeley High School. "We had a great time, we felt, 'Gee, we're doing great here.'" But then he and his MASV co-presenter stepped outside the classroom and observed two boys from that very class physically attacking a girl. "And, you know, we had to say, 'What are we doing?'"

Tim Beneke says that at the time he was sympathetic to the work MASV was doing, but he thought the focus on porn was "very naïve," and the orthodox position that porn turned women into disempowered objects was "awful, intellectually." In his view, conventional *Playboy* porn "was clearly designed to make masturbation into a proud experience. And it was clearly meant to speak to the male condition of shame." If the focus is to be on porn, then why not, in the words of Mark Stevens, take an approach that "offered some compassion for us to talk with guys about pornography without pointing fingers and saying, 'You use pornography, you're a bad, awful person.' It's more like, 'What has that taught you? How has that limited your ability on some level to make some connections with women?'" But the politicized context, and the MASV men's commitment to adopting WAVPM's perspective, pushed to the background the men's understanding of male vulnerability or pain, instead foregrounding male shame and guilt, and a message that viewing porn was nothing less than complicity with rape.

In retrospect, some MASV men believe that their work in public schools did some good; others, like Chris Norton, believe that the slideshows they presented to boys were too often more a projection of their own feminist guilt and need for approval from feminist women than they were a successful attempt to create critical dialogue with boys and young men.

> Back then, it was more sort of like, you know, "men are bad." Andrea Dworkin told us this: we know men are bad, *we* are bad, we're gonna go and tell the high school boys that *they're* bad too, for looking at pornography, and that pornography's gonna make them badder than they already are. There wasn't—I think there's gotta be a *positive vision*. I mean, you don't want to be blind to the bad stuff that goes on, but there has to be kind of some upside for doing this, 'cause I don't think otherwise people are gonna really pay any attention or wanna listen to you.

Larry Mandella reflects on another dimension of the limitations of MASV's antipornography focus:

> I think one of the difficulties during this whole period for me in retrospect was that when men and women are working on these kinds of issues as allies in projects, where it got difficult for me is when the . . . how do I put this?—when the emotions of these issues spilled over and made it harder to remain allies when, when I as a man felt attacked, you know, for being male. . . . What was really kind of in my gut level was I kept feeling and knowing that we needed to do this work from a place of not attacking men, but of supporting them to look at the ways that they had been hurt through sexism, look at the ways in which they were hurting people through sexist actions and realize that it was completely in men's interest to be paying attention to this issue. . . . Sometimes the rhetoric of the movement sounded like it was only about, um, how do I say this?—It didn't take that into account.

The foregrounding of male complicity and guilt also made for rough going within MASV's internal group work.[41] Chris Norton recalls, "We in MASV were more identified with the Dworkin [antipornography feminists]—we, again because of the political nature, because of, you know, wanting to be on the right side—and maybe because of guilt that we were feeling, about our own, you know, attraction to women . . . So it became easier to identify with someone who says, 'Ah, it's all—you're totally bad, you know, what you want to do with women is totally bad'." But Norton also recalls that within the group, "there was some push-back too. I think some of the people, some of the guys would say, you know, 'This is a little ridiculous,' or, 'This is going too far'." Indeed, Santiago Casal says, "Yeah there were a lot [of] little schisms in the group. A lot of it had to do with—with militancy. You know, how militant are you? Some guys were just really, you know, doctrinaire—correct line and all this. So there was—yeah there was tensions."

Robert Allen Feinglass, in his master's thesis on MASV, pointed to the group's "Andrea Dworkin debate" as a "climactic episode" that accelerated the group's demise.[42] Some in the group wanted to discuss Dworkin's 1976 article "Why So-Called Radical Men Love and Need Pornography,"[43] a piece that begins with the claim, "Men love death." Some saw Dworkin's ideas as correct, or at least as important to discuss, while others were insulted and hostile to her claims. The group was "sharply divided from the start," according to Feinglass, on whether even to discuss the article. Greg Ross recalls that MASV's internal political debates about sex and pornography exacerbated his resurgent PTSD:

> MASV got untenable for me, I mean, because what started to happen in MASV was what had happened to me before in Vietnam Veterans Against the War. The communist faction was arguing with the socialist faction, the feminist faction—so what's the primary contradiction? It's sexism, no it's racism, classism, or stupidity-ism, I don't [laughs]. And I just had no patience for any of it, any of it, by then it was all these polemics . . . and I said, "Look, I'm just not going to do it, the rest of these polite, middle-class assholes are gonna, but I'm getting up and I'm leaving."

Some men distanced themselves from the group, others bailed out altogether, and, in Feinglass's words, "the pace of defections accelerated."[44] In November 1980, the group met for the final time and "retired" the MASV name.

All the former MASV men we interviewed saw their work during that short time frame as a crucially important life-shaping experience. And all of them echoed Larry Mandella's words that he was "very proud of what we did." Some of them left profeminist violence prevention altogether. Chris Norton turned passionately to Central America support work, during the U.S. interventions in El Salvador. Greg Ross got trained as an acupuncturist and developed a career in helping veterans and addicts. Others continued in therapeutically oriented men's groups. A few years later, when Larry Mandella became a father, he turned to organizing fathers' support groups. Chris Anderegg realized he was "a finance guy" and developed a successful career as a director of finance for a string of organizations, including the Marin Abused Women's Services, a youth advocate organization in San Francisco, and the Rape Crisis Center in San Pablo. Clearly, even for men who left violence prevention organizing, their work with MASV created a foundation and template for their future work.

But a few of the MASV men continued with profeminist antiviolence work, joining or starting other organizations in the eighties, the nineties, and beyond. And some groups, like RAVEN, not only survived the period of the feminist sex wars but also grew and continue to thrive today. What was different about them?

SURVIVING THE 1980S, PREFIGURING THE 1990S

In closing this chapter, we focus briefly on three stories of survival that signal the antiviolence formations of subsequent decades: RAVEN in St. Louis, two MASV men who have spent their adult lives in gender-based violence prevention work, and psychologist Mark Stevens, whose 1970s and 1980s profeminist violence prevention activism still shapes his work as a campus psychologist.

RAVEN, as we have seen, was started at almost exactly the same time as MASV, by men from similar backgrounds in a similar political context. However, RAVEN did not crumble under the tensions that eventually broke MASV. The most obvious difference was that, from the start, RAVEN focused much more on domestic violence, while MASV focused its public organizing almost exclusively on sexual assault prevention. The men of RAVEN—the core members of which are shown in Figure 2.3—were every

Figure 2.3
Don Conway-Long, Craig Norberg-Bohm, Mick Addison-Lamb, and Mark Benson-Robinson, core members of Rape And Violence Ends Now (RAVEN), St. Louis, Missouri, circa 1980.
Reprinted by permission of Don Conway-Long

bit as immersed in politicized debates about men and feminism as their Bay Area counterparts. But RAVEN's focus on domestic violence nudged them away from the turbulent vortex of the caustic feminist wars about men and pornography that eventually brought MASV down. Concerning the feminist sex wars, Don Conway-Long says RAVEN respected the anti-pornography feminists; however,

> I don't think we ever had a consistent position, so to speak, on that within RAVEN because we had diversity within the group on how we should approach these questions. . . . We would do work and be supportive of the anti-porn events, certainly we did childcare and other kinds of support for Take Back the Night, from the very beginning, I think our first one was '81. We were there as supporters, we did not march in St. Louis, like in other places, we provided support activities. So we distributed fliers along the route, we did the childcare for the women, we guarded the site when they were gone, things like that. We did a lot of supportive work without—trying not to pick sides on the differ- ences among the women and doing our best to kind of figure out the theoretical pieces without letting it take us apart. . . . I think we managed to get through that particular quagmire there, it is one that I know has destroyed some groups.

RAVEN's survival was also due to the group's ability to become institu- tionalized in the community—establishing a physical space for its work, sources of funding, and community legitimacy. As feminist activism shifted the legal system's response to domestic violence, public funds began to flow through the courts to RAVEN, as the place to send men who had committed acts of family violence. Little such funding existed in the 1980s for men who sought to do rape prevention.

In 1977, twenty-three-year-old psychology grad student Mark Stevens had a "feminist epiphany" and joined a men's consciousness-raising group in San Diego. Six years later, employed as a campus psychologist, Stevens joined with the Women's Center at Ohio State University to put together a curriculum to engage college men in "how our training in masculinity con- tributed to the rape culture." His description of these efforts reveals the fine line he was walking in creating a curriculum that linked the privileges and costs of masculinity. At a very concrete level, he was pressed by the need to be accountable to feminist women's leadership, while also creating a curriculum that would have some appeal to young men.

> We knew that we were kind of in a vulnerable position because the Women's Center and many of the women who kind of knew what we were doing—we didn't have carte blanche. We knew that we were going to be held accountable

for what we presented to guys, because the worst thing that could have happened was [for] us to present material that would have looked like we were blaming women, um, for the rape. And, not being, I'm going to put this in quotes: "not being political enough." At that point with feminism, it was really important to see that the rape culture was connected to male privilege. This was a systemic kind of issue—somewhat Susan Brownmiller's work, Andrea Dworkin's work and [there were] some very strong feminists at the Women's Center at that time.

Unlike the men of MASV, Stevens was able to successfully navigate these tensions, even use them creatively to develop a curriculum that was widely adopted by others in subsequent years. Although he was every bit as immersed in the corrosive politics of the time as were the men of MASV—after all, he had served as chair of the National Organization for Men Against Sexism (NOMAS) and as co-chair of the organization's Ending Men's Violence Task Group in the mid-1980s, a time of particular political turbulence—Stevens was perhaps at least partly insulated by his professional position and status as a university psychologist.

But even without such professional insulation, a few of the MASV men—most notably Allan Creighton and Paul Kivel—continued after the dissolution, forming new groups in the 1980s and 1990s that worked with boys and men to prevent violence. What was it about Creighton and Kivel that allowed them not only to survive the messy and painful dissolution of MASV but to emerge with an intact sense of optimism and commitment to being feminist allies in stopping gender-based violence? One key experience Kivel and Creighton point to during the early 1980s is their immersion in community antiracism work. Both of them participated in "unlearning racism" workshops organized by community activist Ricki Sherover Marcuse, and eventually they volunteered for several summers in the "Unlearning Everything" progressive summer camps. Held with 120 kids equally divided by race, gender, and economic background, the camps consciously built a community committed to confronting racism, sexism, classism, homophobia, and ageism.

Though Kivel and Creighton always agreed with the MASV principle that men's profeminist work needed to be done from a position of accountability, they came to conclude, in Kivel's words, that "we had a very simple understanding of accountability in the early days, right? You do what you're told [laughs]." But the antiracism work exposed them to diverse voices and forms of feminism, and "We paid a lot of attention to what women of color were writing about and saying about these issues. . . . And then we stopped to think, 'what does it mean to be accountable?' Of course we operated as one of only a couple of men's organizations in this area with, you know, there were probably fifty women's organizations between the shelters, and rape prevention, and child sexual assault, and all the other things going on—who do you be accountable to? And on what basis?"

Kivel and Creighton formed the Oakland Men's Project in 1980 "to be multi-racial in a conscious and intentional way." The texts they were reading by feminist women of color, and the lessons they were learning from the men of color in OMP, resonated with what they came to see as the limits, or even failures, of their earlier public work with boys in schools.

> We started going into schools with a pretty simple message: you're a young man, you're hitting your girlfriend, stop it [laughs] . . . and the young men weren't all that responsive, not surprisingly, I mean they were pretty direct, and some of them were very articulate, they said, you know, "Sure, we hit our girlfriends sometimes, but there's a lot of violence in our lives, and if you really want to help us sort out the violence, there's gangs, and fights and gay bashing and hate crimes and there's all this level of interpersonal violence, including violence in our families, and the dating violence is just a piece of it." And the other message that especially the young men of color were pretty clear about was that it's not just the interpersonal violence you know, look at the state of our schools, look at the police brutality, we're being hurt, not only harassed but being beaten up by the police all the time . . . you know, if you're serious about helping us figure out the violence, there's all these institutional levels and all these complex interpersonal levels so, so I think that that's—the group began to sort itself out at that point some. And we really had to go back to the drawing boards.

This reassessment of men's violence against women as part of a larger web of violence is, as we will see, part of what sparked the next generation of men's activism. And clearly, for Kivel and Creighton, it was the ability to see violence "intersectionally"—as a product of the intersections of gender, race, and class—that pushed them to develop a deeper sense of what it meant to be accountable allies. Their deepening sensibilities about race became a resource for them in navigating the feminist sex wars and other challenges built in to being profeminist men. They became better able to focus on how boys and men—particularly racially marginalized boys and men—are more likely to pay higher "costs of masculinity," while having less access to privilege. Seen intersectionally, "male privilege" was revealed to them to be mostly white-male, middle-class-male, heterosexual-male privilege. Even though girls and women are still the primary victims of men's sexual and domestic violence, boys and men—particularly those of marginalized and subordinated racial, class, and sexual groups—are vulnerable to emotional and physical violence. In subsequent years this observation was adopted and integrated into gender-based violence prevention curricula.

CONCLUSION

In the 1970s and early 1980s, feminism created a context in which some men—especially men with progressive political views, personal experiences with violence, and positive interactions with feminist women—were inspired to band together to work with boys and young men to prevent rape and domestic violence. This antiviolence work was fraught with strains and tensions: the contradiction built into the project of "men and feminism"; the ways race and class differences created fissures in profeminist men's groups; and as the women's movement itself fragmented around the feminist sex wars, the treacherous challenges that faced men who sought to be accountable to the women's movement in their profeminist work.

Some groups, like the Bay Area's MASV, eventually broke down under these tensions, with members leaving for other sorts of progressive work, and others becoming leaders in the development of new forms of antiviolence curricula and forms of organizing that blossomed in the following decade. Other groups, like RAVEN in St. Louis, successfully navigated the tensions of the early 1980s, and as we will see in the next chapter, helped to pave the way toward institutionalization of men's community-based antiviolence work. Still others—individuals like Mark Stevens—pioneered the transformation of psychology and other helping professions, developing curricula, therapeutic interventions, and national networks of professionals that would begin to change the face of college campuses. In the 1990s and 2000s, a new generation of men joined with these veterans of the profeminist men's movement, helping to reshape the terrain of antiviolence work, navigating some of the same tensions as their predecessors, as well as some new ones.

CHAPTER 3

Digging In: The Bridge Cohort, Mid-1980s to 1990s

Wielding a rifle and a hunting knife, a young man marched into an engineering classroom at the University of Montreal on December 6, 1989, and ordered the men out of the room. Claiming he was "fighting feminism," he began to fire away at the women. Within twenty minutes, he murdered fourteen women, wounded another ten women and four men, and fatally shot himself. The "Montreal Massacre" was quickly viewed in Canada as a "national trauma," and feminists seized the moment, drawing public attention to misogynist antifeminism and the ubiquity of violence against women.[1]

Michael Kaufman, thirty-eight years old at the time of the Montreal Massacre, had roots in left-wing and student movement politics in the 1970s and in those years had become involved with "emerging men's networks, both in the States and in Canada, working with men's groups and profeminist men's movements." As a political scientist he was instrumental in the late 1980s in launching the feminist study of men and masculinities.[2] The year before the Montreal Massacre, he organized a network of men in support of abortion rights, "a little one-shot thing called Men for Women's Choice," that landed his name on mass media Rolodexes as a man who speaks about "women's issues." So when he was invited to join two feminist women on national television in the aftermath of the Massacre, he agreed to do so but felt like "a total neophyte." Though he had done some reading and some writing about violence against women, he realizes in retrospect, "I really didn't have a clue." But he began to learn quickly.

The Massacre of Montreal was a galvanizing moment in Canada, and I've never seen a social discussion change overnight, I've *never* seen anything like this, it was just like—if you watch water suddenly become ice, it was *that* profound . . . basically, twenty years of work by the women's movement galvanized overnight. And literally by the next day, by Friday, the discussions all across the country, including in our Parliament, were about violence against women. Like literally in one day. The women's movement had been sort of turning the soil, turning the soil, turning the soil, [so] that type of *huge* public impact on these issues was just ripe.

But the talk went only so far. A year later, following a series of rapes in Toronto, feminist women turned to their male allies and asked them, "What are you guys doing?" Kaufman took up the challenge, thinking, "Let's do something more, something that's not just a few well-meaning good men making a public statement, but let's try to do something that would allow the majority of men to have a voice—to have a means to speak out against violence against women." Along with colleagues, Kaufman launched the White Ribbon Campaign in 1991, convincing thousands of Canadian men—including members of Parliament, high-profile athletes, and other celebrities—to wear a white ribbon on their lapel on the anniversary of the Massacre, symbolizing their commitment to stopping violence against women.[3]

Over the next couple of years, Kaufman left his position as a university professor and joined with others to build White Ribbon as an organization dedicated to sustaining men's commitment to stop violence against women beyond annual symbolic statements of support. By 1992 the campaign was operating out of some donated office space as a "very low budget organization" with "a lot of volunteers coming through the doors, cutting ribbons—at that time we cut our own ribbons—by the thousands." One day, a man walked through the door and explained to Kaufman that as a religious leader he saw value in getting Christian men involved in the White Ribbon Campaign, but he was also committed to a prolife position. From his point of view, it would be consistent for White Ribbon to oppose abortion as a form of violence. Kaufman recalls this as "a pivotal moment" in determining what sort of organization White Ribbon would become:

I said I was real active in the prochoice movement, and so we sort of looked at each other, and it was for me a pivotal moment. . . . The typical thing to do in a progressive movement was at that point for me to look at him and say, "Boy we're on the opposite side of the fence on a *very* big feminist issue, and a big moral issue, and an issue that is really important. There's no way we can work together." But what really struck me at that point was, I thought, OK, if I say, you know, "There's no space in White Ribbon for someone like you," what I'm saying is that 20 percent of men in Canada—maybe a bit more, who were not prochoice—that'd be saying that the whole Catholic establishment, a network of Catholic public schools, that White Ribbon would not have a place in those schools.

Kaufman pondered his dilemma in light of his experience in the 1970s and 1980s in progressive social movements—years during which he saw how dogmatic infighting over the "correct" political line in the environmental movement, the student movement, and the women's movement had resulted in "a real marginalization, and I was very concerned about what we on the left or in progressive movements had done wrong, and ways that we had perhaps isolated ourselves." He decided on the spot that White Ribbon would not repeat those errors.

> So I basically said to him, "Well listen, I've been active in the pro-choice movement, but could we agree to the following: do we both agree that women should not be beat up by their husbands?" He said, "Yes." And I said, "Do we both agree that women shouldn't be sexually assaulted by a boyfriend, husband, stranger?" "Yes." "Do we agree that women shouldn't be sexually harassed at work? Do we agree that women shouldn't be stalked?" You know, just went through this whole litany of forms of violence against women. And I just said, "So listen, there's a lot that we agree on, that are critical. Why don't we agree to disagree on the issue of abortion, but when it comes to a whole range of forms of violence against women, we can work together."

The result was the building of a broad White Ribbon coalition in Canada, the template for which has since spread to sixty nations. And a key to White Ribbon's success in becoming the world's largest and best-known effort by men to stop violence against women was Kaufman's early strategic decision "that White Ribbon should not be, you know, the revolutionary party that had its position on everything, but was a campaign. And a campaign that had this, as the phrase now goes, 'Big Tent', that it had a place for men across the social and political spectrum . . . to develop a unified men's voice against men's violence against women."

The story of the White Ribbon Campaign's early years introduces several of the main themes of this chapter. By the end of the 1980s the feminist movement's "turning the soil" for two decades had created fertile ground for men's growing involvement in stopping violence against women. However, feminism's internal fragmentation and political marginalization also made clear the limits of a self-defined "revolutionary" social movement. In this context, the strategic decision that Kaufman made in 1992—to shape White Ribbon pragmatically as a broadly popular "campaign" focused on one issue, rather than a deeply political "revolutionary party"—mirrored the strategies other activists were deploying during this "postmovement"[4] transitional period in feminist antiviolence work. And, we will show, these strategies reflect a certain maturation of antiviolence activists' understanding of "being in it for the long haul"; during this transitional period, we see middle-aged activists like Michael Kaufman in Canada and several others in the United States digging in, starting to create organizational structures they hoped would sustain and broaden the work. Some veteran activists—like Allan Creighton and Paul Kivel in the San Francisco Bay Area and Don Conway-Long and Craig Norberg-Bohm in St. Louis—founded community-based nonprofits, linked with women's antirape or domestic violence organizations. Others like Mark Stevens, in Columbus and Los Angeles, created antiviolence specialties within university counseling centers and women's centers and began shaping national networks of antiviolence professionals.

As veterans of 1970s and early 1980s antiviolence work shifted gears from movement-based activism to building organizational structures, a newer Bridge Cohort of men engaged with the work, men old enough to feel the fading reverberations of the previous decades of feminist movement activism but also young enough to have come of age during a time when feminist reforms in the law, politics, and academia and shifts in cultural attitudes about rape and domestic violence had altered the social terrain. These younger men of the Bridge Cohort (including seventeen of our interviewees[5] who fit in the "transitional period" identified in Figure 1.2) brought to the field fresh energy and ideas, in some ways less fettered by the corrosive internal debates that a decade earlier had hamstrung many of their older brothers. But these younger men's entry to the field also introduced new strains and tensions into the equation of men's work as profeminist allies, including grappling with what it means when antiviolence work is severed from a grassroots social movement and becomes a paid job.[6]

ANTIFEMINIST BACKLASH AND FEMINIST ORGANIZATION BUILDING

By the late 1980s, the splintering of the women's movement was widely evident. Perhaps, we can see in retrospect, the idea of a mass movement of women unified by their shared interests in ending patriarchal oppression always contained the seeds of its own dissolution, based as it was on what feminist scholar Maxine Baca Zinn and her colleagues in 1986 called the "false universalization" of white, middle-class women's experiences, interests, and strategies.[7] Moreover, as we saw in the previous chapter, the movement was deeply fissured by the "feminist sex wars," particularly over the wisdom of placing antipornography organizing at the center of feminist antiviolence efforts.

But feminism's challenges came not simply from within; the eventual decline of movement feminism was precipitated in large part by the broadside of antifeminism in politics, workplaces, and popular culture, so powerfully documented by Susan Faludi in her 1991 book *Backlash*.[8] There was also a determined backlash against feminist organizing against rape and domestic violence, starting as early as the late 1970s, emanating from the antifeminist men's rights movement. Organizations calling themselves "The Coalition of Free Men" and the "National Congress for Men" were claiming that men were the true victims of prostitution, pornography, dating rituals, sexist media conventions, divorce settlements, false rape accusations, sexual harassment, and even domestic violence. In their most extreme forms, men's rights agitators argued that feminist ideology and men's shame had combined to cover up massive numbers of men in families who were physically abused and murdered by women.[9]

The grain of truth in the claims of men's rights groups is that boys too are sometimes victims of sexual abuse, women do sometimes physically abuse their male spouses, men are sometimes sexually harassed in workplaces, and some men do get raped. But the numbers of men victimized by sexual harassment, sexual assault, and spousal violence are small in comparison with the numbers of women.[10] Men's rights groups, in their less extreme moments, seized on the silence about gender-based violence against boys and men to assert an empirically false symmetry: women and men, they argued, are equally victimized by family violence and by workplace sexual harassment.[11] As a result, they argued, women's shelters and other community resources devoted to helping women survivors of violence were discriminating against men.

Women's advocacy groups and their allies mostly withstood legal attacks on the still-fragile organizations they were building, but doing so robbed resources and energy that might otherwise have been spent in delivering services or expanding their base. What's more, the claims by men's rights groups of symmetrical victimization in family violence and workplace harassment took hold as a counterfeminist cultural discourse that still today challenges women's shelters and other support services for women.[12]

Men's rights groups were the tip of a much larger iceberg of antifeminist backlash, including organized opposition to abortion rights and a successful effort, culminating in 1982, to block the passage of the Equal Rights Amendment. As early as the start of the 1980s, leaders of the then-embryonic Christian Right such as Jerry Falwell and Phyllis Schlafly began to proclaim the death of feminism.[13] But such proclamations were wrong. By the end of the 1980s, rather than having disappeared, feminism was, in the words of sociologist Jo Reger, "everywhere and nowhere."[14] Although the mass feminist movement had fragmented and become less visible, and backlash had rendered the identity label "feminist" a dirty word for many younger women of the 1990s, most of these same younger women began statements with the preface "I'm not a feminist, but . . ." before stating their agreement with feminist values of equal pay for women's work, equality in childcare and housework, and opposition to gender-based violence. Many core feminist values had become mainstream cultural values that, by the start of the 1990s, were part of the air that young people, including many boys, were breathing.[15]

Moreover, seasoned feminist movement veterans of the 1980s may have left the streets, but they did not leave feminist organizing. Instead, they hunkered down to the hard but less visible work of organization building. Sociologist Patricia Yancey Martin, writing in 1990, observed that rather than disappearing during this time period, feminists had succeeded in creating not-for-profit organizations with mass memberships (e.g., the National Organization for Women or NOW), funded advocacy organizations (the National Abortion Rights Advocacy League or NARAL), and service organizations (rape crisis centers, women's shelters, health clinics). Without a doubt, this institutionalization of feminism introduced what sociologists Lisa Markowitz and Karen Rice call "paradoxes of professionalization": a diversion of focus and energies away from social change activism toward finding sustainable funding sources for service provision, and shifts away from democratic internal group processes toward hierarchic forms of organization.[16] Some veterans of the women's antiviolence movement such as Lois Ahrens, in Austin, Texas, in 1980, expressed alarm that the shift from what began as a radical feminist cooperative domestic violence community coalition to a bureaucratically organized service organization led by a "professional, liberal feminist" board ushered in a depoliticized structure that treated battered women as disempowered "clients" rather than as empowered equals in a mass movement.[17]

Feminist sociologists of the 1980s forged a nuanced view that tempered radical activists' fears of bureaucratic depoliticization and cooptation of grassroots feminism. Suzanne Staggenborg argued in 1988 that, rather than signaling an eclipse of the feminist movement, emergent professionalized "formalized social movement organizations . . . help maintain social movements when environmental conditions make mobilization difficult."[18] After all, by the late 1980s a good number of movement-based antiviolence efforts had struggled and withered under the pressure of antifeminist backlash and the strains of operating mostly with volunteer labor, collective decision-making processes, and small monetary donations. In this context, Martin argued in 1990 against movement purists who feared any diversion from grassroots organizing toward mainstreaming feminism in organizations as a form of patriarchal cooptation: "Feminist organizations . . . have survived for more than two decades despite a purported waning of the movement. . . . Even the most institutionalized feminist organization helps to perpetuate the women's movement through, at the very least, exploiting the institutional environment of scarce resources."[19]

As women began to professionalize and institutionalize their "downstream" work on sexual and domestic violence in the late 1980s and early 1990s, a trickle of the scarce resources devoted to this work was being directed to men's "upstream" violence prevention work. These men grappled upstream with the same dilemma facing the women downstream: how to create a broad, funded, and sustainable field of commitment and action in preventing violence against women, while at the same time retaining the feminist values and goals that had launched the movement in the first place.

DIGGING IN UPSTREAM

As we have seen, Rape and Violence Ends Now (RAVEN), a men's antiviolence organization in St. Louis, was created in 1978, the same year as MASV, its counterpart in Northern California's Bay Area. But RAVEN's eventual trajectory could not have been more different. Whereas by 1981 MASV had splintered and crumbled, RAVEN survived, grew, and continues to thrive today.

Three interrelated factors explain RAVEN's survival. First, as we saw in the previous chapter, while supporting feminist women's efforts in the community, the men of RAVEN managed to sidestep the divisive feminist sex wars of the 1980s by not taking sides in debates about pornography. Second, RAVEN members' relative insulation from the feminist sex wars was possible because, unlike MASV—whose major focus on preventing sexual violence virtually made it impossible for the group not to take a position on pornography—RAVEN focused mainly on preventing domestic violence, thus creating space within which members could remain agnostic about the feminist sex wars. Third (and directly linked to the second point), by the mid-1980s domestic violence prevention in the United States was beginning to be linked to a dollar flow from the legal system, a form of support that was not available for most rape crisis centers.[20]

While MASV members grew exhausted from countless hours of unpaid labor doing rape prevention work in the Bay Area, RAVEN was well positioned to become the main place in St. Louis where the courts sent convicted perpetrators of domestic violence for group therapy; this created a steady supply of clients, and a modest flow of dollars that helped to stabilize the organization. Still, Don Conway-Long explained, in RAVEN's early years there was little money, and everyone worked for no pay:

> All volunteer labor. We were never very good at getting money. And it was also the contradiction of, exactly whose money should we be taking? Because doesn't any money that we take get taken from the shelters? So that was always a problem, we had no idea how to get it. I mean, do you accept *Playboy* money for example? No way, even though they were willing to fund—there were some discussions about those things—no, we won't take it from an organization that actually produces violence against women, supports violence against women, at least serious objectification processes and sexualization.

RAVEN's work blossomed within the next few years to what Craig Norberg-Bohm described as "a pool of twenty, thirty men" whose volunteer work was supported on a shoestring. Eventually, there was enough money to pay a small stipend to the groups' coordinators: "Financially? There were fees charged for the program, and that float[ed] the boat. We wrote proposals and we got grants every so often of small amounts, but we weren't paying salaries. We were covering rent, insurance, lights, phone, and a stipend, so fees can cover that—sliding scale, so men who had good jobs paid more. It functioned off the generosity of the men who would volunteer."

RAVEN started with a small space in St. Louis World Community Center, later moving to what Conway-Long called "a big nice space . . . for a very good price" in a building owned by a RAVEN volunteer. And the group was very busy: "[It] took over so much of our energy, the DV [domestic violence] work—never-ending source of new men, never-ending source of new problems, working consistently." Even for two young men like Conway-Long and Norberg-Bohm, it was sometimes exhausting to be working essentially two jobs—one to pay their bills, and the other, RAVEN, taking up "incredible amounts of time." But they labored for the next decade, building RAVEN into a community institution that, in the words of Norberg-Bohm, "went from a living room to an office, over a couple-of-years period. We went from back-of-the-envelope to accounting and 501(c)(3) [nonprofit status] and fundraising. It went from, you know, strings to a little stronger than that."

RAVEN's story illustrates how, during the 1980s and into the 1990s, activists with their roots in a social movement sustained and broadened their work. First, they needed at least a small, reliable source of ongoing funds. Second, they needed a physical space within which to house an office and the work itself. And third, in order to sustain the funding, the space, and eventually some minimal pay for themselves, they legally defined their organization as a nonprofit, which eventuated a shift away from movement-based volunteerism to an organization led by salaried professionals increasingly concerned with fundraising.

A handful of former MASV members In the Bay Area followed similar trajectories, but in new organizations. Chris Anderegg found work that used his expertise in finance for a string of relatively young community nonprofits, including the Marin Abused Women's Services and the Rape Crisis Center in San Pablo. Allan Creighton and Paul Kivel more directly continued MASV's violence prevention with boys and men through the creation of their own nonprofit, the Oakland Men's Project (OMP). Even before MASV dissolved, Creighton had joined some men in San Francisco to establish Men Overcoming Violence (MOVE), an anti–domestic violence organization that was linking up with similar groups across the nation. "MOVE had a direct connection with Emerge [in Boston]," Creighton recalled, "and with Craig Norberg [and RAVEN] in Missouri and a number of other developing batterers programs around the country."

Following the demise of MASV, Paul Kivel, soon joined by Creighton, launched the OMP, a multiracial nonprofit aimed at educating and mobilizing boys and men to become active in building communities free of violence, sexism, and racism.[21] From the start, MOVE and OMP faced similar challenges to those faced by the RAVEN men in St. Louis, and by the White Ribbon Campaign's founders in Canada: how to build an organization that is in it for the long haul and that can sustain itself financially, while holding true to its feminist foundations. A good deal of this challenge concerned funding. Creighton explained: "OMP started with a small amount of money [from] Paul [Kivel's] mom. And we paid ourselves, you know, fifty dollars a week or something like that. At MOVE, there was no money, and then eventually there was ten dollars a week or fifteen dollars a week." Sustainable funding for these groups, Creighton explained, was an ongoing challenge, especially in terms of their commitments to support and complement, rather than compete with feminist women's antiviolence organizations:

> When we started the nonprofits, we had noncompetitive funding clauses in our organization. We're not going to compete with anything identified as a shelter or rape crisis center—just not gonna happen. And as we started getting to be larger nonprofits, there started to be stuff about, "Are we gonna apply to United Way or not? Are we gonna apply to the San Francisco Foundation or not? How is this gonna work?" So it was ongoing ethical issues that we mostly solved by staying small. I've been associated with rape crisis centers and domestic violence centers for many years [and] it's just engrained, you know: don't do it. We can't do that.

From the start of the 1980s until it shuttered in 1999, OMP specialized in working with boys and young men in violence prevention, and it became an important presence in progressive antiviolence efforts in the East Bay Area. Their work drew national attention, once landing Kivel and Creighton for "fifteen minutes of fame" on the Oprah Winfrey television show. Kivel developed curricula, like his "Act Like a Man Box," that continue today to be widely reprinted and adapted in antisexist and antiviolence education with boys and men.[22] Despite these successes, OMP was confronted with some of the same challenges and limits faced by similar antiviolence men's groups of the 1980s and early 1990s. Allan Creighton described how for him and Kivel, when OMP became a nonprofit in 1984 or 1985, the shift from their familiar collective, movement-based form of organization felt jarring, but necessary: "For me, for both of us, incorporating the Oakland Men's Project and then developing boards and then beginning to have payroll issues, these things didn't seem organic to us but nonetheless we had to have [them]." Kivel agreed that incorporation of the OMP seemed necessary. He described how the context of the early 1980s—the rise of nonprofits against the backdrop of antifeminist backlash and the conservatism of the Reagan years—created opportunities for OMP to grow but also erected huge obstacles to retaining his radical vision of OMP as a catalyst for community empowerment and fundamental social change:

> The whole nonprofit industrial complex was getting consolidated as a major vehicle for what I would say would be managing [laughs ironically] these

issues. Not just around gender but around other things. But a result of all of that was that slowly but quite rapidly, really over a period of five to eight years I think, sexism, patriarchy, white male supremacy were no longer the focus. The focus became male violence, women's empowerment, interpersonal relationships, media images. And a lot of the work became fragmented, partly because there was no longer a women's movement. A lot of the organizations providing services to women were becoming more and more conservative and more dependent on government—not government funding but, you know, nonprofit foundation funding and more intimately connected to the police and the courts. A lot of the batterers programs became much more court-referred-based. So things were shifting around.

Within this more conservative context, OMP found a niche in the community working with teens, mostly in schools. Although Kivel welcomed this work, he concedes that

> It did mean that some of our more ambitious ideas about what we could do in the community had to be really peeled back, [like] mobilizing men to get out for events and campaigns. There were fewer campaigns, I mean there were still Take Back the Night marches and reproductive [rights] marches, but there wasn't a lot of things going on, most women's groups were not so much campaign-focused as service-focused. So there were much more limited ways for men to be hooked into that. . . . So it was education, it was no longer what we would have hoped for at that level with the men, it was individual change, it was no longer mobilization as a community.

As these veterans of the first wave of antiviolence work dug in to the work of organization building, they struggled to retain the radical, feminist, and overtly political roots of their work. They stayed tethered to politics by connecting with national organizations that shared a vision of radical social transformation, especially the profeminist National Organization for Changing Men (NOCM, which a few years later became NOMAS).[23] As psychologist Mark Stevens was setting up one of the first campus-based men's antiviolence groups at Ohio State University and developing anti-rape curricula in the early 1980s, he was simultaneously enmeshed with NOCM. In the national organization, Stevens found like-minded men from around the country such as Craig Norberg-Bohm, with whom he shared ideas and developed strategies: "I was sort of young and interested and passionate and enthusiastic and we started to work together to see how can we make some things happen. And I became a co-chair of the [NOCM] Ending Men's Violence task group and then I moved on to being a co-chair of the whole organization, in 1986 or 1987." For a few years Stevens' professional work on campus and his national political work with the profeminist men's movement enhanced each other. But increasingly he found NOCM as descending into fruitless internal debates and squabbling—about sexuality, pornography, race, men's rights, and the most "politically correct" way to be accountable allies with feminist women. Though he tried to "keep a centrist view" in all of the debates, "I saw a lot of the people . . . getting their energy drained, and it seemed like 50 percent of their life energy was going into arguing with each other. Or trying to grapple with how this men's organization could be a movement that would mesh with the feminist movement and change the world. And so I admired it, I was part of it, but at the same time I felt like 'Oh, gosh, it just seems so draining.'"

NOCM members, in their then-national magazine *Changing Men*, dove head first into the feminist sex wars, with a 1985 special edition focusing on "Men Confronting Pornography," edited by sociologist Michael Kimmel (Fig. 3.1).[24] Curated as a dialogue of differing feminist perspectives on pornography, the magazine included pieces by antipornography activists like John Stoltenberg and Therese Stanton; commentary by "prosex feminists" who argued against the antipornography strategy, like Kate Ellis and the Feminist Anti-Censorship Taskforce (FACT); and an essay by Chris Clark, who asserted what he saw as the liberating value of gay porn. This and subsequent issues of the magazine drew fire from radical feminists, especially antipornography activists in the women's antiviolence community, all of which eventually spelled the demise of the magazine.[25]

Similar divisive debates were taking place within NOCM, *Changing Men* magazine's sponsor organization. By the late 1980s, Stevens had relocated to a job with the student counseling center at the University of Southern California, where he launched "MenCARE," a group of undergraduate men devoted to "Creating Attitudes for a Rape-free Environment" on campus. This work took up much of Stevens' time. And besides, he was getting turned off and drained by "the political correctness that [NOCM] folks were looking for . . . so I started to move away from the group." He shifted what energy remained for national networking to helping to create a Society for the Psychological Study of Men and Masculinity (Division 51) of the American Psychological Association. Essentially, from the late 1980s into the start of the 1990s Stevens remained devoted to the same work—sexual violence prevention with young men—but the locus of his efforts shifted away from a profeminist men's movement base to a profeminist professional base (which he helped to create). Now with a

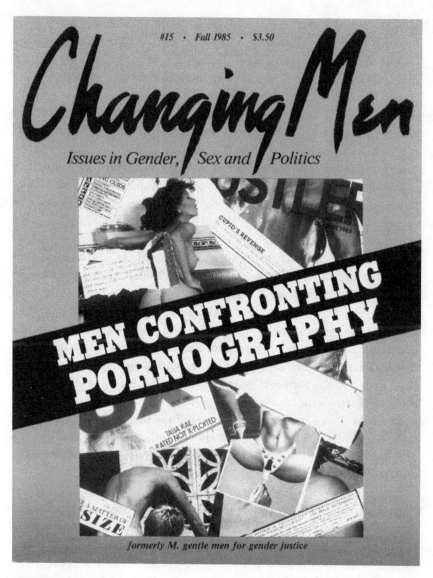

Figure 3.1
Changing Men magazine, "Men Confront Pornography" cover, fall 1985.
©1985 Changing Men Magazine, reprinted by permission of Rick Cote.

full-time job and a growing family—he and his wife had three young children—Stevens pulled back from the national work with NOCM:

> I knew that I could not travel as much as I did before and so I made a decision
> to kind of dig a little bit deeper into my institution, which was to help set
> up MenCARE and helping to create the Center for Women and Men. And so
> it wasn't something that I at all let go, but I didn't do as much at a national

level that I was doing before. You know I was just thinking, USC is paying me, they're not really paying me to do national stuff as much as kind of the local stuff there, so I felt sort of, I don't know if obligated was the word, but it felt like the fair thing to do was to sink my time and energy into my professional home at USC.

Like Stevens, many of the Movement Cohort of men who had initiated antiviolence work in the welter of feminist activism in the late 1970s continued with the work a decade later, but under shifting social conditions. Some started or joined community nonprofits, while others worked to develop niches in the helping professions and carved out spaces on campuses from which to do violence prevention with boys and young men. All of these efforts involved a gradual pulling away from grassroots movements as a base, toward professionalization of the work, including the development of the first standardized antiviolence curricula. And as they began to "dig in a little deeper" in their local nonprofits or campus workplaces, these veterans of antiviolence work also started to mentor a new generation of men, younger men who arrived on the scene equally excited about stopping sexual assault and domestic violence but starting with a different set of formative experiences.

PATHWAYS OF A BRIDGE COHORT

The first group of men who entered antiviolence work in the 1970s and early 1980s (Chapter 2) shared similar pathways into the work. Most of those in this Movement Cohort had some personal experiences that predisposed them to an aversion to violence. Each of them also was involved in the progressive social movements of the 1970s—antiwar, student, environmental, or Civil Rights—which directly or indirectly brought them into contact with feminist women. Inspired by feminism, these men formed men's consciousness-raising groups that, for them, eventually morphed into grassroots antirape and anti–domestic violence activism through which they sought to contribute to a radical, feminist transformation of their communities and the world.

The men who entered into antiviolence work from the mid-1980s through the early 1990s are somewhat younger. Born between 1958 and 1970, the men of the Bridge Cohort came of age during a transitional period when grassroots feminism was fragmenting and declining, and feminist women and men had started to form national and local nonprofits, as well as campus-based women's studies programs and antiviolence centers.

Some of them even see themselves through this sort of generational lens. Jackson Katz for instance, born in 1960, said, "I'm in a weird, I think, kind of bridge generation," locating himself between the older movement activists and younger men who have joined the effort during the current era of institutionalized and professionalized antiviolence work. This Bridge Cohort of men, had a more varied set of pathways into the work than did their older brothers. These multiple pathways into antiviolence work eventually translated into an impressive broadening of antiviolence strategies and tactics, and to a widening diversity of men in the field. They also facilitated a further distancing of antiviolence work from its politicized feminist foundations.

"This is who I don't want to be"

As with many in the Movement Cohort, several men from the Bridge Cohort spoke of having experienced violence in their youth, some in their family of origin, some in their neighborhood or school. But not all of them: Marc Rich says that his antiviolence perspective is rooted in having grown up in 1970s New York in "a Jewish household . . . around lots of other Jewish folks where there's definitely a spirit of questioning and challenging." One of the challenges young Marc faced was from his father, who as a boy "was physically abused by his parents . . . but really went the other direction. So he really went to a space of talking to me pretty consistently about treating women with respect . . . he's just a very gentle man, he's respectful of other people."

Several other members of the Bridge Cohort, however, did not benefit from such positive examples of adult manhood. Quentin Walcott's mother and father divorced in 1972, when he was two years old. Though his mother never liked to discuss the reasons for the split, years later she explained to Quentin, "My father was abusive in the sense that he would [use] the children as a weapon. One of the reasons that she had to get out of that relationship is because he would hold us out over the train tracks, just to scare her." Keith Smith, as a young boy growing up in New Jersey and New York in the late 1960s and early 1970s, saw "lots of violence against women," first in his own family, and then later in his teens, among his peers.

> I saw a lot of domestic violence in my own family. And around me, it was just the *norm*. And I tended to have a lot of female friends, so sometimes I would have female friends who were in violent relationships. In college, I saw a lot of

abuse of women by men, I saw a lot of men being verbally abusive, I saw a lot of taking advantage of women, women being seen as less than men. And I never understood—I didn't understand the dynamic. . . . I didn't understand why men were doing it. I think that's where this all originated, I think that's where I sort of at a young age developed empathy for women.

In his early twenties, Tim Love's empathy for women grew exponentially when, he says, roughly half of his women friends disclosed to him that they had been subjected to violence, mostly sexual violence and some domestic violence. He recalls feeling stunned by these revelations. "I remember . . . a whole range of emotions around that. Anger, helplessness, anger at rape in general, anger at the perpetrators, frustration, and helplessness around like not being able to really do anything about it."

Jackson Katz's biological father died of a heart attack in 1960 before his mother gave birth to Jackson. She remarried and young Katz grew up "with a stepfather who was a very damaged human being." His grandfather—a war hero and former professional football player—was the family patriarch whom Katz both looked up to and eventually used as a negative example of manhood:

> My grandfather had a reputation of being a real tough-guy Jew, who would fight and beat up and defend Jewish kids against, you know, Irish, Polish, Italian kids would pick on Jewish kids. But while he was protecting other Jews from violence, among the Jews that he failed to protect from violence were members of his own family, who he failed to protect from his own violence. So while he was publicly a big successful military and sports figure, he was brutal to his family, who were reduced—all of them—to caricatures in some ways. My stepfather was one of them, and he was emotionally absent and physically and emotionally brutal at the same time. But so, I always saw him as a model of what I didn't want to be, you know, and I could see that early on, "This is who I don't want to be."

Growing up in the San Fernando Valley in Southern California in the late 1960s, Frank Blaney was "exposed to domestic violence at an early age." And though he thinks in retrospect that his empathy for his mother "kind of on a subconscious level fed my whole understanding" of gender-based violence, he also credits his later interest in antiviolence work to his youthful concern with "preventing violence against myself . . . Growing up I was the victim of violence pretty frequently. I grew up in kind of a rough neighborhood and got beat up a lot." Gary Barker was a teenager in suburban Houston in the late 1970s, and he witnessed a classmate gunning down another boy in the high school cafeteria. Though at the time he could not make sense of this as "male violence," a few years later he came to understand how he fit into a larger field of gender, violence, and power. He recalls as a freshman in his college dorm one night witnessing "an overly drunk girl that several guys were probably having nonconsensual sex with." The next morning, when he heard groups of guys laughing and joking about the incident, he recalls feeling shocked and puzzled.

> We didn't even have words like "date rape" yet, you know, [but] I looked at those guys with a certain degree of, I can't understand where you're coming from on that, that you somehow think that's OK, I can't understand how you're talking, but again not necessarily having words or anything to put to it. So, I guess in thinking of myself as different, I think part of it was [realizing] there's some way of being manly out there that I just don't feel like I fit into, and I'm not sure what the version is that I do fit into, but there's something about this version that's out there and makes the most noise that I definitely don't fit into.

Barker's description of his distaste for the dominant male culture in his college dorm, and his incipient but as-yet-unformed sense of himself as "different," hints at a potential—a psychological and emotional predisposition—to oppose the form of masculinity that perpetrates and celebrates violence against women. Barker's story—like the accounts of Frank Blaney, Quentin Walcott, Keith Smith, Tim Love, Jackson Katz, and others of the Bridge Cohort—also describes a growing well of empathy for women. Although they felt as boys and young men that they did not fit in, that they abhorred violence against their mothers and women friends, that they themselves wanted to be safe from men's violence, their stories also illustrate that they had no idea what to do with their feelings of anger, frustration, and dis-identification with men's violence. As with the Movement Cohort, the Bridge Cohort's antiviolence psychological and emotional predispositions did not automatically translate into antiviolence activism. And as with the cohort before them, these younger men's actions were shaped by the social and historical context in which they came of age.

Reverberations of a Movement

By the time the men of the Bridge Cohort started to engage with antiviolence work, the backlash against feminism was in full force, and the women's movement was fragmenting. But this is not to say that the feminist movement was gone. For one thing, feminist women had become a powerful force in other social movements. Feminist ideas, values, and collective decision-making processes reverberated in the 1980s environmental and peace movements.[26] As a college student in the early 1980s, David Lee was "very active in the peace movement, and sort of came to a realization of—you know, sort of encapsulated by the bumper sticker 'World Peace Begins at Home'—that the violence that happens in our everyday lives influences the conditions that create a world where violence is normalized." Lee's developing micro-macro understanding, his ability to grasp the link between violence in intimate relationships with mass state violence, did not come automatically, just because he was a smart Yale student; it came because of feminist women's powerfully active presence in the peace movement.

Ben Atherton-Zeman was a twenty-year-old college student in 1986 when he joined in the Great Peace March, a walk for peace that stretched across the continent, from Los Angeles to Washington, DC. During the eight-month March, during long hours of walking and in their evening camps, Atherton-Zeman was educated by feminist women.

> These women on the Great Peace March explained to me about men's violence against women, domestic violence, dating violence, sexual violence, sexual harassment, sexism, pay equity issues, and just talked about their own lives as women. And it really made me mad. Hearing how much their lives sucked had a huge impact on me, and it made me mad. And the women on the march were like, "Well, if you're mad, you should do something about it. It's great that you're on this walk across the United States for peace, but as you can see, we have people doing that. What we don't have are men saying 'I'm a man against sexism, I'm a man against violence against women.'" So I decided I would. It sounded like it was needed, so I said I'll do this.

This awakening during the Great Peace March translated into a burst of activism for Atherton-Zeman during his subsequent college years, and eventually to a lifetime of commitment to antiviolence activism. Most of the men of the Bridge Cohort, though, did not experience their first sparks of feminist awareness within the context of direct social movement activism. There are two general pathways into antiviolence work for the men of the Bridge Cohort. First, several learned about feminism and about antiviolence activism initially through experiences in college—both in the classroom, taking women's studies courses, and through campus organizations. Second, several others came to antiviolence work following college, routing through nonfeminist organizations or occupations that sparked their awareness of the topic. Whether their interest was triggered in college or after, most of these men found their way to anti-domestic violence or antirape nonprofits that had recently been created. The work of the Movement Cohort may have become less and less visible as a national movement in the streets, but a generation of feminist activism continued to reverberate powerfully on college campuses and in community organizations. Here, the men of the Bridge Cohort found not only partly transformed institutions but also valuable feminist mentors, experienced veterans of the movement who inspired, challenged, and guided a new generation into the work.

Women's Studies and Campus Organizations

Arguably, academia is the site of the greatest successes by the women's movement in bringing about meaningful institutional change. Feminist reforms of colleges and universities lie in the area of academics—both teaching and research—and in the creation of campus women's centers and sexual violence specialties within college counseling centers. As college students, the men of the Movement Cohort may have taken social science courses on poverty or social inequality during the late 1960s and early 1970s, but these courses tended to focus entirely on race and class; at best, such courses would include a token mention of "women's issues." By the middle to late 1970s, that had started to change. A generation of mostly younger women scholars, fighting against derision and outright opposition from senior scholars and administrators, began to challenge the blind spots and distortions of scholarly research and curricula that implicitly focused on men's lives, experiences, and perspectives, while ignoring women or deploying sexist caricatures of them.[27] The first U.S. and Canadian interdisciplinary women's studies programs appeared in 1970.[28] By 1977 there were 276 women's studies programs in U.S. colleges and universities, and the number swelled to 585 by 1989.[29] In addition to interdisciplinary women's studies programs, feminist courses also multiplied within traditional academic disciplines (including history, anthropology, sociology, psychology, political science, literature, and classics) and in professional schools (social work, law, education, and counseling psychology among them).

By the mid-1980s, feminist scholars were already bemoaning the less-than-revolutionary impact of women's studies.[30] But there is no doubt that the scholarly beachhead created in women's studies and within some academic disciplines set up a very different educational field for students of the Bridge Cohort. David Lee entered Yale in 1980 and eventually became a women's studies major—something unheard of just a decade earlier. On the opposite coast in the late eighties and early nineties, Marc Rich experienced a "big light bulb that went off" when he "started taking more courses that looked at feminist scholarship and women's studies issues [that] pushed me to start looking at masculinity in different kinds of ways . . . that was the first thing that opened the door for me."

Robert Jensen "meandered through my twenties in journalism," and then returned to graduate school in 1988 at the age of thirty, where he "landed on the feminist critique of pornography, which—if you remember at the time was politically pretty much on the way out." Still, Jensen's decision to commit to antipornography activism came "through a purely academic entry point," his conviction that Andrea Dworkin and Catherine MacKinnon, "that whole generation of radical feminists," were correct about the links between pornography and violence against women. Soon, Jensen found himself enmeshed with feminist activists who were doing antipornography public education, where he found "not only a sense of the ideas, but the practice and politics in a feminist context."

As a teen Jackson Katz had been turned off by the violent, tough-guy masculinity of his grandfather. However, he also identified in some ways with it; after all, Katz himself entered college as a football player, and in retrospect he can see that "Football for me was a positive outlet for my rage and anger that I could constructively channel on the football field and get rewarded for it." But the feminist ideas he began to hear in the college classroom just seemed to be "making so much sense." Katz became the first man at UMass to minor in women's studies, where he found ideas that helped him make sense of his own ambivalences and discomfort with conventional violent masculinity. As a nineteen-year-old sophomore writing for the student paper, he attended a rally for better lighting on campus, which led to the first in a lifetime of public feminist statements: "I actually wrote an opinion column about it, it was called something like, 'A man can't understand,' and it was about if I were a woman and I had to worry about being raped on a regular basis I would be, you know, ticked off about it."

As the words of Marc Rich, Robert Jensen, and Jackson Katz imply, women's studies classes provided an intellectual spark for a developing feminist consciousness for many men of the Bridge Cohort. From the start, women's studies programs also emphasized an activist, social change component to the curriculum. Majors and minors in women's studies were placed in internships—in campus women's centers, community-based domestic violence shelters, or rape crisis centers—that joined academic feminist knowledge with action. Men sometimes found barriers to participation, as many women's shelters or rape crisis hotlines did not welcome men as volunteers or interns. For instance, by the early 1980s, the Los Angeles Commission on Assaults Against Women had developed numerous community services to support women who were victims of sexual and domestic violence. Following four years as a volunteer, Patti Giggans became the executive director of LACAAW in 1985, a position she still held when we interviewed her in 2012. LACAAW sought men's financial support in those early years, Giggans said, but they did not think it was appropriate for men volunteers to staff the hotline, or to participate in the actual running of the organization: "We were founded by feminists, we were a women's organization working on quote 'the women's issue of violence against women.' At that point there was no problem about saying it was a women's issue, because it was. We were women, it was our issue, we were dealing with it. You know, we wanted men to help, we wanted them to write checks, but you know, we weren't putting men on the board."

By the late 1980s, however, LACAAW began to find appropriate ways to use the few men—usually young college students—who wanted to help. Male volunteers were put to the task of community education with boys and men, work that eventually morphed in the 1990s and beyond (as the organization changed its name to Peace Over Violence) to vibrant community- and school-based violence prevention education with youth. In addition to organizations like LACAAW creating a niche for men volunteers, the growing number of campus-based groups like the ones Mark Stevens started at Ohio State University and USC, and the burgeoning community nonprofits devoted to violence prevention with boys and men, like RAVEN in St. Louis, MOVE, and OMP in the Bay Area, and the Men's Resource Center and Emerge in Boston, became outlets for men who wanted to link their feminist studies with action. For instance, when Ben Atherton-Zeman was a student at Hampshire College and UMass in the late 1980s and early 1990s, his classroom education, which included an entire course on acquaintance rape, was organically linked with his activism on campus, with community organizations, and with a growing national network of feminist women and men working against violence.

I formed a [campus] group for men against sexism, called WIMPS, Wild Intrepid Men Protesting Sexism. Isn't that neat? And we had another group called Men Against Violence, so we did lots of stuff together, the two groups, including being allies to women for Take Back the Night. Which at the time was a women's-only march, so we would help to organize—along with the [Boston] Men's Resource Center, we would all organize the men's vigil part of the TBTN march. We'd have like a send-off, "bye" type of thing, and then we'd sit as a discussion group . . . and then greet the women as they came back. And that was fun for me. In the middle of that is when I first discovered NOMAS. I think 1992, the Men and Masculinity conference in Chicago was my first, and I went there and was blown away that so many men cared about these issues.

Jackson Katz also linked his classroom feminist awakening with campus activism and organization building. Following an undergraduate experience with peer education at UMass, he attended a graduate program at Harvard, where he studied existing antibullying curricula used in schools and adapted these curricula to what would become Katz's signature contribution: the "bystander approach" to violence prevention with male college athletes.[31] In 1991, he created a pilot program, eventually in 1993 securing a paid position running the Mentors in Violence Prevention (MVP) program at Northeastern University, the first institutionalized campus-based violence prevention program for male athletes, using the bystander approach. MVP became not just a workplace for Katz but a locus for recruiting other men into antiviolence work, and a template for other such programs nationwide.

Some men of the Bridge Cohort experienced their initial spark of interest in stopping men's violence in women's studies courses and campus organizing; others passed through college focusing on other topics and began working in various professions that had nothing to do with gender-based violence.

Occupational Pathways to Antiviolence Work

Tim Love started college at the end of the 1980s studying engineering and then shifted to English. A self-described "late bloomer," he was not sure what he wanted to do after graduating, so he worked in a restaurant for a while and then decided he'd try teaching. A twenty-three-year-old white man from an upper-middle-class family, Love got a job with AmeriCorps in Atlanta, and he was placed in a "fairly poor, primarily African American school," and it was there he "got to start to see inequality at work." His education about social inequality grew when AmeriCorps placed him with the Task Force for the Homeless in Atlanta, and here he eventually found his calling in antiviolence work: "I was seeing people who were working, who still weren't making enough money to live someplace. And then also [I was] starting to meet a lot of families that were being torn apart by domestic violence—sexual violence [also] being an issue that split apart families—that women who were homeless were also experiencing."

Tim Love "wanted to do something" about the "sense of injustice" he felt in this setting, so he "got some training [with] some specific focus around domestic and sexual violence. In addition, a woman that was in charge of the organization was just one of those people that you meet that your life is forever changed after that. She was involved nationally with a lot of different movements around civil rights for homeless folks, housing rights, economic justice, and quickly brought me into all of that. So I spent about three and a half years working there at that organization, kind of learning."

Love subsequently landed a position with the Texas Association Against Sexual Assault—first in San Marcos and then at the statewide TAASA office in Austin, where we interviewed him—conducting youth education around sexuality and violence issues.

Tim Love's story is typical of the subset of men of the Bridge Cohort who routed into antiviolence work via occupations, rather than directly from their college education or campus experiences. And for most of these men it was not just any sort of occupation that sparked a commitment to stopping violence against women. For Love and for others, it was typically working in occupations that served kids or adults from racially marginalized groups, from poor families and neighborhoods, kids who were defined as "troubled" or "at-risk," adults already "in the system" because of drug and alcohol addictions, that triggered an awareness of how domestic and sexual violence were part of a larger pattern of danger and oppression. In a very real sense, this subset of men of the Bridge Cohort came to "gender work" via "race and class work." This race/class-to-gender pathway describes the occupational trajectory of Tim Love, a white man, but it was especially common for the men of color among our interviewees.

Of the seventeen men of the Bridge Cohort in our sample, six were men of color. None of these six reported that college women's studies courses sparked their interest and eventual commitments to working against sexual assault or domestic violence. As many critics in the 1980s pointed out, women's and gender studies was still, perhaps implicitly, speaking primarily to white people's concerns, not yet embracing racial/ethnic and class diversity in ways that would speak to the concerns of most women of color (much less to men of color).[32] For instance, starting at the end of the 1980s, Quentin Walcott, an African American, had been a student activist at City University in New York, working on issues of racism and political prisoners. Following college, he intended to go to law school with hopes of doing constitutional law, but "as a way to pay my tuition" he took a job "running groups and leading workshops" with young people in Queens.

Here, he began to see connections between the race and class marginalization of these kids, with domestic violence: "Typically [the] kids that they sent to me [were] quote-unquote the bad kids. I found that they weren't really bad at all, they were just . . . I dug a little bit deeper, and I found that many of these children were witnesses to domestic violence in the household, so they were really acting out behaviorally, they were diagnosed as ADHD or what have you, some were given medication, but it was really that they were acting out behaviorally because of what they experienced in the household."

Walcott sought out "appropriate curricula" on family violence to integrate into his workshops with adolescents. He learned of the Urban Justice Center's Abusive Partners Intervention Program and signed up for a two-year training in batterer intervention. Before long, and for the next fifteen years, he was running groups for men who batter.

Tony Porter followed a similar path to antiviolence work, though it was longer and more circuitous than Walcott's. Porter was employed for a few years as a corrections officer in a youth facility in upstate New York, working with "troubled youth . . . all young boys," and eventually he shifted to an adult maximum security facility for the criminally insane, "a knock-em-down, drag-em-out, be-a-tough-guy kind of job." Part of his job was to take the men to AA and NA meetings. This sparked his interest in learning to become a substance abuse counselor—"at that time, in that place, there weren't many black counselors"—and he worked for the next twenty years as a substance abuse counselor at Nyack Hospital in New York, eventually as director of addiction services. Through this work, he began to see that "the large majority of the women I had were victims of DV [domestic violence]. A large majority of men were perpetrators." Porter was educated about domestic violence and eventually recruited into anti–domestic violence work by women in the community, especially Phyllis Frank, from whom he learned "all about male domination and sexism and patriarchy and what we know about domestic violence . . . Phyllis Frank taught me very very well, back in those early years." Before long, Porter was traveling the country helping to educate men about domestic violence prevention, and eventually in 1997, when he was forty years old, he started his own antiviolence organization, A Call to Men.

Geographic Hubs and Movement Mentors

As a new cohort of men began to move into antiviolence work, it made sense that many of them gravitated to geographic areas where such work had already been established: Boston and New York on the East Coast, San Francisco–Oakland and Los Angeles in the West, St. Louis and Austin in the heartland, Toronto in Canada.[33] In these hubs of feminist activism, antiviolence organizations were taking root and community coalitions were forming. Our interviewees' descriptions of their pathways to antiviolence activism paint a clear picture of the common characteristics of these activist hubs: one or more colleges and universities that spark interest and feed activists into the community; feminist rape crisis and domestic violence organizations putting down roots in the community; emergent routes for men's participation in campus and community education and prevention; a growing national network of antiviolence activists and professionals; all grounded, crucially, in the continued work of an established group of women and men, seasoned veterans of the movement, who inspired, educated, and initiated a new cohort of antiviolence workers.

David Lee's life of antiviolence work gestated in two major hubs, the Boston area and then California's Bay Area. After leaving college in 1984, Lee worked for several months with Men Against Domestic Violence, a New Haven group that had spun off from Emerge in Boston. One day, canvassing for a battered women's shelter, he knocked on a door and a young man answered: "I said what [organization] I was with and he then disclosed to me how he had just beaten his girlfriend the day before. And so I put my clipboard down and I talked with him for the next hour. And then I realized—that was my prevention epiphany—I need to really get involved in how to prevent this. . . . But that became how I got really interested in the prevention piece, and thinking about moving forward. I also had gone to some of the [national] men and masculinity conferences."

Later that same year, Lee moved to California and took a job in San Francisco with the Children's Self-Help Center, where he met former MASV member Chris Anderegg. For the next ten years, Lee also volunteered with MOVE, where he crossed paths with Allan Creighton and Paul Kivel: "When I moved to California in '84, I had already owned a Men Overcoming Violence bumper sticker, and so I called them up right away and so I got to meet Allan Creighton and the other men there, and then eventually Paul Kivel. At the time they seemed like they'd been doing the work for so long because the work of MASV started in the '70s. You know, I got here [and] fell into that network."

Several men of the Bridge Cohort, like Lee, mention Movement Cohort activists—Allan Creighton, Paul Kivel, Michael Kaufman, Craig Norberg-Bohm, Don Conway-Long—who mentored them in local organizations, or in the context of national networks and organizations. Most also mention feminist women of the Movement Cohort as key mentors.

Ben Atherton-Zeman's early community antiviolence work in 1989–90 was in Amherst and Boston, with the Men's Resource Center's High School Education Project on dating violence. But he credits much of his growth in the work to the tough feminist mentoring he received from Phyllis Frank, whom he first met in 1992 at a national NOCM conference. Atherton-Zeman was one of several men we interviewed who mentioned Frank as an important early and ongoing feminist mentor. A 1970s pioneer in the national feminist shelter movement and an organization builder, Frank was one the first feminist women to see the importance of nurturing and challenging men to become active feminist allies. "When men began to filter in," to antiviolence work the early eighties, Frank recalled, "the question was should it be women-only, and some organizations said yes, some said no." When men did start to get involved, she says, it was "a very mixed bag."

> A discrete number of the men who were involved understood how crucial it was to listen to the voices of women. So many of the men who were beginning batterer programs and running them would trample on women and women's voices—the very women who they were saying they were going to be working on behalf of. Because of sexism and the nature of the way sexism works, some of the very same men who were our best allies, according to them, were causing women great havoc. . . . Very often the men who are most progressive, who think they've done the work, who think they're already fixed, are not open to hearing the impact of the ways they manifest patriarchy and sexism, they're not open to hearing how women are experiencing them. And if you want to tell them, they use the very strategies that are in the culture for men to silence and shut women up.

Frank, however, saw early on that if violence against women was to be stopped, men had to be a part of the solution, so she committed herself to working with men, at both a local level and in her ongoing work in the national profeminist men's movement. Ben Atherton-Zeman described the importance of Frank's tough-love feminist mentoring when he met her through NOCM: "I mean, it's a real gift, right, for a woman to be the one to educate men on sexism. I mean, here was Phyllis Frank, this feminist woman, educating me on my sexism. Huge gift."

Tony Porter also credits Frank as "the primary one who engaged me" in antiviolence work. His words paint a picture of a process of collective mentoring from a generation of "hardcore feminist women":

> They taught me a lot, and that sits at the foundation of my work. I've had experiences that most guys coming into the work today just haven't had, sitting

at the feet of twenty women in the room, and every one of those women have been in the movement for thirty years—I'm talking thirty years back from 1990. Women who really had their hands on the pulse of pushing the envelope with men and these issues. Women who were clearly part of the battered women's movement, when they were hiding other women in their basements, in the spare rooms in their homes—there were no shelters at the time—women who were dealing with issues at a time when police officers were just doing whatever the hell they felt like doing. I'm talking about women who were truly truly the battered women's movement.

Like Tony Porter and other men of color in the Bridge Cohort, Juan Carlos Areán came to gender work through a network of community political engagements, "mainly antiracism stuff, anti-imperialism stuff," first in his native Mexico, and eventually in the Boston-area hub. When he moved to the United States in 1981 at age twenty to study music, he carried his social justice commitments with him, "but I kind of left the political work aside a little bit." In New York City he met the woman he would eventually marry. "We talked about politics and social justice and she said, 'What about women's rights? Where do you stand with that?' And I was like, well, what about them? I never really thought about it, never had been aware of those issues." Areán "sought to meet with other men who were kind of struggling with the same issues. . . . I ended up living here in Amherst, Massachusetts, which happened to miraculously be kind of like a center where, back then in the late 1980s, was kind of a hub of that. And I met a few people like Steven Botkin and Rob Okun and so on and got involved in the work of what became later the Men's Resource Center of Western Mass." In 1991 Areán took a training from the MRC and started working batterer's intervention groups: "I was really taken by the work, I was fascinated by it . . . and little by little I got more involved and I ended up working there."

The words of Ben Atherton-Zeman, Tony Porter, Juan Carlos Areán, and others describe how their antiviolence commitments and understandings were sparked and mentored by feminist women of the Movement Cohort, given organizational form within the growing local hubs of feminist antiviolence activism that were simultaneously linking up in national activist networks.

TRANSITIONAL OPENINGS, EMERGENT TENSIONS

Thus far in this chapter, we have traced the dynamics of a period of transition in antiviolence activism, roughly the mid-1980s to the mid-1990s.

During this time, four key shifts were set into motion that created opportunities for a broader and more sustainable field of activism but that also simultaneously generated new challenges and obstacles. First, there was a shift from grassroots feminist movement activism "in the streets" to the creation of offices and professionally run organizations on campuses and in communities. Second, new antirape and anti–domestic violence curricula was strategically shaped and deployed to appeal to boys and men. Third, this transitional period is characterized by the entry of a new and decidedly more diverse cohort of men into antiviolence work. And fourth, we will argue, this period ended with the passage of landmark legislation that started a flow of state funds to violence prevention work.

From Movement Activists to Professionals

The feminist movement, especially in its visible and radical in-the-streets manifestations, fragmented and faded into abeyance by the mid-1980s. But feminism did not disappear. Rather, savvy Movement Cohort activists dug in, successfully building national and community organizations, and fighting for reforms in the legal system and in higher education. As a younger cohort of activists entered the field in the late 1980s and early 1990s, they found feminist-created organizations in place, and they benefited from the inspiration and mentoring of movement veterans.

Although the creation of antiviolence organizations is surely evidence of partial (and meaningful) success of the movement, the "paradoxes of professionalization" were also becoming apparent by the late 1980s.[34] In 1986, sociologist Paul Lichterman studied Men Overcoming Violence (MOVE), the San Francisco–based anti–domestic violence group that Allan Creighton helped to form and that David Lee joined after moving to California from Massachusetts. Lichterman observed that the founders of the group were "remnants of a radical leftist subculture," men who defined their work as an "enactment of antisexist politics." However, Lichterman argued, this political orientation to antiviolence work came into conflict in the group with the "increasingly therapeutic themes" brought about by an "occupational change" in the work. Namely, the newer recruits to MOVE tended to be men who routed to antiviolence work not from radical movements but from the university-based human services fields. The goal of these new volunteers was a professional one, to get graduate degrees and to develop a "men's specialty" in the growing field of counseling psychology.[35] This professional orientation, according to Lichterman, led to MOVE's declining emphasis on public education aimed at violence prevention, while fueling its emphasis on clinical work with men who were referred to the group by the courts. For the founders of the group, the fear was that MOVE was "becoming just another counseling agency"[36] shifting away from the radical vision of social transformation shared by the MOVE's original members, especially considering their foundation in the grassroots group MASV. As we will see in the next chapter, activists continue to grapple with the ongoing tension between professionalized approaches to antiviolence work in sustainable funded organizations, with a continued vision of substantial radical social transformation.

Curricular Appeals to Boys and Men

We saw in the previous chapter that the first movement-based attempts to do rape and domestic violence prevention work with boys and men were limited in part by what many activists in retrospect see as a "politically correct" approach that loaded guilt onto boys and men, most likely closing them off to seeing feminism in a positive light. As veterans of the Movement Cohort transitioned into building sustainable organizations, they also strategized to develop curricula that retained a feminist critique of male violence and helped to build empathy for women, while also appealing to men to think of themselves not as bad guys but as part of the solution.

Thanks in part to national networking, men all over—from the White Ribbon Campaign in Canada, to RAVEN in St. Louis, Emerge in Boston, and MOVE and OMP in California—were developing educational interventions that were more "guy-friendly." Mark Stevens was deploying this approach when he wrote one of the first curriculum manuals for violence prevention on college campuses in 1983 at Ohio State University. It was still a moment of intense feminist debates about violence and pornography, and Stevens didn't want to appear to be "not political enough . . . it was really important to see that the rape culture was connected to male privilege, so we had to kind of dance with, be able to market something that guys wouldn't just say, 'no' and shut us off, but also having some political correctness at the same time." Stevens developed a curriculum that eventually was widely adopted with college women's and counseling centers, and his words describe a sophisticated strategy:

> We had to hook the guys in that they have something to gain by reducing the rape culture. And in some ways that was very political, because we started to develop exercises that allowed them to see male privilege—allowed them to

see that they're getting something out of the rape culture, but they're also paying a price by being in the rape culture. So we developed some exercises that
they got a chance to reflect upon it. We hooked guys in to how they were taught
to be sexual beings and the pressures that they had to score. And what it meant
not to score . . . and some of the pain that's connected to the pressure to score.

As Stevens was developing his curriculum at Ohio State, and then later
in California, Jackson Katz was shaping a similar curriculum that would
become foundational in the next decade: the bystander approach. Rather
than positioning high school boys, fraternity brothers, or athletes in a violence prevention workshop as potential rapists, and risking putting them
on the defensive or turning them off immediately, the bystander approach
appeals to boys' and men's better selves, encouraging them, pushing them to
actively intervene on the street, at a frat party, in a bar, when they see their
peers engaged in behavior that seems likely to result in an acquaintance rape.

The new curricula developed during this transition period have the benefit of appealing to a broader group of boys and men, drawing them in by
telling them that feminism (or, at least opposing violence against women,
even if it is not overtly defined as "feminist" action) is good for them, and
that it's the right thing to do. This shift in emphasis, though, introduces
another dimension of the same tension set into motion by professionalization of the work: its appeal to the good in men potentially broadens
the field, making antiviolence work more appealing to more men, but this
very broadening risks severing antiviolence work from a deeper political
engagement with a foundational cause of violence against women—men's
institutionalized power and privilege. The new curriculum broadens the
field, but at the same time it nudges men's antiviolence work a step or two
away from its roots in the feminist movement, potentially thinning men's
accountability to women's leadership.

A More Diverse Field of Action

The Movement Cohort of antiviolence men was mostly white (often Jewish)
and middle-class, but we have seen in this chapter how antiviolence work
began to draw a more diverse cohort of men, starting in the late 1980s.
Although white men of the Bridge Cohort mostly routed to the work first
via college women's studies and campus feminist organizations, the men
of color tended to come to the work some years after college, through professions that sensitized them to how violence against women was linked
with other forms of oppression and violence in poor communities and

families of color. The entry into the work on the part of men of color was facilitated by the growth of community-based antiviolence organizations, coupled with how the work of a generation of feminist women was reverberating not simply in antirape or domestic violence organizations but in a growing network of community organizations. This created new pathways into antiviolence work for men of color.

Brown and black men, on account of their differing life experiences and pathways into the work, brought contrasting concerns and perspectives, potentially broadening and deepening antiviolence work. White men by the late 1980s might have been learning about the intersections of race, class, and gender in some of their women's studies classes; men of color were bringing a kind of *organic intersectionality* to antiviolence work—an understanding of violence against women as already and always connected with the everyday violences of race and class subordination in their own lives. Among other things, this meant that the men of color who entered the field during this time were already sympathetic to the new curriculum's focus on how boys and men not only perpetrate but are also victimized by violence. In Tony Porter's words, "looking at intersections of oppression, we're not just talking about ending violence against women, we're talking about ending violence against *all* women. We're talking about not just holding men accountable but we're talking about the healing of men."

A key part of the diversifying of antiviolence work during the transitional period involved active recruiting and mentoring by veteran activists, most of them white. As we have seen, several of the men of color discuss being mentored by older feminist women. Don McPherson, a man of Jamaican descent who is often assumed to be African American, was recruited and mentored by Jackson Katz near the tail end of the transition period. As a college student and football player at Syracuse University in 1987, McPherson finished second in the Heisman Trophy voting for the best football player in the nation, and he was already active in public education, volunteering with Athletes Against Drunk Driving. Following a successful professional football career, in 1994 he went to work for Northeastern University's Center for the Study of Sport in Society, running a program called Athletes in Service to America. It was there that he met Katz, who had recently started his MVP Program. Soon, Katz recruited McPherson into violence prevention work with athletes, and McPherson's education about feminism, masculinity, and violence was nurtured in the vibrant hub of the Boston area:

> I was sitting in the back of the room and listening and learning about social
> construction of masculinity and the link to violence [against] women and

bystander behavior and listening to Jackson . . . talking about all these different aspects of masculinity as it relates, not just to violence against women, but to a whole host of other issues from one of the brightest guys around on those issues, on masculinity and gender. . . . Being black, and growing up in the seventies in New York at the tail end of the civil rights movement, being black was such a shaping element to my life, and as to my gender, I had never even had one conversation about it. And so I was, it was like a heroin addict the first time, I was hooked the first time, and that was it, that's how I got started.

McPherson went to work for MVP, where he developed into an important national figure in antiviolence work with athletes and college students. He entered the field just as it was expanding in a number of ways.

VAWA and the Institutionalization of Antiviolence Work

On September 13, 1994, President Bill Clinton signed into law the Violence Against Women Act (VAWA). The culmination of years of feminist public education and political maneuvering, and following failed attempts to create federal legislation a decade earlier, the VAWA was drafted and introduced in 1990 by then-Senator Joe Biden and a broad coalition of feminist advocacy groups.[37] Despite opposition by fathers' rights and other anti-feminist groups, the bill was passed with bipartisan support and signed into law by the president four years later.[38] The VAWA institutionalized support for responses to violence against women, creating the Office on Violence Against Women within the U.S. Department of Justice. Of the $1.6 billion originally budgeted by the VAWA, the lion's share was directed to improving law enforcement, and a sizable chunk went to creating and sustaining services for battered women's shelters. A small amount of money was designated for violence prevention work.

The VAWA was a watershed moment in the United States for those who had labored to build local and national organizations to stop violence against women. According to feminist scholars Mueller and McCarthy, the passage of the VAWA "represented years of state-level lobbying by radical feminists who abhor the state."[39] Some radical feminists may have seen the VAWA (and any such maneuvering within the liberal state) as a deal with the devil; others saw it as a major victory that could help to stabilize fledgling local and state organizations that continually ran thin on funding, while exhausting their base of volunteer and very-low-paid labor. Movement veteran Patti Giggans reflected on both new opportunities and increased tensions that came with the passage of VAWA:

Big difference. That's a real shift, in the engaging men. It's a project funding stream out of Violence Against Women Office, VAWA funding. . . . When
that funding source came, I mean there was talk about it for a bit, you know
there's always been a tension about the programs for victims and the prevention programs both being underfunded. So the idea that men's groups
could come forward and get funding, it was, yeah, I think that's part of the
uneasiness, the suspiciousness. There's a whole joke as well: when men get in
the movement, the salaries for them will get higher. After women have, you
know, created this industry. It's an industry now.

Giggans' words—"It's an industry now"—and her naming of tensions
that emerge when federal funding opened space for men in antiviolence
work, point to major issues we will discuss in the next chapter when we
look at the current time period. The VAWA ushered in this new era, further shifting the ground on which antiviolence activists did their work,
in three ways. First, according to legal scholar Rose Corrigan, because of
the emphasis on funding domestic violence shelters, the VAWA initially
helped to legitimize and institutionalize work against domestic violence,
while leaving "sexual assault—and all of its uncomfortable, inconclusive,
sexualized implications—again out of the picture."[40] Second, in creating
a funding stream for antiviolence work, often in the form of competitive
grants for providing community services for survivors of violence and for
prevention work, the VAWA helped to usher in a professionalized model
of violence prevention, resting increasingly on an "evidence-based" health
model of prevention, and further pushing feminist political forms of
organizing to the margins. And third, in creating a small but meaningful stream of funding for violence prevention work with boys and men,
the VAWA further institutionalized the creation of paid positions for
men in state and local programs. As we will see in the next chapter, the
shifting terrain of antiviolence work in the late 1990s and beyond creates
an ever broader field of participation for men to engage with prevention
work, while continuing to stretch that field thinner in terms of its political
depth and potential for radical social change.

CHAPTER 4

Plugging In: The Professional Cohort, Mid-1990s to the Present

On October 25, 2006, the Los Angeles Commission on Assaults Against Women (LACAAW) made a big announcement at its Annual Humanitarian Awards Dinner: the thirty-five-year-old organization was changing its name to Peace Over Violence. Held at the exclusive Beverly Hills Hotel, the black tie gala featured Hollywood celebrities Harrison Ford, Calista Flockhart, and Steve Martin, with attendees donating from several hundred to thousands of dollars a plate. The LACAAW of 2006 bore little resemblance to its 1971 origins, when a half-dozen women responded to sexual assaults in the community by posting antirape alerts on trees and at bus stops, performing guerilla theater, selling antirape bumper stickers, and eventually forming a volunteer-staffed rape and domestic violence hotline run out of a Hollywood living room.[1]

Thirty-five years after its founding as a grassroots feminist group, LACAAW had blossomed into a 501(c)(3) community nonprofit with a professional board of directors, an annual budget of more than $2 million, several salaried employees, and a steady flow of volunteers. The organization provided an expanding range of direct services to survivors of sexual assault, stalking, and domestic violence (including services targeted to specific Latina, LGBT, and teen communities), legal and policy advocacy work, and community education. LACAAW had also recently expanded its violence prevention programs, launching in 2005 a "Men of Strength" program in local high schools, aimed at empowering young men to stop sexual assault and rape.

"We had outgrown the name," explained long-time Executive Director Patti Giggans. But it was not just the organization's impressive growth that had made the LACAAW name obsolete; it was how it had grown within a shifting social context, morphing from a grassroots feminist organization to a nonprofit run by paid professionals and funded largely from foundation grants. Giggans had been with Peace Over Violence since the early 1980s and as such could take the long view on how the organization had navigated changes in the larger public sphere. She conceded that the name change to Peace Over Violence in 2006 was partly strategic, better positioning the organization with potential funders: "The more we got connected to the outs[ide], to the corporate world, people from other than nonprofit, other than movement, a lot of my board members [would say about LACAAW]: 'This name, I try, [but] I can't get it through the door [of] my corporation,' you know?"

It wasn't just corporate funders who may have been put off by LACAAW's name. Frank Blaney, a main facilitator of POV's Men of Strength program in LA schools, says that the new name makes his job working with high school boys a bit easier: "When we used to be called the L.A. Commission on Assaults Against Women they would announce who we were and a chill would go through the room because these stereotypes of what feminism was about would start popping up in either youths' minds, or adults', or whoever we were talking to. Since we changed to Peace Over Violence it doesn't happen quite as much."

After a good deal of discussion about potential new names, the board decided to rebrand the organization as Peace Over Violence, with the slogan "One on One, One by One." It may on the surface seem puzzling that a successful and longstanding organization would make such a move, but LACAAW's name change to POV in 2006 was far from an aberration. During the first decade of the millennium, several other well-established antirape and anti–domestic violence organizations changed their names, and in most such cases "rebranding" included removing "women" from the organizational name and replacing negative terms such as "rape" with positive language that pointed to peaceful futures. In 2010 Northern California's Marin Abused Women's Services became the Center for Domestic Peace. The Seattle-based Men's Network Against Domestic Violence was renamed the Northwest Men's Project, and in Massachusetts, Help for Abused Women and Their Children (HAWC) in 2009 was renamed Healing Abuse, Working for Change. Begun in the early 1980s, the Family Violence Prevention Fund grew into a national nonprofit with an operating budget of around $16 million; in 2011, it changed its name to Futures Without Violence.

In a 2011 blog, David Lee, head of the California Coalition Against Sexual Assault (CALCASA) listed a half-dozen other organizations just in California that had recently undergone name changes. Lee, who like several members of the Bridge Cohort now holds a managerial position in antiviolence work, speculated that the recent name changes reflect organizations' growing desire to create a positive image that emphasizes what they "are working *for* instead of what they are working *against*."[2] Lee's speculation about the growing positivity of antiviolence organizations' public faces certainly rings true, but we also see the flurry of name changes as the public symbolic face of organizational strategies to adapt and compete in a rapidly shifting institutional context of antiviolence work.

The passage of the 1994 Violence Against Women Act (VAWA) signaled the end of what we described in the previous chapter as a transitional era of antiviolence work, navigated by a Bridge Cohort of activists. The organizational name changes that followed the VAWA a decade later crystallized a historical moment characterized by several interlocking trends: first, the eclipse of feminist movement-based antirape and domestic violence organizing by a growing network of antiviolence nonprofits, operating increasingly under an ascendant public health model of violence prevention; second, a state- and foundation-funded marketization of antiviolence work that presses community nonprofits and campus antiviolence organizations constantly to seek grant support and to justify continued funding with evidence-based research that testifies to their effectiveness; and third, the professionalization of the work itself, including an influx of men doing violence prevention work.

In this chapter, we will first describe medicalization and marketization of antiviolence efforts in the late 1990s and 2000s, with an eye to how members of the Movement Cohort and the Bridge Cohort navigated and also helped to shape this context. Then, we will examine the pathways of a younger and increasingly diverse group of men, the Professional Cohort, into violence-prevention work, focusing especially on how professionalization of antiviolence work and routinization of curricula created opportunities as well as tensions in working with boys and men. And we will end the chapter with a discussion of how antiviolence organizations and workers discern whether their work is having an impact.

FROM A MOVEMENT TO A PROFESSION

By the early 1990s, activists of the Movement and Bridge cohorts had launched campus- and community-based organizations that were developing sophisticated local violence prevention strategies, while linking up regionally and nationally with other antiviolence activists and professionals. All of these organizations struggled with the twin challenges of doing good and useful community work and finding ways to broaden and sustain the work.

By the late 1990s, three interlocking social changes had begun to create fresh opportunities and new challenges for these organizations. First, growing public awareness of domestic violence, sexual assault, sexual harassment, and other forms of gender-based violence had fueled a dramatic growth in demand for antiviolence efforts in various institutions, including K–12 schools, colleges and universities, fraternities, workplaces, organized sports, prisons, and the military. Second, this exploding demand was coupled with impressive (though still less-than-adequate) supply-side growth in the form of multiple sources of funding for antiviolence work, especially from the federal government and from a swelling base of private and corporate foundations. And third, many antiviolence organizations, by the mid-1990s, had formed themselves into 501(c)(3) nonprofits, positioning themselves legally to seek government and foundation funds with which they could then deliver services to survivors of gender-based violence, and to launch violence prevention efforts that were increasingly defined in terms of public health.

The VAWA has provided steady funding streams for antiviolence work in the United States. Conservatives ceaselessly forge efforts to defund or chip away at the VAWA's modest annual budget of $412.5 million (in 2013). (To put that amount into perspective: the federal government in 2013 also budgeted $8.6 *billion* for federal prisons, and $682 *billion* for the military.) Of the $412.5 million, small fractions are allotted to prevention programs that are distributed to states and local domestic violence and rape crisis centers through the Centers for Disease Control and Prevention (CDC) and to regional and college antiviolence efforts through the Department of Justice (DOJ). This very institutional sourcing of VAWA funding helped to shift the language and work of violence prevention away from its feminist movement roots, toward a language of disease and/or crime prevention.

A 2010 Ms. Foundation study observed that financial support from the VAWA had "transformed what was a scattered presence of shelters and programs into a more cohesive safety net for women throughout the country." However, the Ms. report warned, VAWA funds were spread very thin, given the huge and multifaceted need for antiviolence work. Further, the continuing political vulnerability of VAWA funds to cutbacks or elimination left local agencies vulnerable; "Foundation support," the report asserted, "is more critical than ever."[3] From 1994 to 2008, the Ms. study revealed, the number of foundations supporting gender-based violence work had expanded from 199 to 484, with the total amount of money increasing during this time from $16.4 million to $80.3 million annually. Of these funds, the lion's share—about 60 percent—was devoted to domestic violence agencies, with smaller portions directed to sexual assault and other issues. Most of the foundation funds were earmarked for direct services for survivors of violence; smaller portions were allotted to violence prevention work.

Nonprofits have flourished over the past two decades. Geographer Jennifer Wolch has argued that the rise of nonprofits constitutes a "shadow state" that arose largely to address the gap in social services to the poor, the elderly, and others left abandoned as liberal New Deal and Great Society programs were reduced following the early 1980s.[4] Critical race theorist Ruth Wilson Gilmore agrees that today's roughly two million U.S. nonprofits "stepped up to fill a service void," but she observes that their very legal definition as nonpolitical narrows the work and pushes paid staff (despite their knowledge or intentions) to "become in their everyday practice technocrats through imposed specialization."[5]

Large social changes are never monocausal, but the growing public awareness and demand for institutional change, the existence of VAWA and expanding foundation support for antiviolence efforts, and the rise of antiviolence nonprofits can be seen as impressive historic accomplishments of the women's movement. Feminism as a mass public movement had largely disappeared by the 1990s, but we can view these social changes and institutional reforms as constituting a historical moment of *professionally institutionalized feminism,* in which feminists actively work not only in antiviolence organizations that they created but also to some extent in government and foundation funding agencies themselves.[6] Professionally institutionalized feminism has created wider opportunities to address violence against women "from the inside" of institutions, rather than simply criticizing it from the outside. It also makes the work more sustainable, in large part by supplying funds for antiviolence workers to earn salaries for their efforts. However, professionally institutionalized feminism's collaboration with the state,[7] and its grounding in what Gilmore calls "the nonprofit industrial complex," limits the depth of antiviolence work, casting it less as a movement to bring about fundamental, feminist social change and more in a medicalized language that eclipses feminist language, analysis, and strategies.[8] And too often it turns leaders of antiviolence nonprofits into fundraisers.

Listening to professionals, especially those who administer antiviolence nonprofits, we heard dizzying descriptions of multiple and shifting sources of funding for their work and agonized renderings of the amount of time and energy they devote to organizing events and campaigns aimed at generating support from individual donors, and cobbling together short-term grants from foundations and the federal government. Nina Alcaraz, the deputy director of the Monterey County Rape Crisis Center, explained, "sexual assault money is funded through [the U.S. Department of] Homeland Security, as rape is being viewed as an act of terrorism, so then those moneys get passed down to California and they disperse it through various rape crisis centers throughout the state. That's for intervention. Prevention work is funded also through the California Department of Public Health, but a lot of it, I would say, is you have to go to private foundations and donations." In St. Louis, RAVEN continues to thrive as the go-to agency for court referrals of domestic violence perpetrators, but it takes constant effort, according to Executive Director Janeen McGee, to maintain a flow of funds: "We are fortunate that we get some state funds that help support us, through the Department of Public Safety. There's also some state foundation funding, from the Missouri Foundation for Health, we have a large grant through them—we do some ongoing grant writing, some donor solicitations."

Antiviolence professionals are cognizant of the need to pitch their grant applications in language that resonates with donors' values and goals and meshes neatly with the emergent institutional context of public safety and public health. Domestic violence and sexual assault are less likely to be framed today in feminist language of social movements to end patriarchal "violence against women" and are recast as an "epidemic" of violence framed in language similar to that used to address other behaviors that have been targeted as public health problems, such as obesity, smoking, or drug addiction: antiviolence organizations now frame their work as professional "primary prevention" interventions that aim to isolate violence "risk factors" and to promote "protective factors."[9] As Tony Porter told us, even the terms used to refer to battered women have changed: "we used to call them 'women who were being battered' and later, hopefully, 'survivors.' Now we have a tendency just to call them 'clients'." Melding the corporate language of many of their board members to this public health frame, leaders of antiviolence organizations increasingly refer to the broader community (including potential funders) as "stakeholders."

The growing flow of funds for antiviolence work has had another important outcome: the creation of paid jobs in antiviolence work, in local rape-crisis and domestic violence centers, in statewide organizations like the California Coalition Against Sexual Assault (CALCASA) or the Texas Association Against Sexual Assault (TAASA), in social work and counseling, and on college campuses. But few of these jobs pay very well, especially by the standards of professionals who hold graduate or professional degrees. Craig Norberg-Bohm spoke of both the organizational and individual limits of the low levels of financial support for antiviolence work:

> Most of our organizations struggle. We are not well funded. There are a lot of $300,000 organizations, $500,000, a lot are even smaller and doing this work with a few staff. And an executive director making six figures is lucky. They're mostly making high five figures, as a rule. A person who's got a family to feed isn't going to do this work much, they can't be the sole income provider almost anywhere in the field, even at the top. And that's one of the reasons that men aren't in the field. . . . Therapy, private practice, academic teaching, those are the places where there is money enough to make a living. You go to work for a crisis center, you'll be lucky to make 30K. You know? You can't raise a kid on that.

Indeed, although a couple of longtime executive directors we interviewed reported annual salaries a bit in excess of $100,000, many of the younger service providers reported salaries in the $20,000 to $40,000 range, while some of the more established professionals reported earnings ranging from $40,000 to $80,000.

Many of our interviewees said that they considered themselves fortunate to be paid to do work that they find meaningful and important. But few considered themselves to be well paid. And a small number—notably central members of the Bridge Cohort, Jackson Katz and Don McPherson—eventually left organizations they had helped to form and struck out on their own as independent contractors. In the 1990s and 2000s, Katz and McPherson became active speakers on the college campus circuit, consulted with local and statewide antiviolence agencies who were forming or revising their prevention efforts, and contracted with large organizations like college and professional sports teams and the U.S. military to shape and administer violence prevention campaigns. In Chapter 5, we will revisit this phenomenon, with an eye to how activists in the field view both the promise and dangers that inhere when individual men go solo as independent antiviolence entrepreneurs in a field built by, and still largely supported by, women's labor.

Disappearing "Women"?

In recent years, the term "gender-based violence" has largely supplanted "violence against women," both in organization names and in descriptions of the work that they do. This change in language helps to make visible the reality that boys too are frequently the victims of sexual abuse, and that sexual assault and domestic violence are also problems in same-sex relationships. As a result, antiviolence organizations have shifted a fraction of their resources to working not just with women survivors but also with boys and men survivors.

This broadened "client base," coupled with an expanding emphasis on prevention contributed to a growing sense that an exclusive focus on women did not accurately reflect the broadening nature of antiviolence work. When the Boston-area Help for Abused Women and their Children (HAWC) changed its name in 2009 to Healing Abuse, Working for Change, one of the main reasons was that Massachusetts had recently legalized same-sex marriage, and the thirty-year-old social service agency wanted its work with hospitals to reflect this change in ways that helped them better to deliver services—domestic violence shelters, counseling, and support groups—to individuals and their children in same-sex families.[10] Trina Greene, who manages POV's "Start Strong" violence prevention program for middle-school children, echoes this sentiment: "We shifted from calling it violence against women to just the violence prevention movement, because men are impacted by violence one out of six, you know? So One in Six[11] is an organization that we work with . . . there are men victims and survivors who also need support. So I feel like we're coming to a change in the tide and I think that sometimes that change is always scary."

People we have spoken with in the field agree that it is important for antiviolence organizations to go beyond "violence against women" to create a broader symbolic face and expanded services that better meet the needs of boys and men victimized by sexual and domestic violence. But many would also agree that such change is "scary." Creating gender-symmetrical language risks rendering women invisible—and women are still by far the most common targets of sexual and domestic violence, still most in need of support services. Gender-neutral language also risks obliterating the history of antiviolence work as a social movement initiated and built almost exclusively through the efforts of feminist women. Put simply, the change to "gender-based violence" properly connects antiviolence work to an expanding "client base," while making less visible the roots and continued extent of violence against women. The shift to gender-neutral language also makes sense strategically, as a way of connecting with funding agencies that might balk at overt expressions of feminism, but this strategy has the effect of further depoliticizing the work, shifting it from a social movement base to a social service profession.

Depoliticization of Antiviolence Work

The professionals who administer antiviolence nonprofits work hard to compete for and to exploit scarce available resources, and they appreciate the government and foundation support for their work. But most of them—especially the veterans of the women's movement who still work in the field—are wary of how the health and criminal justice frameworks within which they work can limit or even subvert the work they do. David Lee, who has a background in public health and now heads up CALCASA, said that "taking on violence as a public health issue does not always work . . . we get a little bit trapped in that—we recognize what public health can bring, but also recognize what its limits are."

One of the major limits noted by several people we interviewed is how institutionalization and professionalization have depoliticized antiviolence work, with criminal justice and medical approaches eclipsing feminist approaches. Patti Giggans told us, "I really feel so connected to a movement, I grew up in this movement in a way, you know?" But she is aware of how the very growth of professionalized antiviolence work threatens the existence of the movement: "Women have created this industry. It's an industry now. We've created a profession, and we're professionals now. Okay, well what does that mean? Where does the movement fit into that? Can you have a movement made up of professionals?"

Several veterans of the Movement and Bridge cohorts asked similar questions. Chris Anderegg continued to work with community antiviolence nonprofits well into the 2000s, but he bemoaned the loss of a radical, social-change impulse in the work. When the work got institutionalized, and government moneys started to flow in the mid-1990s, Anderegg said, "it got focused on service delivery because the people who are giving the money want measurable services. How many people did you give counseling to? How many beds did you provide? . . . Back [in the 1970s] we were part of a movement, even though there was a very small amount of men who were involved in it, it felt like we were part of a movement, and now all the feeling is gone." Paul Kivel saw things similarly. He had continued his work with boys and men into the 1990s and 2000s, but in 1999 he discontinued the Oakland Men's Project's nonprofit status, in part owing to how such work had become increasingly depoliticized:

A lot of the work became fragmented, partly because there was no longer a women's movement. A lot of the organizations providing services to women were becoming more and more conservative and more dependent on govern- ment—not government funding but, you know, nonprofit foundation fund- ing and more intimately connected to the police and the courts . . . there was no broad sense of movement building or long-term political change . . . the nonprofits were doing much more time-limited, much more narrowly focused [projects with] major government funding for women's programs, which really tied them even more tightly and intimately into the whole health services and nonprofit model. More corporate money came in to fund these things so it became less and less possible to do more radical work within these kinds of programs.

To be sure, activists of the Movement and Bridge cohorts had labored and lobbied to create the very institutionalization of antiviolence work that threatens to depoliticize their work, ironically further severing it from its movement roots. Juan Carlos Areán spoke with pride about how the organization he works with, the National Violence Prevention Fund (now Futures Without Violence), had helped to pass the Violence Against Women Act, but he is also troubled with the implications of his organization's strategy of doing "bipartisan" work in the nation's capi- tal: "When you go up to the Capitol, I have learned that there are some things that usually don't go very well, and one is talking about femi- nism. I don't think our politicians really relate to that language. They don't even relate to the gender equality necessarily. It's much easier to talk about violence and for everybody to agree that violence is wrong than to, you know, revive the Equal Rights Amendment talk." We saw in the previous chapter how Michael Kaufman had made a similar decision in the early 1990s to shape the White Ribbon Campaign as a single-issue men's antiviolence campaign with wide appeal, rather than as a radical organization that sought to connect violence prevention to other femi- nist and progressive issues. The strategy worked, and it helped to build White Ribbon into the world's largest men's antiviolence organization. However, Kaufman laments that in shaping White Ribbon in this way, the organization becomes "looser, you certainly lose a rigor . . . you lose a depth of analysis," especially one that connects an understanding of violence against women to other social issues.

White Ribbon, you know, you could be someone who doesn't have a clue about [what causes violence] and just say, "Oh yeah, I'm against violence against women." . . . You lose that depth, those linkages. White Ribbon doesn't speak out when a government cuts back social services, [and] my guess is that that will lead to more violence against women. I'm assuming that. But White Ribbon, because of the nature of what it is, isn't going to come out against cutbacks in, you know, unemployment insurance. We don't. We wouldn't come out as White Ribbon against the use of violence in war, against U.S. or Canadian involvement in Afghanistan, because we would differ within White Ribbon on, you know, should we be there? Although *I* would say, if you're a country that's trying to develop this sort of warrior culture, warrior mentality, it's going to be a culture in which there's more gender-based violence.

Ramesh Kathanadhi, who works with Men Stopping Violence, a national institute that provides training and curricula for regional and local antiviolence groups, shares Michael Kaufman's frustrations with how current organizations seem incapable of connecting with other social issues: "The national agenda around teen dating violence doesn't challenge at all the school environments that are completely being gutted and eviscerated and also how in communities of color and in poor communities, [they are] being real pipelines into prisons. The frustration I have with so much of prevention work and so much of the dialogues that we're having around it is that it is inherently ahistorical. It requires us to completely divorce ourselves of the realities that are right in front of us."

Areán, Kaufman, and Kathanadhi are describing an antiviolence field that, by sustaining itself through professionally institutionalized feminism, has surrendered its radicalism (defined here as the ability to address an issue—like violence against women—so as to connect to confronting its root causes in male dominance, the decline in public support for schools and the poor, and militarism). The community face of antiviolence organizations—especially perhaps when they are in fundraising mode—can also compromise or even surrender their feminist identities. Scholar-activist Robert Jensen sarcastically described two "comical" fundraisers:

I've seen fundraisers for rape crisis centers—a silent auction, where one of the prizes is cosmetic surgery.[12] So you have a feminist movement that tried to make the argument that women should not, you know, conform themselves to male expectations—all of a sudden, giving cosmetic surgery gift certificates as a prize in a silent auction, that's kind of weird. In Houston, the Houston Astros baseball team has a group called Wives of the Houston Astros. One of the fundraisers they do for the Houston Area Women's Center was a fashion show. So you have women defined as adjuncts to men in male sport, who put on a fashion show to benefit an allegedly feminist organization.

Feminism: Disappeared, Eclipsed, or Implicit?

A major feature of the "industry" that feminist activists helped to create is how antiviolence nonprofits are now joined at the hip with institutions that feminists once saw as the enemy: the government, the medical establishment, the police, and courts. To be sure, feminist engagements have created meaningful reforms within these very institutions, thus making it possible sometimes to create effective collaborations. However, the sheer size and power of these institutions can dwarf their smaller feminist partner organizations, raising fears among activists that feminism will be absorbed, be co-opted, or simply disappear, like a drop of purple dye in the ocean. These institutional links are viewed as useful, necessary even, but as Patti Giggans explains, they also become reasons to further push feminism to the background: "I don't talk about [Peace Over Violence] being a feminist organization. I feel like we have a feminist perspective [but] we also have the public health perspective. We also have a criminal justice perspective. Obviously, we use the police, we try to hold the abusers accountable. . . . So to say that we're a feminist organization, I personally feel is a misrepresentation."

Feminism, our interviewees suggest, has been eclipsed by the alliance of antiviolence nonprofits, the state, and foundations. We purposefully use the term *eclipsed* here, rather than "eliminated" or "obliterated." A solar eclipse conjures images of the moon temporarily blocking the direct light of the sun from reaching the earth; however, even during a "total" solar eclipse, the earth never falls into total darkness. The sun is still there, its corona of light spilling around the edges of the moon, indirectly lighting the earth. So too, feminist antiviolence activists today work behind parameters set by depoliticized and medicalized approaches to rape and domestic violence prevention, while creatively strategizing to influence public policy, to shine feminist light onto antiviolence curricula and on-the-ground prevention efforts.

There are several ways in which activists creatively inject feminism into antiviolence work. First, although they recognize the limits, some also see aspects of the current institutional configuration of antiviolence work as providing space for progressive organizing. Allan Creighton, for instance, sees the field of public health not simply in terms of how it imposes limits on radical organizing but as a political field that can be reciprocally influenced by feminist activists and organizations. The word *public* in public health, according to Creighton, opens space for an antiviolence strategy that "draws away from working victim by victim by victim and moves towards the community by community by community."

In short, Creighton argues, the public health field creates opportunities to creatively apply more radical, feminist, and multiracial approaches to addressing violence issues. The longtime movement activist said that having a salaried job leading the violence prevention effort in the UC Berkeley student health center is "a social justice thing . . . and that's how I justify [it]—I have to say, 'Oh it's a job, good, I can get a job.' I'm not so fond of the public health stuff all the time, but when I get that far in thinking about it, I'm thinking, 'Yeah, it's community organizing, that's really what we're supposed to be doing,' then it really makes sense to me."

Longtime activists from the Movement Cohort, like Creighton, continued to mentor younger people entering the field, teaching them about their history by infusing a feminist understanding of the sources, consequences, and solutions to violence against women. After Don Conway-Long helped to start RAVEN in the late 1970s and 1980s, he pulled away from the group for several years, focusing on other political work and on his teaching. When we interviewed him, he had recently reconnected with RAVEN as a consultant and was surprised at the extent to which RAVEN's former "highly politicized profeminist analysis . . . is not there among the men," having been supplanted by "this therapy kind of dynamic." But Conway-Long took it upon himself to bring some feminist mentoring to RAVEN: "I'm kind of persuasive [laughs], that's a big claim. Well I will try to be persuasive anyway. I intend to talk about my history, the history of RAVEN, what the issues meant to us in the beginning, what we hoped that the organization could become. Even though it's so different now, we can still go back and re-seize on some of those early principles, *if they choose to do so*."

Clearly, as we will see in the second half of this chapter, the younger generation of activists who have entered antiviolence work in recent years continues to benefit from the mentoring and experience of activists from the Movement and Bridge cohorts. There is also, of course, the question of what happens when the older generation of activists leaves their jobs, or dies? Ben Atherton-Zeman points to dangers implied when feminist pioneers of antiviolence work retire, or are edged out by boards of directors who seek more "professional" managers:

> There's this tendency lately for us as a movement to be hiring executive directors who are not from the movement, who are not feminists. Our boards are looking to people to raise more money now that we no longer have a staff of three, we have a staff of thirty in our agency, and instead of an annual budget of a hundred thousand, it's become an annual budget of two million. Boards of directors are responsible fiscally for that, and so they get scared and hire

somebody who has experience managing, but no experience as a feminist. No people from the movement. So that's, I think, an unintended side-effect of our finally getting some funding through the Violence Against Women Act and other things, is that we now have people in this movement who aren't just passionate advocates. We have people doing this 'cause they want a job.

Robert Jensen sees similar dangers: "The people, and they're mostly women, at the top of those organizations really do see themselves as CEOs and fundraisers. Their job is to manage a hierarchy and make sure there's money coming in." But Jensen also sees a strategic deployment of feminist strategies by activists on the ground, who he says, "are bristling because they want to keep a more politicized edge to the work, they don't just want to do service provision, they want to do public education. And a lot of them are quite radical. They're the women who are the most consistently radical in feminist circles in the United States today. But often they're working with CEOs and VPs who don't even consider the rape crisis center a feminist enterprise; it's a social service delivery system."

The actions described above—Allan Creighton using a student health job to do community organizing, Don Conway-Long nudging younger activists to re-incorporate more radical and feminist analysis into their work with domestic violence groups, Robert Jensen describing efforts by women activists to conduct feminist rape crisis work even when working for organizations with corporate leaderships—describe a range of progressive strategies by savvy feminist activists who are limited but not smothered by the constraints imposed by the health model of violence prevention, and by the professionalized and increasingly corporate funding system of the nonprofit industrial complex. Sociologist Danielle Giffort introduced the term *implicit feminism* to describe how feminist values (but not feminist labels or language) sometimes shape strategies deployed by leaders or workers who are operating in antifeminist or postfeminist organizations.[13] So too, today's feminist antiviolence activists on the ground, and even some longtime feminist leaders of antiviolence organizations, may see it as imprudent or even perhaps not fully accurate to explicitly label their organizations or their work as "feminist." But the feminism is still there—even if sometimes only "implicit"—and is being made available to a new and younger cohort of activists. But Don Conway-Long's words "*if they choose to do so*" raise an important question, not only about intergenerational transmission of knowledge but also about how the shifting institutional landscape differently shapes the Professional Cohort's pathways into antiviolence work, as well as its challenges.

PATHWAYS OF A PROFESSIONAL COHORT

Born between 1971 and 1991, the twenty-four younger men[14] we interviewed belong to what we call the Professional Cohort, men who engaged with antiviolence after the mid-1990s, when the work itself had become highly professionalized. This is not to argue that each of these men shares a professional class status, or defines himself as a professional (though many do). Rather, we use the term *Professional Cohort* to highlight how these men's moments of engagement with antiviolence work occurred in a historical context of institutionalized (and increasingly networked) organizations with built-in professional occupations—executive directors of nonprofits; salaried prevention specialists in schools, universities, and community organizations; gender-based violence niches in counseling psychology and social work—and also a number of internships, volunteer positions, and low-paid part-time jobs young men can plug into, sometimes temporarily, sometimes leading to longer commitments and careers.

This range of volunteer, job, and career positions in the field of violence prevention expanded the space for men's involvements. And the complex networking of government, foundations, nonprofits, helping professions, and universities created a multidimensional geography of criss-crossing pathways into (and sometimes out of) antiviolence work. The men of the Movement Cohort came to antiviolence work mostly through their political activism in the social movements (especially the women's movement) of the late 1960s and early 1970s. The men of the Bridge Cohort engaged during a time when movement feminism was fragmenting and activists were building community nonprofits and starting to professionalize antiviolence work. These changes created strains between professionalization and politicized feminism, while also broadening the field of action, a major indicator of which was an influx of more men of color into antiviolence work.

The men of the Professional Cohort come of age during a time of a dramatic deepening of three patterns that were just starting to become evident for those of the Bridge Cohort. First, as some aspects of feminism were being successfully integrated into institutions, feminism as a grassroots social movement was further receding from public view. Sociologist Jo Reger refers to today's college students as "Generation Fluoride" to describe their relationship with a feminism that appears to be both "everywhere and nowhere." On the one hand, feminist ideas and values are "everywhere," like fluoride in public drinking water, permeating the culture in a way that leads younger people to take for granted, for instance, the idea of equal opportunity for women. On the other hand, with a grassroots women's movement in largely in abeyance, feminism is simultaneously "nowhere," largely invisible,[15] thus feeding a "post-feminist" sensibility premised on the idea that the work of the women's movement is done, that feminist organizing for social change is no longer necessary.[16]

Second, the Professional Cohort continued and expanded the Bridge Cohort's increasing diversity, both racial/ethnic and sexual: of the twenty-four men we interviewed in this cohort, nine identified as men of color (four as African American, three Latino, one biracial, one South Asian), and nine identified as something other than heterosexual men (five as gay, three bisexual, one queer transgender). And third, the Professional Cohort came of age during a time of expansion in the number and range of pathways into antiviolence work, facilitated to a great extent by a dramatic integration and networking of funded organizations, careers, jobs, and internships in violence prevention work. Next, we sketch the two most common patterns of entry into men's contemporary violence prevention work: pathways through a network of feminist education, campus and community organizations; and intersectional (race, class, and sexual) pathways.

Pathways in a Networked Field

We spoke to Joe Samalin in a Manhattan diner, near where he earns a modest salary as the coordinator of training and technical assistance for the Washington DC–based Men Can Stop Rape. The stocky thirty-six-year-old has a boyish face, and his friendly and enthusiastic demeanor was unabated through the interview. Samalin said he and his girlfriend, who works with a human rights nonprofit, were hoping soon to purchase their first house. Samalin's pathway to his job is typical in many ways of those of the Professional Cohort, especially the white men we interviewed. As a teen, Samalin experienced the pain of seeing his mother "recovering memories of the ridiculously horrific amounts of sexual abuse of children that existed on her side of the family, going back two generations, and herself as a survivor." For young Joe, this was "a big deal . . . part of my family story." In college from 1994 to 1998 at SUNY New Paltz, Samalin "fell in with the rowdy crowd of feminists, I took an intro to women's studies course or two, but mostly it was the activism and the organizing . . . I was the token guy in the women's group on campus." For Samalin, attending his first campus Take Back the Night event was "pivotal." He recalls "three to four hundred women" who participated, and there were also "between twenty and thirty men on the march, which was cool." But at the march's end, "some of the guys were upset" when they learned that the speak-out was to be women-only: "After the march, at the speak-out area, the doors got closed in all our faces. I turned around, and for the first time realized, 'Oh! I've got thirty men here, pumped up from the rally, and don't know what to do with them.' So I took them all over to the corner, we all sat down and talked about how it was to be at the rally, and how it was to be guys doing something on this issue, and said 'Hey, let's all meet again, next week. Wednesday, anyone?' "

The men's discussion at Take Back the Night sparked a new campus men's organization. A few years later, Samalin hoped to replicate such an organization when he arrived at Columbia University to work on a master's degree in East Asian Studies; "I thought coming into an Ivy league institution I'd have to start the men's group there, and I was all excited to do it—turns out they'd had one for ten years before I got there, so that was pretty exciting. And humbling." For the next few years, Samalin co-ran Columbia Men Against Violence, working in conjunction with the campus women's center. His postcollege employment record is a string of jobs in the antiviolence field, starting with a position for three years in New York with Day One, "recruiting and then training college students to be peer educators in issues of interpersonal violence and domestic violence at campuses and in their neighborhoods." From there he moved to a job with Safe Horizon, "New York's largest victim services agency, [working] specifically with their anti-stalking program," after which he took his current position with Men Can Stop Rape.

Joe Samalin's Take Back the Night story from the late 1990s echoes a similarly fraught moment two decades earlier, when radical feminist women tried to bar the men of MASV from participating in the first-ever TBTN march in San Francisco. Both groups of men had to figure out how to navigate the tensions built into what it means for men to be working as allies with women. What's different for men of the Professional Cohort is how the organizational context provides ready-made avenues for men like Samalin to plug in and participate. By the time Samalin started college, Take Back the Night was already an institutionalized tradition at SUNY, overseen by a campus office. When he arrived at Columbia University, Samalin found a men's antiviolence organization already existed, as did a range of networked community nonprofits and a number of professional opportunities that were potentially open to him once he entered the job market.

Comparing the stories of the men of the Professional Cohort with those of earlier Cohorts, what is most striking is just how much institutional infrastructure is already in place on campuses and in communities, and how well antiviolence organizations and professionals are networked. Patrick Donovan's story illustrates this point further. As a high school student at the end of the 1990s, Donovan's best friend was a girl, and he was appalled with "the level of sexual harassment that she got walking through the campus." In his freshman year at Boston College, he was given the option to focus his first year community service on women's issues, soon "got connected with the Women's Center," and was asked to link the BC campus efforts with those at the Boston-area Rape Crisis Center. By October, he was helping to organize the annual Take Back the Night event, a transformative experience for him: "When the time came for the open-mic, a lot of my friends from the club then went up and spoke about their own experiences with violence and abuse. So that's when it went from becoming a political issue to more of a personal issue for me, with names and faces and stories. And, I wanted to get more involved and stay with it."

Donovan did "stay with it" after graduating, moving to jobs in youth violence prevention with a YWCA rape crisis center in San Jose, California, and then with HAWC, in Seattle. Professional Cohort men who followed a similar college-to-jobs antiviolence trajectory also talk about the importance of mentors. Like those of the Bridge Cohort, the younger men often talk of women professors or community organization leaders who inspired and taught them. And more so than those of the Bridge Cohort, these younger men speak of the centrality of male mentors in their lives and work. Rob Buelow was twenty-seven years old when we interviewed him, and he had already served a two-year stint as violence prevention coordinator at the University of California, Irvine, before returning to Harvard to do graduate study. Buelow attributes much of what he now teaches about sexual consent to lessons he has learned from older men such as Harry Brod and Jackson Katz, veterans of profeminist work. As a college student at Penn State University in the mid-2000s, Buelow describes himself as "taking on a very sort of dominant, masculine role as an individual," and then he took the advice of a woman friend to take a women's studies class: "[I] went into it with my preconceived notions of what women's studies was going to be like and what feminism was all about . . . stereotypical, and traditionally, probably wrong (laughs), senses of butch women and angry people. So I go into the class, not skeptical, but I had a sense of what it might be like. And my teacher walks in, and it was Brian [Jara], and immediately my preconceived notions, stereotypes, and schemas were blown up. Like, whoa, there's a guy teaching this class, that's not what I expected."

We have seen that the men of the Movement Cohort had few or no women's studies classes or professors available to them in their college years and that several men of the Bridge Cohort benefited from the growth of women's studies in their college years. For the men of the Professional Cohort, women's and gender studies courses, majors, and even some graduate degree programs were routinely available. And although most gender studies professors are women, over the past decade or two a growing number of men have entered the field.[17] At the point in his life when he walked into his first women's studies course, Rob Buelow suggests, learning about feminism from a man opened his eyes, revealing a burst of connections between what was going on within and around him.

> Then I started to see it all around campus, you know, with the drinking culture, particularly pertaining to sexual violence and the way that men talked about women and expectations of relationships, and what were my own expectations of relationships and all those sorts of things. And then I saw it in my friends and the language that they used and the things that they prioritized and the things that we talked about as guys—it just all of a sudden seemed to inundate my world.

The emotional impact of these revelations soon drove Buelow to action: "I felt bad. I felt like I was part of the problem, and I wanted to do something about it." Along with a woman graduate student, Buelow formed a One in Four men's rape prevention group on campus, which eventually merged with the ongoing Men Against Violence organization. His active student leadership role at Penn State started him on a professional pathway in campus-based violence prevention work.

The trajectories of Joe Samalin, Patrick Donovan, Rob Buelow, and others of the Professional Cohort reflect the common themes outlined by sociologists Erin Casey and Tyler Smith in their study of contemporary men's pathways to antiviolence work. Casey and Smith point to three common moments in the pathway: first, an initial "sensitizing experience" (often a personal or second-hand experience with violence), followed second and third (in either order) by an opportunity to become engaged in an antiviolence organization or event (it is striking in this regard how often our interviewees mention campus Take Back the Night events as pivotal moments), and by a shift in the personal meanings of gendered experiences in their own lives (facilitated by women's studies courses, campus organizing, and feminist women friends).[18] However, not all of the men we interviewed followed this pathway, which most closely applies to the experiences of white college-educated men. Tal Peretz studied two very different men's community antiviolence groups in Atlanta—one a group of Muslim black heterosexual men; the other, a group of black gay and queer men—and found that their experiences diverged both subtly and dramatically from the pathway described by Casey and Smith.[19] So too, the men of color and non–heterosexually identified men in our study describe pathways that are complicated and enriched by intersectional engagements with race, class, and sexuality.

Intersectional Pathways

We interviewed Emiliano Diaz de Leon in a conference room of the Texas Association Against Sexual Assault, where he had worked for the past three years as a primary prevention specialist. On the walls of the TAASA office were fliers and posters for antiviolence events, a framed portrait of Dr. Martin Luther King, and a bulletin board on which people had thumb-tacked short handwritten and often humorous phrases about their work (e.g., "I'll straighten out their homophobia" and "We just can't stop preventing things, we are preventioneers on a rampage"). Thirty-six years old when we interviewed him, Emiliano earns a modest salary with TAASA and lives in Austin with his wife, a teacher, and their young child.

Emiliano Diaz de Leon grew up in a "working poor" family in Austin. His mother worked hard at "barely minimum wage" to support Emiliano and his siblings. Early on, "there were really no positive men at home [or] on the street . . . two men while I was in high school came in and were abusive to my mother, and were also drug addicts and alcoholics." Young Emiliano was troubled with witnessing domestic violence at home, and by the time he was in high school in the early 1990s, he says, "I was already perpetrating dating violence . . . I was becoming like my step-dads, you know, the abuse was beginning to escalate." His life trajectory turned dramatically when as a sixteen-year-old sophomore he was recruited to Expect Respect, a group for boys at his high school, run by Cisco Garcia, the man who became Emiliano's mentor and role model: "Here's this Latino man who's living this kind of really nonviolent life—this is the first time that I've seen this loving, nurturing, caring man—who treated me with a tremendous amount of respect, and really believed in me, believed in my ability to transform my behavior."

Emiliano stayed with the group for the duration of high school, reading Paul Kivel's book *Men's Work* along the way, joining the Boy Scouts, and working as a youth minister at his local Catholic Church, all of which "helped me survive, get off the street, [and] graduate from high school."

Following high school, Emiliano met his future wife Cindy, who "knew my story [and] made it crystal clear that she wasn't going to be with me if I was going to be abusive in any way. That was a condition of our relationship, that it needed to be healthy and nonviolent." Cindy suggested he apply for a job at Safe Place, a shelter for battered women and their children, so at the age of twenty-one and for the next five years Emiliano worked as a children's advocate there, where he was mentored and challenged by women supervisors and co-workers. He thrived in this work and began to speak publicly about his own experiences with violence, even appearing on the Oprah Winfrey television show. Eventually, he moved to a position as the children's advocate at the Domestic Violence and Sexual Assault Center in Harlingen, Texas: "I worked with the children of battered women. . . . I really began meeting a lot of boys that, like at the shelter here in Austin, were also abused primarily, you know, by men. And really began thinking about, how do we prevent that, especially with Latino boys and men? And how do I personally kind of do that work? How do I move from an institution to actually a community setting? And primarily from kids who have already experienced domestic violence to really working to prevent domestic and sexual violence?"

In 2008, Emiliano got his chance to do prevention work, moving to his current job in Austin with TAASA, where he helps to coordinate violence prevention work with boys in schools and provides "training and technical assistance primarily with rape crisis centers that are doing primary prevention of sexual violence work."

What is most striking about Emiliano Diaz de Leon's story, comparing it with others we have discussed above, is the extent to which college is not a salient part of his pathway. He did take some college classes, earning an associate's degree, but the turning point in terms of consciousness and activism for him came in high school, catalyzed by a male mentor and an antiviolence program for boys. And, like several other men of color we interviewed, such as Gilbert Salazar, whom we profiled in Chapter 1, Emiliano Diaz de Leon's passion to do prevention work with boys and men emerged out of his previous work with youths who had been victimized and abused, and with whom he empathized in light of his own family experiences. His perspective on antiviolence thus emerges from a place of moral outrage with men's (including his own) violence against women, but also from a place of sympathy for the vulnerabilities of boys, particularly poor Latino boys.[20]

Sean Tate was working as an academic counselor for his alma mater, the University of Texas, when we interviewed him, and he came to this job from a position with the Texas Council on Violence Prevention. The thirty-one-year-old Tate's story resonates with those of other men of color in our study. Early on in life, he recalls being very aware of racial oppression, but "there weren't many conversations happening" around him about the oppression of women. Still, witnessing how poorly his mother—the sole provider in his family and "the smartest and most hard working person I know"—was treated at work, he began to see connections.

> Seeing what it's like for an intelligent, very capable woman trying to make it in a quote-unquote man's world. You know, you couldn't miss it . . . as an African American, as a black guy in this country, like, you know, [laughs] you get used to the idea of injustice and how people in positions of power can oppress people who aren't. So there's an automatic identification with gender rights struggle, to civil rights [and] race equality. So it's not a far stretch, you know what I mean? [laughs] Like it's a, it's just like well, yeah man, I can totally understand that.

Clearly, not all African American men make the sort of "automatic identification" between racism and sexism that Sean Tate did. However, recent research suggests that he may not be an aberration. Among the black professional class men she studied, sociologist Adia Harvey Wingfield found a common tendency for such men to draw from their experiences of racial oppression to become allies with women for workplace equality.[21]

Our interviews with the two youngest men in our sample, twenty-two-year-old Jamonte Pitts and twenty-one-year-old James Campos, hint at an emergent pathway to antiviolence work for younger men of color. During their high school years in Los Angeles, Pitts, an African American, and Campos, a Latino, were both involved in "My Strength" campus groups, set up and facilitated by Peace Over Violence. Following high school, they were both recruited to paid positions with POV, helping to facilitate high school My Strength groups.[22] When he was in his early teens, Campos told us, he found out that some of his family members "were abused sexually by a family member," and early in high school he found out that his "girlfriend at the time, she was raped and that was like the climax. It was like, I need to do something." He joined the My Strength campus group, at first participating without much enthusiasm, but eventually he found it resonated with his concerns and empowered him to act.

> I guess I needed extra credit for a health class. . . . [My Strength] wasn't appealing to me until the point where my mother was getting abused by my step dad at the time. So it was kind of like, this is happening in my house, these people are helping out, giving all this information and it kind of reinforced my

wanting to be there. Ever since that, from ninth grade on to where I am now, I've been committed to POV and the work they've done. I've taken it to school, to church, to my own family right now, and it's a great benefit.

Campos' and Pitts' youth, their life experiences and generally shared social location with poor boys of color in Los Angeles schools, in addition to their own positive engagements with My Strength, made them valuable resources for POV's continued work in local schools. This direct recruitment of young men of color into antiviolence jobs (often part-time and for lower pay than for the college-educated professionals they work with) may with time develop into a different sort of pathway, possibly as a first step that leads to college, and to professional careers in violence prevention.

The pathways of Emiliano Diaz de Leon, Gilbert Salazar, Sean Tate, Kevin Hawkins, and James Campos differ from those of most of the white men of the Professional Cohort, in three ways. First, though many men of color share with white men early sensitizing experiences of violence in their own families, the combination of racism and (often) struggling working-class family contexts makes possible an organically intersectional standpoint for understanding violence as a multifaceted phenomenon, grounded in race, class, and gender. Second, young men of color, once sensitized to the problem of violence, find generally different organizational pathways to violence prevention employment—sometimes as early as high school, and sometimes by being recruited right out of high school for jobs working with "at-risk" youths. And third, an intersectional understanding of violence frequently stimulates men of color to create varying approaches to antiviolence prevention with boys and men.

Kevin Hawkins says that in the work he does now, his identity as an African American male of working-class background allows him to better identify with the mostly working-class and African American men who are sent by probation and parole boards to his RAVEN groups in St. Louis: "The majority of them are 'me' in identity. I understood where they were coming from. And I just found myself really feeling the need to provide help in ways that they're able to relate to and understand." Sean Tate echoed this statement. Working with African Americans, he said, you have to deal first with the reality that these young men suffer from the "psychological burden" of knowing "there's a 30 percent chance . . . you're gonna go to jail or you're gonna die. You have to be sensitive to that experience before you can ask that person to be looking out for other people, you know? And I think that on the whole, African American men feel incredibly neglected and ignored. They got their own set of issues [and so] if you're dealing with the issue of race, you can [then] make that connection to the issue of gender."

Kevin Hawkins' and Sean Tate's words speak to the importance of having men of color working in the antiviolence field. Their life experience often situates them to better understand and empathize with boys and young men of color, and this informs their ability to focus on race and "make that connection to the issue of gender" in their violence prevention efforts. It can also mean that they bring a different orientation to working with young white people. Keith Smith, an African American counselor who does violence prevention with fraternities and other groups at the University of Vermont, a primarily white campus, says he is aware that there's a considerable amount of racist fear projected onto him by white students, and he strategically uses this to educate them: "If I'm working with a group of white men and we're talking about sexual assault and rape, and maybe I start talking about rape myths, I'll talk about how there's this myth about black men being, you know, these sexual predators—and even if I'm working with white women, I also will talk about that, as a way of getting them to think a little more broadly about the stereotype."

Men's organically intersectional engagements with antiviolence work can also emerge from experiences of sexual and gender oppression. The gay, bisexual, and queer-identified men of the Professional Cohort described pathways that were distinct in some ways. Todd Henneman worked for several years as a journalist, and then doing corporate diversity training for Disney. In 2000, at the age of twenty-nine, he was recruited to a job as assistant director for the University of Southern California's Center for Women and Men, his primary job to restart and administer MenCARE, a student violence prevention group.[23] Previous to taking the position, Henneman says he had no experience working in the field of gender-based violence. His rapid self-education included lots of reading, and a training session with Jackson Katz. Despite his lack of background in the field, Henneman feels that he was predisposed to understand many of the issues MenCARE would confront, thanks to growing up gay, "feeling different, like this otherness and being afraid of coming out as an adolescent . . . kind of like my whole access into the world of male privilege—because I didn't feel like I fit in there."

Similarly, Stephen Philp told us that as a young gay man, "I understand discrimination." As a freshman at USC in 2006, he got drunk and blacked out at a party. When he awoke, he realized a man had sexually assaulted him.

> I obviously never gave my consent to what happened, but I was taught to
> feel really ashamed about that experience, to not identify that as sexual
> assault because that's just what happens in the gay community, like you get

drunk to the point of blacking out, and somebody takes advantage of you and that's what happens, and you asked for it, and that's how the gay community works. And it's like: No, not at all, that's not acceptable, that's not an acceptable culture . . . as I processed the experience more and came to terms with what it really was and named it, which was sexual assault, yeah, this is a problem . . . and we need to address that problem.

In 2006, Philp joined MenCARE, where he was mentored by Henneman and was inspired "to develop that program about gay, bisexual, and transgender male, male-identified people and sexual assault." That same year, two thousand miles away, John Erickson's pathway to antiviolence work was sparked when he "was hate-crimed" as a first-year gay athlete by some of his teammates on his University of Wisconsin-Whitewater volleyball team, who "got very drunk one night and they smeared feces on the hotel room door that I was staying at." Erickson transferred to another college, where he was drawn to women's studies, and eventually into antiviolence work with a campus women's center.

Although the men of color in the Professional Cohort narrate pathways that express an organically intersectional understanding of race, class, and gender violence, the gay and bisexual men in the study express another sort of organic intersectionality, using their own experiences of sexual marginality, subordination and violence to broaden engagements with gender-based violence. Tal Peretz argues that for the gay, bisexual, and queer men he studied, "there may be a special salience to sexual and gender-based oppression: a non-normative sexual or gender identity not only invites investigation and explanation, but encourages these *in reference to* gender."[24]

Robbie Samuels, thirty-six years old when we interviewed him, identifies as a "white queer Jewish transman," and his story illustrates an amplification of the sorts of salient connections between gender and sexuality that Peretz refers to, and to the development of a radically intersectional engagement with violence. As a lesbian college student in the early 2000s, Samuels was immersed in "dyke culture" and active in feminist and LGBT campus groups. While transitioning in 2003–04, Samuels applied his political understanding of power to himself, and realized that as a man,

My voice was going to carry both a greater privilege and a greater responsibility, and that I needed to do some self-reflection, because the way I moved in the world as a very brass, loud, opinionated woman, dyke, in woman-centered spaces was one thing, but to now be that guy–like, *that guy*... A lot of it was realizing that the behavior I had when I was identified as female, and I was being loud, and I was being obnoxious, and you either loved me or hated me, that's who I was and whether you agreed with me you loved me or hated me—wasn't always the best behavior. I was silencing people, I was taking up airspace, I was taking up physical space, I wasn't being a good leader. All the things that now I'm like, "Oh, that I couldn't get away with as a man."

Samuels' words reflect sociologist Kristen Schilt's findings in her study of the experiences of transmen, who in their workplaces experienced escalating status and respect, sometimes even higher pay and position compared with how they had been treated as women. Their experiences helped them to understand the many ways male privilege still operates, often mostly as subtle interactional processes.[25] Schilt observed, however, that not all transmen were equally escalated. Black transmen, in particular, noted that some of the same interactional styles and traits they had exhibited as black women—such as the use of a loud voice and boisterous body language—were now interpreted as threatening, now that they were black *men*. Samuels understood that "I needed to be race-conscious at the same time that I need to be gender-conscious . . . because not only did I realize that I was going to be perceived as *a man* in the world, but I immediately was like 'I'm going to be a *white* man.' My race had not been a conscious thing up to that point . . . just that, like, I'm *the man*. Like, I'm going to be, capital T, capital M."

Samuels searched the Internet and found a local chapter of NOMAS, an organization he says expressed a sensitivity not just to gender and power but to race as well. With NOMAS Boston, he found a supportive political community. In 2006, Samuels founded SoJust.Org, Socializing for Justice, an online site that, like Samuels, is radically intersectional in how it connects progressives in the community to organizations and events that are working against violence and more generally to build social justice.

Thus far, we have illustrated how the experiences of men of color with race (and often class) oppression and gay, bisexual, and queer men's experiences with sexual oppression can create predispositions for intersectional understandings and engagements with gender-based violence. However, we do not want to give the impression—and here, we are paraphrasing a memorable title from an early 1990s black feminist text[26]—that all the gay and queer men are white and all the black and brown men are straight. In fact, among our Professional Cohort interviewees, Gilbert Salazar identifies as Latino and bisexual, Brian Jara as multiracial and gay, and Kevin Hawkins as African American and gay. When we interviewed Hawkins, he was working with RAVEN in St. Louis. The thirty-nine-year-old had routed to work with the domestic violence prevention group through several jobs with organizations that are part of a progressive community network: with the Red Cross doing HIV/STD prevention with youths; for eight years as the youth advisor with Growing American Youth, St. Louis' oldest LGBT support group; with Planned Parenthood for four years, coordinating men's services. Together, he says, these jobs allowed him "the opportunity to just really incorporate a lot of what people referred to as 'feminist approach' to the work that I was doing with LGBT youth, with urban inner-city low-income youth, with young women," and now with adult men who batter. This quick summation may make Hawkins' trajectory appear more seamless than it really was, but it is easy to see in his story how his own intersectional identifications—black, male, gay— meshed in various ways with progressive St. Louis organizations that are also increasingly concerned with making connections between race, gender, class, and sexual issues.

RESPONSIBLE BYSTANDERS, GOOD MEN

As violence prevention work with boys and men became professionalized over the past twenty years, two innovations first introduced in the 1990s by pioneers like Mark Stevens, Jackson Katz, and Paul Kivel were institutionalized into the standard prevention curricula. First, preventionists deployed some version of the bystander approach, which addresses men in groups—sports teams, college fraternities, the military—and encourages them to actively intervene in situations that appear to be heading toward a sexual assault. Jackson Katz said that "everybody loves the bystander approach because you're not targeting perpetrators, you know, you're saying, 'everybody has a role to play,' and so I think it takes the defensiveness away from them." Seth Avakian agrees, saying that the bystander approach gets him in the door to do sexual assault prevention with men's sports teams and "finals clubs," Harvard University's informal fraternities that "throw lots of parties": "If you're at a party and you see a guy with a really drunk woman, how could you step in? So its really talking through the steps of how could you do this? And I think there's a lot of social pressure to not be the quote-unquote cockblock. And it's to get them to realize that they're not just potentially helping the woman involved, they're also helping the guy getting himself in a bad situation. . . . if we've gotten someone to take that step, that's a small win."

As Avakian's words suggest, part of the logic behind the bystander approach is that it harnesses men's sense of responsibility to the male group; intervening in a potential sexual assault preserves the integrity of the team, the frat, or the military unit by preventing men in the group from getting into trouble. The bystander approach, in effect, attempts to flip 180 degrees men's sense of responsibility to the male group away from a traditionally sexist male bond that too often enables—even rewards—assaults of women and then envelopes perpetrators in a protective "code of silence."[27]

The bystander approach deploys a second innovation of working with boys and men: appealing to them as "good men." Too often, as we saw especially with the pioneering work of the Movement Cohort, boys and men in prevention workshops or classes responded defensively, feeling perhaps that they were being treated a priori as guilty of sexual assault, simply because they are male. David Lee says that in retrospect, "in the '70s and early '80s it was not male positive work, it was very critical of what men did—and I think we as men carried guilt and shame." Another longtime veteran of antiviolence work, Craig Norberg-Bohm, is enthusiastic about the positive turn in today's approaches: "What's the positive? What is a healthy relationship? And what's good in men's culture? It's not all bad! What are the babies in our bathwater for maleness? What do we want to promote? That's very rich. Because we want people to feel motivated and positive. It doesn't feel good just to be 'Oh, I'm a crud because I'm male.'"

Indeed, today's antiviolence curricula strategically position high school boys, men in fraternities, athletic teams, or the military, in Tony Porter's words, as "being good men, being healthy men." Similarly, Jackson Katz attempted to creatively subvert traditionally patriarchal connotations by naming one of his early groups "'Real Men' for the purpose of deconstructing the whole notion of a real man." Jimmie Briggs says that when he named his youth antiviolence organization "Man Up," it drew "a lot of pushback from feminists," but he insists that "just as the campaign is seeking to redefine the landscape of this issue, we're also seeking to redefine the phrase 'Man Up'. Our inspiration comes more from the urban hip-hop meaning: to represent, to not back down, to stand up, to face your fears, to face your challenges. That's how we define Man Up in this context."

Working with groups of men can be harrowing at times, with pushback coming from individual men in the groups. But Jeffrey Bucholtz's story of an incident in a workshop he co-led for three UC Santa Barbara fraternities also speaks to how the male group, once positioned as "good men," can become active and responsible bystanders in the context of the workshop itself: "So Chris is reading [aloud] the penal code where it says a woman who is intoxicated to the point of incapacitation is unable to consent, and I'm like: 'So basically what we're saying is if a girl is passed out you need to respect that,' and this big guy stands up: 'You fuckin' faggots! That's fuckin' bullshit!' I mean, Chris and I were literally looking for the exits because this guy was amped up. What was interesting was watching the guys around him tell him to sit down and shut up."

The combined bystander/good-men approach to violence prevention seeks to "get in the door" with boys and men, and then eventually to "get them on board" to change their own practices and to challenge the culture of the groups to which they belong. However strategically smart this approach is, many practitioners recognize that it has its limits, and even, some would say, dangers. First, the approach risks projecting the problem of sexual assault on to "other" men, not any of the "good men" in the room. Second, the bystander/good-men approach risks pulling violence prevention further away—perhaps even severing it—from its feminist roots. In positioning the male group and the individual men in the group as inherently good, and only in need of mustering some (traditionally masculine) strength and courage, a key feminist insight is potentially lost: that sexual objectification, conquest and domination of women—"scoring"—is a central organizing principle of many such male groups, not an individual aberration. The nationally popular "Men of Strength" curriculum illustrates both the promise and the limits of the bystander/good-men approach to violence prevention.

Men of Strength

Promoted in the early 2000s by the Washington, DC–based group Men Can Stop Rape, the most publicly recognizable face of the "Men of Strength" campaign was its series of "My Strength Is Not for Hurting" posters, developed by long-time antirape activist John Stoltenberg. The posters, distributed widely in schools, public places, and on the Internet, use social marketing strategies to symbolically project the values of a bystander/good-men approach to sexual violence prevention. Visually, the posters deploy gendered tropes commonly seen in advertising: a close-up shot of a young and conventionally attractive male-female couple, the man looking directly and confidently into the camera, and the woman gazing (often adoringly) at the man, or looking into the distance. At the top of each poster (such as those depicted in Figures 4.1 and 4.2) is written "MY STRENGTH IS NOT FOR HURTING," and each poster highlights a statement by the young man, e.g., "When she was too drunk to decide, I decided WE SHOULDN'T," and "So when she changed her mind, I STOPPED," and "So when I wasn't sure how she felt, I ASKED."

Figure 4.1
"MY STRENGTH IS NOT FOR HURTING" poster.
"My strength is not for hurting" poster copyright © 2014 by John Stoltenberg, reprinted by permission
(Contact: media2change@gmail.com.) Photography by Lotte Hansen.

Figure 4.2
"MY STRENGTH IS NOT FOR HURTING" poster.

"My strength is not for hurting" poster copyright © 2014 by John Stoltenberg, reprinted by permission (Contact: media2change@gmail.com.) Photography by Lotte Hansen.

The My Strength posters have drawn criticism from some feminists for how they visually and textually reproduce a traditional patriarchal positioning of men as active subjects, while silencing the voices of women, treating them as reactive objects.[28] Contrarily, other feminists see the posters as cleverly drawing men in with their appeals to male strength and responsible leadership, while subtly pivoting around to the idea that women are in fact *not* passive objects; rather, the message of the posters is that good men listen to and respect women as active and fully human sexual subjects.

The men we interviewed had a range of opinions on the content of the My Strength posters, but there was a strong consensus that educational posters, by themselves, are unlikely to have much impact. Stephen Philp's comment was typical: "[Posters] can be an element of a campaign. A smart poster campaign can actually do a great job spreading the message, but if that's not reinforced by education, outreach, face time, activities, and some other forms of actual engagement, then you can't change attitudes about something as serious as sexual assault off of a poster."

In fact, the My Strength posters were never intended to be a stand-alone effort to end sexual violence. Though, as Paul Kivel laments, "social marketing became a big buzzword not just in this movement but in the nonprofit sector," antiviolence activists see posters and other media as, at best, supportive of on-the-ground efforts. David Lee was hired in 2005 to oversee CALCASA's development of a major Men of Strength campaign, mostly in California high schools. From the start, Lee said, he saw the My Strength posters, t-shirts, radio, and Internet campaign as "brilliant." However, he believed they would be effective only when coupled with the other part of the program, the creation of Men of Strength Clubs (which CALCASA changed to "My Strength Clubs"), the goal of which was "for young men to become leaders in their community, standing up and speaking out against sexual violence." Working with local rape crisis centers, Lee and CALCASA first piloted six of these groups:

> We were blown away with how wonderful it resonated. So we had black "My Strength" wristbands and t-shirts and things like that. We had these materials to try to saturate the environment, we did radio ads, we did a whole bunch of Internet stuff. . . . The goal is that those men who would go to that club would then take community action, do community action projects. And the theory is that through the range of these activities, that would then lead to some of the changes of the norms in the community. . . . We started with six the first year. We've got between forty and fifty clubs in California now.

Peace Over Violence hired Frank Blaney in 2005 when it was designated by CALCASA as one of its six organizations to run My Strength pilot programs in Los Angeles schools. Blaney also sees a stand-alone poster campaign as "kind of superfluous," but he came to love facilitating My Strength groups because "it resonates with the boys" when he shows them alternatives to the narrow and violent conceptions of masculinity they see around them: "The selling point is not just the fact that a lot of their sisters and moms have been abused. The thing I'm selling, and how I hook 'em, is you can express your full personality without having to kowtow to these stupid male stereotypes. They've been locked in that box. And here for one period a week or however often I meet with them, they can really to a greater degree show who they really are. That's intoxicating to them. They just run with it. Give them the freedom, the permission, the safety to break out of that box."

This strategy worked well for Jamonte Pitts, who as a high school student spent two or three years in one of Frank Blaney's My Strength groups: "I loved it! It enlightened me about a lot of issues and a lot of things that I was uncomfortable expressing or talking about. It helped me open up and know what was right and what was wrong without feeling ashamed about it." Following high school, Pitts was recruited to work with POV; "It was something that I wanted to teach guys and other young males about."

Some men, however, expressed frustration with the limits of the My Strength curriculum, and more broadly with how they see violence prevention curricula as reflecting a deradicalized approach, shaped by the nonprofit industrial complex. Ramesh Kathanadhi told us that he and others in the field are responding to the "neutral" and "bland" curricula by infusing "social justice" values into the work through what he called "strategic subversiveness and disruptive engagements." Gilbert Salazar, for instance, told us that the My Strength curriculum he was required to take into the high schools was not always the most useful way to engage the mostly poor, working-class, and primarily Latino boys he worked with in Salinas, California: "[The boys'] feedback to the [My Strength] images was not very positive. The images to me seemed very polished. They didn't seem quite, you know, *real* enough for me. . . . I don't really use them very often, I don't really show them to boys very often. . . . I feel that in teaching boys about masculinity, it has to encompass all forms of violence, [not just] sexual violence. Particularly in this community, where the violence that gets the most attention is gang violence."

Salazar creatively melded aspects of the My Strength curriculum with strategies he developed through his interest in "theater of the oppressed," a form of radical community theater intended to build group consciousness and transformative social action.[29] Combining creative writing with theater, he said, was "very transformative with the students." Salazar was not the only man we interviewed who used theater in his antiviolence work. Ben Atherton-Zeman has been doing "Voices of Men" theatrical performances on men and feminism since the 1990s, and more recently Marc Rich adapted theater of the oppressed methods in his college sexual violence prevention work[30]: "We want the fraternity guys and the athletes in the room to look at our guys on stage and like them. Because for me the turning point of the show is for them to go, 'that guy's cool, I'm just like that guy, that guy's just like my roommate—oh my god he raped someone, what does that say about me?' "

Other forms of "creative subversion" in violence prevention work involve using "culture jamming" and humor. Brian Jara said his Men Stopping Rape group at Penn State inserted into campus urinals "intentionally provocative" splashguards on which was written, "You hold the power to stop rape in your hands." While organizing a Men Against Rape group on his campus, Jeffrey Bucholtz said he came across a group called "Jugglers Against Rape. They were cool. Yeah. They wore antiviolence t-shirts and did juggling stuff." From the Jugglers, he learned that it helped for the work "to be fun and guys had to find a way to enjoy what they were doing and that we had to be able to laugh," though he conceded that "there's a fine line there. It can be very easy for a group like that to turn into: we make jokes about what's going on and don't do anything about it. But our strategy was: no, we're going to use the jokes to do something."

What Bucholtz defined as a "fine line" between having fun and taking on the serious work of violence prevention has blurred considerably (and controversially) in recent high-profile public antiviolence events like "Walk a Mile in Her Shoes" and "Slutwalks." As a freshman at Western Washington University, Dillon Thompson joined Western Men Against Violence, which was mostly a men's discussion group, but they did one public event: "Walk a Mile in Her Shoes, where we all get high heels and walk a mile." Created in 2001, Walk a Mile in Her Shoes is a theatrical public event intended to raise public awareness of men's commitment to ending violence against women. The playfulness of these events can draw men like Dillon Thompson, giving them a venue to make public their otherwise less-visible antiviolence commitments (see Figure 4.3). But, as sociologist Tristan Bridges has pointed out, Walk a Mile events also revive longstanding feminist questions about the politics and meanings of men's drag performances: by theatrically disrupting a sexualized gender binary, does men's drag undercut male privilege, or does it simply caricature the oppressive aspects of women's subordination (like the physical

Figure 4.3
Men at Walk a Mile in Her Shoes, 2013.
Walk a Mile USC 2013, reprinted by permission of Kaya Masler.

debilitation of wearing high heels), thus reinforcing the bodily and social superiority of men?[31]

Slutwalks raise even broader questions. Sparked in 2011 when a Toronto police officer stated that women could steer clear of being sexually assaulted if they would "avoid dressing like sluts," Slutwalks—massive public marches of mostly scantily clad young people promoting the in-your-face message that no matter how much one embraces a "slut" image sexual assault is never justified—soon erupted in cities around the globe. Slutwalks were fully inclusive of men, had a carnivalesque atmosphere permeated with an air of ironic humor and a youthful third-wave feminist sensibility about celebrating women's sexual pleasure and empowerment (see Figure 4.4). All of this, including especially marchers' seizing and valorizing the epithet "slut,"[32] contrasted sharply with second-wave feminist Take Back the Night events that traditionally emphasize how sexualized images of women are linked to sexual dangers.

The radical inclusiveness and sexual playfulness of Slutwalks and of Walk a Mile in Her Shoes events clearly appeal to many young activists today and provide public venues for men to make public statements about their opposition to violence against women. Feminist sociologists find that women at Slutwalks are encouraged when they see men participating, but they also raise critical questions about the limits and dangers built into these events: Might all the public sexual playfulness trivialize the depth

Figure 4.4
Man at a Slutwalk, Carbondale, Il, 2012.
Photograph by Kristen Barber, reprinted by permission.

and seriousness of the problem of gender-based violence? Will the centrality of men in these events marginalize women's voices? Might the ironic
humor expressed by men's wearing heals or writing "slut" on their bare
chests ultimately, in the words of sociologist Kristen Barber and Kelsy
Kretchmer, "be reactionary and antifeminist"?[33] These sorts of questions
speak centrally to the need to assess the actual impact of men's growing
roles in violence prevention efforts.

PLANTING SEEDS, MOBILIZING MEN

A major development in antiviolence organizations' growing links with
government and foundation funders has been an expanded need for measurement and accounting. Chris Anderegg, the former MASV activist,
found an employment niche in the 1990s helping feminist antiviolence
organizations seek funding and balance their books, including serving eleven years as director of finance and operations for Marin Abused
Women Services. "When I was working at MAWS," Anderegg explained,
"I was basically working with federal and state funders to be sure that we
were complying, and getting the money. . . . This grant will pay for this,

but not that. You have this enormous spreadsheet to track, so you can also demonstrate to the funders—'OK, we spent your money as prescribed'."

Funders understandably want to see evidence that their money is well spent, that the antiviolence efforts they have funded are effective. Many antiviolence professionals share funders' desire for evidence-based research; they too want to know what works, and what does not work. However, violence prevention professionals often lament how their curriculum, pedagogy, and goals are shaped and narrowed by the need to document results—usually in quantitative terms—when actual (especially long-term) results are in fact very hard to measure. This is especially so for violence prevention. David Lee explained that when it comes to delivering services for violence survivors, at least an agency can document "how many people we sheltered, 'cause at least I could say, 'These many lives got a respite for a period of time'." However, Lee explained, "For prevention it's harder . . . we don't expect things to change instantly, that I can do some magic formula and then reduce instantly the rates."

Pressed to show evidence of change, prevention professionals in recent years have developed before-and-after questionnaires and other measures of short-term effects of their interventions on, for instance, college men's beliefs in rape myths or their adherence to attitudes and values that are known to be correlated with acquaintance rape.[34] Antiviolence organizations frequently use the findings of similar studies to promote their work to funders, and to various constituencies. The University of Southern California's MenCARE,[35] a group of men students who do peer education workshops with fraternities, men's athletics, and campus residence advisors to reduce sexual assault, stalking, and partner violence, states on its webpage that researchers from the USC Rossier School of Education have "tracked the results of MenCARE. Pre- and post-test data collected across a number of years indicate the effectiveness of the MenCARE method."[36] As an undergraduate in 2006, Stephen Philp was enthused about being part of MenCARE, in part, he told us a few years later, because "since we were part of a study, we've been proven to be effective, and it's great to feel like you're doing something that actually has a positive effect on your environment."

Most people we interviewed—especially veterans of antiviolence work—were less sanguine about what such studies—especially paper-and-pencil pre- and posttests—could actually tell them about the impact of their work. There are good reasons to be cautious. A three-year ethnographic study of a batterer intervention program by sociologists Douglas Schrock and Irene Padavic suggests the need for deeper and more sophisticated ways to measure impact. Schrock and Padavic observed that, on the one hand, the men in the program "honed their rhetorical skills in present-ing themselves as egalitarians who take responsibility for past harms and who are committed to anger control and nonviolence"—precisely the sort of standard posttest measure that might be used as an indicator of a suc-cessful intervention. On the other hand, Schrock and Padavic note, "the version of manhood most honored in the program—emotionally inex-pressive sacrificial breadwinners entitled to women's deference—con-sists of qualities that research has linked to men's violence, which may explain why the . . . evaluation study of this program found completers to be equally as likely as dropouts to continue battering women."[37]

Since many foundations limit the duration of their funding to one-year grants, it stands to reason that the sorts of evaluations meeting this need are measuring short-term attitudinal change, rather than longer-term changes in behaviors, relationship dynamics, or community mobiliza-tion. Though antiviolence organizations must develop such studies to justify support for their continued efforts, activists on the ground have their own ways of assessing the impact and effectiveness of their work with boys and men.

Near the end of each interview, we observed that sexual assault and domestic violence are still huge social problems, despite several decades of feminist antiviolence mobilization. Confronted with the enormity of the problem, we asked each man, "What keeps you going?" This question evoked deep reflection on how to draw on hints and signs of change, in order to maintain optimism and commitment in the face of continued frustration with the slow pace of social change. Nearly every person, when asked this question, acknowledged that it is very hard to assess the impact of violence prevention work. Frank Blaney analogized his work to "that of a farmer, where you're planting seeds and you never know what the final effect is going to be. You're just out there doing it and doing it."

Mark Stevens estimates he has given workshops with "twenty thou-sand people, maybe more over the years," but besides taking "some credit for there being a movement on college campuses," he can rely on "only anecdotal information" to assess the impact of his life work. Many spoke of the satisfaction of a young man approaching them a year or five years down the line, and telling them that the work had changed his life. Gilbert Salazar smiled as he told us of a boy who had been in one of his high school My Strength clubs writing in a letter to Salazar, "'I'm not gonna get a girl drunk to get laid like I usually do'. That's like, that's *huge,* you know?" Many shared such individual success stories, which, they said, buoyed their hopes for continuing the work over the long haul. Michael Kaufman loves to tell the "absolutely wonderful" story of a man in the mid-1990s who approached him to ask permission to make multiple copies of an antiviolence TV ad that the White Ribbon Campaign had run before the Super Bowl. "It turned out that his job, he was a VCR repairman. He made dozens of copies of this short ad, and whenever he fixed a VCR, he would put a cassette into the machine and return it to the person." Keith Smith chuckled as he recalled the satisfaction of a small victory for his efforts in bystander intervention work at the University of Vermont: "A guy was talking about being in a store, seeing some sort of domestic abuse thing going on, and dropping a jar of pickles, which distracted the whole thing. Yeah, it was very creative."

Longtime activist Craig Norberg-Bohm understands the need for activists and professionals to keep themselves going with anecdotal success stories. But he warns that this "ray of hope syndrome," especially in trying to reform domestic violence perpetrators, can hold the danger of "raising false hopes." He also agrees it's difficult—even with long-term programs like RAVEN, or My Strength Clubs—to measure to what extent violence prevention programs are actually changing men's attitudes and actions. Norberg-Bohm argues instead for moving beyond anecdotal stories or unreliable impact studies, toward a radical shift in how success is defined and measured:

> We haven't yet gotten to the point where we can measure that that guy doesn't hit anymore. How do you measure that that kid doesn't grow up to be a hitter? That he grows up to be a lover, you might say? How do you measure that? That's tough. We're not sure if that's working. [But it's] clear to me that [we need] a community that welcomes those men to be changed. So then you can say, "how can we get more mobilization to happen?" So let's measure mobilization. That can be processed. When a man says "I can't do anything about that problem" [changing] to "I absolutely have something I can do about that problem," that's a nice shift. You can measure mobilization, because you've got to count how many feet show up at things. It's the measure. We can also do things like count [media] coverage; we want this to be visible, so are we getting visible?

Of course, professionals in antiviolence nonprofits and in funded campus organizations are constrained by the need to justify continued funding by providing "hard evidence" that their work is changing the boys and men who are targeted by their programs. But Norberg-Bohm's idea to "measure mobilization" holds the promise of reinfusing political organizing into a context defined less and less in these terms. Joe Samalin is thinking the same way: "The work we do now, MCSR, is about creating a core group of men in a community that can stand up and be present and be visible allies on this issue, to women." Todd Henneman says that his MenCARE program provides personal growth benefits for the ten to fifteen men who participate every year, and he argues that the group's visibility makes an important statement on campus: "I don't know if it really changes attitudes and behavior but we're kind of like a tent pole on the campus. Even if everything else we do, like the workshops and our posters and Take Back the Night and things like that like don't change things, I think we're at least holding kind of a line, like: This is an issue that guys should care about."

Violence prevention workers today, we have shown in this chapter, labor within a highly professionalized field that has progressively broadened its scope; this is due in large part to the successes of previous cohorts in wresting concessions from the state, and building community-based antiviolence nonprofits, campus organizations, and professional fields. This broadening field expanded opportunities for young men to plug in as volunteers, to get paid jobs and careers in antiviolence work. But, we have argued, this very institutionalization has stretched antiviolence efforts away from their feminist political foundations. As a result, the men and women in the field today navigate—often very creatively—ways to retain or re-infuse the work with feminist, antiracist, and social justice values.[38] They are also forced to navigate another rocky road in this terrain: What does it mean for men to be working as allies with women, to stop rape and domestic violence?

CHAPTER 5

Earning Your Ally Badge: Men, Feminism, and Accountability

Over the past four decades a succession of men have joined with feminist women, seeking to be allies in stopping rape and domestic violence. From the start, these men were few in number, though in recent years their numbers have grown. And from the start, men's "upstream" violence prevention work has been fraught with contradiction. When men work to prevent sexual assault and domestic violence, they are simultaneously enabled and constrained, rewarded and criticized, given premature star status and critically scrutinized, all because they are men who are carving out space as feminist allies, doing work previously assumed to be the province of women.

Feminist activist Phyllis Frank has for decades been a catalyst—mentoring, criticizing, and encouraging men who enter the field. Several of the men we interviewed expressed appreciation to Frank for the energy, intelligence, and passion with which she has mentored them. She was one of the first feminist activists to embrace the importance and necessity of men's violence prevention work, and more broadly in working with men as feminist allies. But she is also well aware of the built-in contradictions of men's ally work. Once, she told us, she took a phone call from a distraught woman, the partner of a man in her batterers program. "She was saying to me 'I need you to fix him, I need you to get him to stop. You gotta do something'." The woman was crying, Frank recalled, and "my heart was breaking," but on the spot, Frank drew from her years of experience in talking with women who were in abusive relationships:

And what I said to her, which is the truth as best I know it, is that "I so wish that I could do that, but there is nothing that I can do that will guarantee or even make it most likely that he's going to stop being abusive to you. Even if he stops hitting you, he will still likely be assaultive or horrible to you." She screamed at me, literally at the top of her lungs, and she said, "I can't believe it, I can't believe it. You're taking away my hope!" And in that moment, I said, "Oh, please, I don't want to take away your hope. Even hospice tells us not to stop hoping. But it is crucial that you make your plans based on the man you know you have, not on the one you hope he someday will become."

Frank realized that her spontaneous advice—to "make your plans based on the man you have, not on the one you hope he someday will become"— was an "elegant turn of a word" based on her years of experience in shelters and hotlines, taking "hundreds of calls from women." Subsequently, she taught this statement to everyone in her program, including a man she was mentoring who later went on to become a "famous" violence preventionists: "[He] worked very closely with me, and actually affirmed what a wonderful statement that was, because I do trainings all the time. And several years later, I got a newsletter, because he's now famous and I'm not—he's far more famous than I am—and he's quoted in the newsletter with that quote." Frank's feelings were mixed. It was good to see her idea being widely disseminated. But it also rankled that the man implicitly took credit for the idea. "It was very painful for him not to say, 'Phyllis Frank once taught me this'."

Phyllis Frank told this story not because she is someone who demands praise or fame for coming up with a good idea, but because it served as an example of both the promise and the dangers of men's growing presence and public stature as antiviolence leaders. Men, because of their privileged social positions *as men,* are more likely than women to be listened to when they speak in opposition to violence against women. And everyone in the field—including especially the women who have labored so long doing the downstream work with survivors of men's violence—agrees that it is crucially important for boys and men to hear the antiviolence message conveyed by these male allies. But men's growing visibility and status also risks rendering women's historical roles as activists, institution builders, and mentors less visible, their voices silenced. Frank described this paradox as a "slippery slope of a problem": "Men are getting involved in greater numbers. Many men are getting involved and making money, and I always worry about capitalizing and making money on things that women have been doing and saying for a long time and not making money, so that's kind of a negative. Men get more appreciation—listened to better, often credited with what women have said—that happens over and over again. But the truth is, they are saying something incredibly important for men to say. So, you kind of [say], 'All right, all right.' "

Phyllis Frank's refrain—"All right, all right"—captures the collective sense of the women we interviewed, that even though men's growing presence in the antiviolence field can be problematic, their work also plays a crucially important role. To put it simply, and as many women stated it, "We need men as allies."

What does it mean to be an ally? The *Merriam-Webster* dictionary definition ("a person or group that gives help to another person or group") tends to imply a symmetry that does not pertain with social movement allies.[1] Sociologist Daniel Myers argues that in social movements there is a built-in asymmetry between *beneficiaries* ("rank-and-file activists who hail from the population that would expect or wish to benefit from the movement's activities") and *allies* ("movement adherents who are not direct beneficiaries of the movements they support and do not have expectations of such benefits"). Allies "share a political stance" with movement beneficiaries and "define problems and solutions similarly," but they "have a different field to negotiate." As "insider-outsiders" in the movement, Myers explains, allies "are members of the activist community but not members of the beneficiary population that underlies the collective activist identity and in fact they are, by definition, part of the enemy."[2]

Whites who ally with people of color to stop racism, heterosexuals who ally with LGBTQ people to oppose homophobia and heteronormativity, and men who ally with women against the various manifestations of patriarchy are aware that as movement "insider-outsiders" they are not working on a level playing field. In particular, such activists are beginning from a position of privilege that, by the very terms of calling themselves "allies," implies that their actions aim to undermine and end these privileges.[3] So, even though the identity "ally" might carry some morally positive weight—one is, after all, working to make the world a more peaceful, just, and egalitarian place—it also necessarily includes some morally ambiguous baggage that raises critical questions and scrutiny concerning the depth of an ally's commitments to social change. Sociologist Matthew Hughey observed, for instance, that white antiracism activists' identities are premised on what he calls "stigma allure," where allies operate from an understanding of "whiteness as racist" and "manage self-perceptions of stigma by not only accepting a 'spoiled' identity . . . but by embracing stigma in forms of dishonor, pathology, and dysfunction as markings of moral commitment and political authenticity."[4] We heard some such expressions of "spoiled" and stigmatized "masculinity-as-sexism" from the men in our study, but this was far more common among the men of the Movement Cohort. Joined at the hip as they were with the highly politicized feminist movements of the 1970s and early 1980s, these men's self-definitions and their outreach to boys and men in those early years were often couched in terms of male shame. By the 1990s men's antiviolence activism had stretched away (though it never fully disconnected) from this politicized feminism, and from antiviolence strategies that emphasized the refutation of masculinity. The pathways and actions of the Bridge Cohort and the Professional Cohort were shaped increasingly by medicalized and professionalized discourses and pragmatic strategies premised on creating honorable definitions of "good men" and "healthy masculinity." By the late 1990s, with these positive self-definitions built into curricula (e.g., the bystander approach), men doing antiviolence work could increasingly distance themselves from stigma and male shame. This had the effect of broadening the appeal of antiviolence work for men, and it also helped to open the gates for a few men to become "stars" in the violence prevention field.

In this chapter, we draw from our interviews with women such as Phyllis Frank, and with all three cohorts of men, to probe the contradictions of men's ally work. First, we look at how men—simply because they are men—are frequently given more attention and respect, basically for saying the same things that women have been saying for years. We examine how for men this "pedestal effect," as Tal Peretz has called it, manifests in unearned praise, and sometimes in rapid and premature escalation to leadership status and higher pay, and we probe the debates surrounding the small number of men who have ridden this escalator to rock-star status as individual antiviolence contractors. [5] Second, we examine the other side of the pedestal effect: men who enter antiviolence work are frequently subjected to a high level of skepticism and critical scrutiny, often from feminist women leaders and colleagues. We show that young men of color often experience especially acute forms of this critical scrutiny. Third, we look at how male allies in an increasingly diverse field—often using strategies learned from women mentors—consciously navigate the twin challenges of unearned privilege and critical scrutiny. A key factor, we argue, is how these men define to whom they are accountable in this work.

THE ESCALATION OF MEN

In many ways, male allies in violence prevention experience the pedestal effect, a level of praise and escalating status men receive in feminist spaces that far outstrips what a man has actually accomplished or contributed. One of the most common mechanisms of the pedestal effect is men's voices and ideas—even when they are repeating things that women have been saying—being "heard" by audiences who tend to ignore or dismiss women's voices. Men of the Movement Cohort recognized this right away and sought to strategically use this male privilege. Don Conway-Long, for instance, said that in the early years of RAVEN, the men did a lot of public speaking about violence against women, often paired with a woman speaker from a local shelter: "When we said the same thing they did, the men would hear it, but they wouldn't hear it if the women said it." Conway-Long concluded that he would use this aspect of male privilege to get men to hear feminist messages: "If you'll just listen to me, and I'll say the same thing [she] just did, and it's, 'Oh! That's interesting!'"

More than three decades later, a new cohort of male activists face a similarly contradictory field of action, even when they try to mitigate the pedestal effect by pairing with a woman cofacilitator. Jeffrey Buckholtz explained how, when co-speaking with a woman colleague to a university class about sexual violence, his pedestal effect "light bulb went off":

> A queue of people, after class, forms for me. A queue to talk to me and ask me questions. They were so excited by me. At that point I'd really learned everything I knew from Carol about this stuff. She was the one who talked about all the programming and yet they were asking me questions about what she talked about. And at that moment it was like, the light bulb went off and I went, Oh, shit! I can say it a million fuckin' times: I recognize the privilege, I've learned this from women, you can say it 'till you're blue in the face, it does not change the applause. It does not change the people going "that was awesome!" It doesn't change the reward structure.

Jeffrey Buckholtz's words reflect an understanding that male privilege is not merely an individual attribute that, like a pair of shoes, can be removed and discarded; it is also built into the fabric of institutions and organizations.[6] Men in the field routinely experience this form of public adulation, and rather than engaging in fantasies about shedding or "giving up" such male privilege they wonder, discuss, and strategize what they should do with it. Part of the challenge is that, especially for men who might have experienced marginality from not living up to honored forms of masculinity, all of the positive attention feels good; but it can be simultaneously troubling. Allan Creighton said that starting in the 1980s, when he was working with women's shelters, "On the road, you get these incredibly appreciative audiences who are most all women and, 'Oh you men are so wonderful, it's so great that you're doing this.' It was a little intoxicating to get the attention." Mark Stevens had similar experiences: "the reactions from women have been incredibly positive, thankful, and sometimes I felt almost idolized in ways that made me feel uncomfortable." Frank Blaney expresses this same ambivalence about getting praised, mostly by women: "Every time I go to a conference and get up and speak and maybe there's a hundred people in the room and three males and I get up and say something that is anti-sexist, they think I'm Jesus Christ, Moses, and Santa Claus all wrapped up in one. I do appreciate when I get respect from women who have been involved in this work. But then again, because it's so rare for males to be involved, sometimes you get too many accolades."

Women in the field are not fully comfortable with the disproportionate accolades that men receive, or with the fact that antiviolence messages are more readily heard when spoken by men, fearing that this interactional dynamic reinforces long-standing aspects of male supremacy and women's public invisibility—precisely what feminists hope to dismantle. But on the other hand, they see the dissemination of the antiviolence message as crucially important; they concede that putting men forward to speak to boys and men is a strategic compromise. Danielle Lancon, Todd Henneman's supervisor at USC's MenCARE, observes that Henneman "probably does get a different level of respect because he's a man, but I think in this case it just sort of works out well [laughs ironically] because—it's advantageous for him, it's advantageous for the community, for our office, for the campus."

Similarly, Shira Tarrant,[7] a national leader in working with younger feminist men, finds men's "premature congratulation problem" to be "annoying," but she views it as needing to be tolerated for the greater good:

> I see it happen in the classroom, I see it happen in media and blog attention. So, yeah they get to be the good guys and then the women, there's still that issue of like, "Why are you so angry?"—that kinda thing. Or still twice the work to get half of the recognition . . . At the same time, well, but what is our end goal? Strategically speaking, what is our goal? And so if there is a little bit of extra congratulation along the way—annoying, needs to be addressed, we can hash that out—and if it means that some guy gets extra attention because of his biological sex, I'm like, then *fine*. Because if it means minimizing the rate of rape and reducing sexual assault, that's the goal.

Although most women we spoke with were consciously willing to make this same strategic compromise in hopes that it would help to lower men's violence against women, they were less sanguine with how the pedestal effect plays out within their workplaces. Janeen McGee described a recent training session at RAVEN: "I can remember a time recently with Kevin Hawkins, who's our program manager—he spoke up and talked about why the anti-oppression piece in our recent training was so important and . . . and there was just, you know, *awe* over what he had said and how helpful it was. And I know there were women at the table who had also been involved in that training who said, you know, 'He said the same thing I've been saying at these meetings all along, but now all of a sudden it's taken as a good thing and without question.'"

Trina Greene describes similar interactional dynamics taking place at Peace Over Violence, where she works: "I've had experiences in a meeting and maybe I've said something, right? And then there's not much feedback—OK, nod, OK, OK, I get what you're trying to say, or I get what that woman is saying. And then a male says the same exact thing, you know, just with the man's voice, that's about it. 'Oh my gosh, that is a great idea! We have to write that down.' And it's like, are you kidding me, we all said the same shit? What are you talking about?"

This overvaluation of men's voices in antiviolence workplaces can be viewed through the lens of what sociologist Arlie Hochschild called a gendered "economy of gratitude."[8] When men do even a small fraction of the work that women have shouldered in the past—for instance, "helping" with housework or childcare—they frequently receive lavish praise for doing so. The "going rate," to use Hochschild's term, on men's contributions to this labor is so low, men who make even token contributions stand out as rare men who are then showered with praise and gratitude. There appears to be a similar (perhaps even more extreme) gendered economy of gratitude for men in the antiviolence field. Leiana Kinnicutt recalls a recent gathering of organizations by the Office on Violence Against Women, where "they made all the men stand up and we all gave them a round of applause for being there. I mean, that happens a lot. Part of me is glad that they are there, but . . . it's just, it's a little much." Shelley Serdahely takes this a step further: "There's been an element of [her voice trumpeting fanfare] 'Dah-duh-dah! The men are here now, the women can step aside, we're gonna save the day!'"

Part of this workplace dynamic, Phyllis Frank speculates, is attributable to women's socialization to support and "lift up" men: "Women fawn all over them. Women, that's how we are with men. Everybody lifts men, and wants men's attention, and women are taught to compete for men's attention." Serdahely agrees, worrying that "Women have become caretakers in some ways to men who are doing this work, you know, making sure that men feel good about it and know how special they [are]." Serdahely is troubled when antiviolence organizations recreate these sorts of gender dynamics between women and men: "We're not reflecting the change we're trying to create in the world." Beyond this emotional "caretaking" of men in antiviolence work, women also point to their own socialized tendency to defer to men, even men with less experience. Gwen Wright finds it "disconcerting [that] here are all these really brilliant and extraordinary and sometimes exceptional women, and suddenly, the man's in the room and they reverted back to what they do naturally, which is, there's a man in the space, he should be the person in charge."

Indeed, we gathered a good deal of evidence from our interviews, with both women and men, that the pedestal effect and the skewed economy of gratitude in the antiviolence field results for many men in a rapid—even premature—escalation to positions of leadership and public visibility. Phyllis Miller laments that occupational gender inequality within the antiviolence field works similarly to that in other professions: "It's like, 'Wait a minute, I've been here twenty years, why is he coming in here with less experience, making the same salary?'" Serdahely spoke of a man she works with who "is wonderful, and I don't want to take that away from him," but after working in the field for only "a couple of years . . . he was invited to meetings at the CDC, and that just doesn't happen for women. It just doesn't. You don't have to earn your stripes as much if you're a man. You're more unique so there's a smaller pool, you'll be a bigger fish in a smaller pool."

This sort of upward mobility for men in a predominantly women's occupation is similar to what sociologist Christine Williams described as a "glass escalator."[9] Williams observed that male elementary school teachers and nurses were routinely afforded more respect and status than their female co-workers and commonly were "escalated" to supervisorial positions, such as school principal. Reflecting similar tendencies, several of the women and men we interviewed in the antiviolence field gave examples of men earning higher pay than even more experienced women. Sean Tate, with a tone of outrage in his voice, described "an interesting sort of paradox" where he was given a higher honorarium than "a woman who probably has twenty more years of experience than me. If I go speak at a national conference on violence against women, I'm gonna make more money than the women. And I'm not just *saying* that; I've seen it. I've seen the checks cut."

The escalation of Tate's status and pay in the antiviolence world may have as much to do with race as with the fact that he is a man. Unlike African American men in other female-dominated occupations, who have been found by sociologist Adia Harvey Wingfield *not* to benefit from a glass escalator effect,[10] in antiviolence work men of color are actively recruited and sometimes rapidly pushed forward as leaders and public spokespeople. This recruiting and escalation of men of color has much to do with the perception among professionals and the general public that young boys of color are especially "at risk," that their schools and communities need to be targeted with violence prevention, and that the most effective leaders in this effort will be men of color. With an incredulous chuckle, Tate related the irony of "finding yourself in alpha male position by talking about [laughs] how men shouldn't be in the alpha male position": "I was working for TCFV [Texas Council on Family Violence] for like four months before I was around the country—you know what I'm saying?—talking to people who have been in this work for thirty or forty years, you know? There's a huge reward in it. There's so much reward and so much power in talking about dismantling power [laughs]. . . . When you're a guy and if you're out here talking about these kinds of things, you get put up on a pedestal immediately."

Tate was not the only man of color who expressed a sense of irony and discomfort with his own escalation. Jimmie Briggs said he is frequently "invited to speak at all the conferences and panels, to do lectures," and was given honors by *GQ* magazine and *Women's E-news*. This recognition is good for his organization, Man Up, and Briggs says that the attention makes him feel "honored, but uncomfortable." Ramesh Kathanadhi wondered aloud what it means in terms of race relations for him to have been publicly pushed forward as a spokesperson: "Being a person of color in a predominantly white community of feminists, I'm what proves to them that they're not racist. Or that they've brought in people of color as allies genuinely. And I'm the male that also proves, 'look how far we've come'."

Kathanadhi's words might give us pause before concluding that a combination of race and gender makes antiviolence work a rare occupation in which men of color are multiply privileged, over women and white male colleagues alike. This is an oversimplified view. As we will see later in this chapter, men of color may benefit in some ways—including the few younger men who have been actively recruited into the work with little formal education or professional experience—but they also frequently receive an extra layer of critical scrutiny, their motives and their actions called into question in the workplace.

GOING ROGUE, OR USING THE MASTER'S TOOLS?

By the mid-1990s, a combination of factors created space for a few men to become independent contractors in violence prevention. Antiviolence nonprofits, many of them founded by members of the Movement and Bridge cohorts in the 1980s and 1990s, became launching pads for anti-violence careers, but the salaries in these positions remained modest—low, in fact, given the level of education held by many people in the field. Simultaneously, large organizations—universities, the military, professional and college sports leagues, and corporations—began to funnel funds toward prevention of sexual harassment and domestic and sexual violence, paying generous honoraria to speakers and workshop facilitators and contracting with longer-term consultants to create on-site prevention programs. The small handful of men who had led the way in starting nonprofits, developing violence prevention curricula, and building their own public profiles as national leaders in the field were positioned to meet the growing organizational demand for men's leadership in violence prevention. Juan Carlos Areán expressed a concern, similar to that voiced by several men we interviewed, about the men who did "go solo" becoming "big stars":

> I am aware that we men get a lot of kudos for being in the movement and for doing the right thing. I see some men in the movement that seem to be forgetting that, and it makes me uncomfortable sometimes. I think there are a lot of men in this movement that have chosen to go solo, and I sometimes wonder how much checks and balances they have. They might have some, I don't know. And, some people become big stars, which in itself is not a problem, but I know that a male speaker charges like three times the equivalent of a female speaker. So, obviously that's perpetuating the problem, right?

Todd Henneman echoes this concern, saying that although he understands that some people rely on speaker fees to make their living, it still makes him "worried" and "will rub me the wrong way sometimes" that people he contacts about giving presentations on his campus "get too caught up in getting credit for something, or like what they're going to be paid . . . I don't want to name any names but there's some people who every time I've heard him speak I've heard him say the same thing. And it's like, well if I'm paying you like $5,000 to come to our campus, why should I pay you $5,000 to say the same thing that you said last year?" Tim Love sees the emergence of individual antiviolence rock stars as a logical but unwelcome outcome of the more general glass escalator for men in his field: "We've seen a lot of men get involved in the movement and then being very quickly kind of pushed to the top, promoted within organizations [and then] going off on their own and doing like consulting work, and getting paid more than women for doing the same kind of work. So even within our movement there's [what] we refer to around here as that 'rock star status,' that like, 'Ohh, you're a *man* who's doing this work, that's so *wonderful!*' "

Jackson Katz is the quintessential rock star in men's violence prevention work. Katz, we have seen, is a key member of the Bridge Cohort, a former football player who helped to launch the bystander approach to violence prevention with the Mentors in Violence Prevention (MVP) program at Northeastern University in the early 1990s. By the end of the decade, Katz had left his job at Northeastern to become an independent contractor. By then he was the go-to guy for campus lectures, workshops, or antiviolence consultations. With his rebranded MVP Strategies he became the central professional contractor working with all branches of the U.S. military, developing their version of a bystander intervention program.

Everyone we interviewed in the field knows Jackson Katz. Some were trained by him, most have seen him speak, some use his *Tough Guise* film in their educational interventions, all of them have thoughts about his high-profile leadership role in their field. Katz is a bit of a lightning rod for two general issues concerning men's roles in antiviolence work. The first question regards what it means when a man leaves organizations— be they campus-based or nonprofits—and decides to go solo. The second question concerns how conventionally masculine men like Katz both benefit from and strategically use this masculinity in antiviolence work.

Katz knows that some people in the field raise questions about the kind of money he makes doing antiviolence work. He emphasizes that when he first started doing this work, he made "Not *one penny*, for ten years of full-time activism. And so when people are critical of all of these men [who] are making this money, it's like—I was in it way before I made *a penny*, and it was a commitment, not a job, you know what I mean?" Katz concedes that now, however, "I get lots of rewards, right, for my work. And so what am I supposed to do with that? Am I supposed to not do the work because I'm getting acclaim for it and it's illegitimate for a man to be getting acclaim for work that quote unquote women have been doing for all these years with no acclaim? It's like, what do you do with this?"

Not surprisingly the women in the field are aware of the male rock-star phenomenon in general, and of Katz's role as the most celebrated rock star in particular. Some of them, like Shelley Serdahely, express concern over this gendered inequity: "There are hundreds of women doing this work, and they're not given the same kind of star status that men are. They're not paid as much for speaking engagements." Most of the women we interviewed, however, see this inequity as something they can and should live with. Leiana Kinnicutt, for instance, noted that, "there's still a little bit of tension in the field around men getting a lot of spotlight. I mean, if you look at who charges what to do speeches, like a Jackson Katz will charge $5000, whereas my executive director wouldn't charge anything. So I mean, there's a whole lot of that kind of tension, but I think [there's a] realization, especially in our organization, that men not only need to be a part of this, as an essential ingredient, but that their involvement should be welcomed and celebrated."

Some might see statements like Kinnicutt's as a feminist capitulation to male dominance in her field, but hers is clearly a strategic decision, akin to what development studies scholar Deniz Kandiyoti once called a "patriarchal bargain," through which women hope to achieve some of their goals—in this case, violence reduction—within the parameters of still-existing systems of male privilege.[11] Similarly, Patti Giggans' words are those of the savvy feminist strategist: "Jackson Katz gets an amazing amount of attention, all right? I mean, he's a rock star. But he's been such an ally, you know in some ways I feel like, yeah, he deserves it. You know what I mean? Buy his books. Support him. You know? And I bet that their salaries are all higher than at the traditionally women's organizations, yeah. So there's going to be that kind of genderized resentment that's just going to be there. You know? It's just part of it. We're going to—you've got to live with it."

In addition to a "genderized resentment" of male rock stars felt by some women in the violence prevention field, there is also a generational tension that is felt most acutely by younger men who are trying to carve out a space in the field as independent contractors. Jeffrey Buckholtz is nearly two decades younger than Katz and also sees himself as a feminist ally who seeks to make violence prevention his life's work. Early on, he realized he did not want to work for a nonprofit. "My wife at the time," he says, "was working for a nonprofit at a rape crisis center and she was just drowning, getting paid like $25,000, just absolute crap. And I'd watch so many people in the nonprofit and NGO [nongovernmental organization] structures and just—if you're not in the upper tiers of management or directorship, it's very hard to sustain a living, you know?" Buckholtz and his wife were "not OK with" living on such low income, and he also determined, "I don't want to be a nonprofit because I don't want to be sucking up to donors all the time and always scrambling for grant money." He and his wife decided to form "a violence prevention business." He likes the fact that as co-director of We End Violence, a "social business,[12]" he is not subject to the constraints of the nonprofit world. But he also feels the strain of having to generate business and maintain a flow of income. That's especially hard to do, he says, when veterans like Jackson Katz and

Ben Atherton-Zeman have the inside lane for invitations to deliver key-note addresses, run workshops, and do performances.

> There is a handful of these Men Can Stop Rape guys who are in the public sphere and have been doing this for a while who have developed these relationships and there is kind of a good ole' boys. . . . Now, I'm not like wounded by this or deeply offended, but I swear there is a piece of me that's wondering: when do the guys that have been in the spotlight—and god I want to hear from them, I've learned so much from them over the years—but there's like an ownership over some of it and not wanting to let go of that and share it. And at the same time they do a great job, so I don't want [to be] critical of that, but . . . there's a generation of these men who created a movement, but a piece of me is like, when are you going to hand some of it over and start setting it up so that it's not all in your hands? And you've got all these young guys who are fuckin' *ready*, it's like we're ready to go, ready to make a life out of this, a career out of this.

A second tension viewed by Buckholtz and several other men concerns how the field's rock stars display their masculinity. Many male feminist allies who enter antiviolence work grew up as boys who could not or would not "measure up" to conventional masculine standards. From their experiences as marginalized boys and men, and from a feminist analysis that points to conventional masculinity as a major source of gender-based violence, they see their violence prevention work as aiming to open space for different forms of expression for boys and men—including embracing traits traditionally disparaged as feminine—rather than slightly reforming, and then celebrating, conventional masculinity. By contrast, the field's male rock stars tend to be men who embody, display, and benefit from being conventionally masculine men—Jackson Katz and Don McPherson, for instance, are former high-level football players, and this very masculine status gives them access to, and a level of legitimacy as bridge builders[13] to male locker rooms, board rooms, fraternity houses, and military bases. Katz and McPherson told us in various ways that they feel right at home in such male groups, and they rise to the challenge of using their athletic bodies, voices and masculine legitimacy to challenge these men to be better men. Jeffrey Buckholtz outlined the tension in this approach:

> If you ask me do I like working with fraternity men, I'd say absolutely not. Will I work with them? Sure. Have I worked with them? Yes. And some fraternity guys are fantastic. But Jackson Katz, Don McPherson, they go in there and

they have a different feeling about that crowd. I do think they have a different, more universal approach and I think sometimes that they do a better job than I do at getting access to some of those more masculine guys. At the same time, my strategy is to push and question what masculinity can be like if it is based around this image of don't be like women. What does masculinity do to men?

A few of the less conventionally masculine men we interviewed said they felt that the celebrated and rewarded masculinity of the field's rock stars made them feel further marginalized, and they wondered whether this approach promoted anything close to the kind of change imagined by a feminist vision of equality between women and men. Katz, however, sees his masculine attributes as situating him better than other men in the field to approach—and change—men who hold power and privilege: "In my experience over the last twenty-five years, a lot of the men who get involved in antiviolence work and [are] supportive of feminist organizations are men who are alienated from the hegemonic culture because they were not successful in it, or they were policed by it, or they were abused by it. And I come from a very different place 'cause I come from . . . being completely unintimidated by the male sports culture and the jock culture . . . it empowered me, my success in that field empowered me, rather than the experience of a lot of these other guys."

We asked Katz if he was implying that only masculine men like himself could successfully do the sort of antiviolence work he does, and he replied by referencing—and disagreeing with—the iconic social justice leader and writer Audre Lorde, whose oft-repeated statement reads, "For the master's tools will never dismantle the master's house. They may allow us to temporarily beat him at his own game, but they will never enable us to bring about genuine change."[14] Certainly, in men's antiviolence work with boys and men, embodied athletic masculinity is the adjustable power drill in the master's toolkit. Is it possible to use this tool to dismantle the privileges of masculinity? Or might we expect that the use of the master's tools will, at best, poke some holes in or file off some of the jagged edges of masculinity, while reinforcing the privileges of those who embody it? Katz understands this tension, but long ago he chose to strategically use his masculine privilege.

I've used it my whole activist career, to good end, as far as I'm concerned. I've self-consciously used my sports background and credibility to do the work that I do. . . . I know this gets complicated and I appreciate it, and I've *always* been self-reflexively thinking about, "OK, I'm using hegemonic masculinity to deconstruct hegemonic masculinity," which is what I am doing. I always took that quote from Audre Lorde, "You can't use the master's tools to take apart the master's house," and the first time I heard it I thought, "This is completely wrong, this is completely wrong." It's like, Audre Lorde is a writer, *she's* using the master's tools—writing is the most dominant tool of the hegemonic culture—to deconstruct the master's house. So it's internally contradictory in addition to being problematic as a political strategy. So even though it makes you think, I think it's wrong.

Women we have spoken with recognize this tension too, but on the whole they are grateful that Katz has cracked the surface of these masculine bastions and are hopeful that he can catalyze change within them. Asked about Katz's work with the military, for instance, Shira Tarrant said, "I think he's the guy to do that work because he is, you know, physically and in his presentation, his style, he can speak that language and so it's very effective. . . . So they can hear him, and he says all the time, you know, 'Is it right that other men can hear me in those ways? It's not right but it is effective,' and so until that changes, I'd rather have him—I'm glad he's doing the work."

There is no question that Katz's use of the master's tools—his own athletic masculinity—has at least gotten him invited in to the master's house, shrines of male privilege and institutionalized violence like the locker room and the military. Whether his and others' work in these houses has been effective is an open question that we will take up in the final chapter.

NAVIGATING THE PEDESTAL

Male allies know they are hypervisible in the work that they do, and most of them have developed simple techniques in their workshops, presentations, and counseling groups to deflect the unearned praise, extra attention, and kudos that men in the field routinely receive. Joe Samalin deploys strategies that he hopes will at least partially preempt the pedestal effect: "It feels really good when I'm on the radio, when I'm on TV, when I'm getting credit for doing this kind of work, [but] I temper it [by saying] that everything I learned about this work, I learned from women. Except for the few things that I learned from some men, which *they* learned from women." Seth Avakian finds himself put on a pedestal not just for the feminist work that he does but also for being an active father with his young child. When this happens he tells his admirers, " 'Thanks a lot, but it's really nothing more than women have been expected to do forever, so I'm certainly not brave or a hero for doing it. I just think I'm trying to be a dad.'" His strategy is "Not [to] minimize what I'm doing, just make it seem like it should be normal."

Juan Carlos Areán said that in addition to being ready to deflect unearned praise, he works with his female co-trainer to "model" respect for women's ideas within an "equal power" relationship. Areán tries to be ready to react to the common gendered dynamics that silence or marginalize women, while putting men on a pedestal: "Sometimes my female colleague will say something and it will go over people's heads, and I will say something similar or amplify for them and everybody is like 'Wow, that's amazing'. So, as is appropriate, I use that as a teaching moment. I point it out." Similarly, when Tim Love realizes he has been given credit for saying something that a woman has previously said, he responds in the moment; his strategy is simply to "deflect back to, 'Yeah, I'm really glad Morgan came up with it!'"

Even when a man is working alone, Ben Atherton-Zeman explained, he can model respect for women: "One of the things we should be saying, as we speak up, is 'Hey, why are you just listening to this from me? Plenty of women have told you this in the past, why not listen to them?'"

Sometimes strategizing against the pedestal effect also involves carefully thinking through the public symbolism through which men's anti-violence groups promote their work. Men who are newer to the work, who may be seeking ways to appeal to broader swaths of men who have not yet thought about the issues, can sometimes inadvertently amplify how men in the field are positioned as rare men and heroes. Todd Henneman explained how he preempted one such potential mistake when MenCARE, the campus group he supervises, was coming up with ideas for its first generation of promotional posters: "And one of the ideas that they had was literally to kind of make this cartoon character that was superhero-ish-looking. And I was like, 'Wait, wait, wait—like, that is, *no*.' It's not that guys are being the heroes swooping in; they're just being like decent guys [and] this is the expected standard of conduct. So they shouldn't be getting some sort of accolades; they're not like rescuing the damsel in distress."

Men, especially those new to the field, can easily fall into basking in the adulation they receive, especially from women. They are unlikely to come up with smart strategies to counter the pedestal effect, simply from out of the blue; instead, they tend to learn these strategies from their mentors. Tony Porter says that when he talks with younger men entering the field, he tells them it's important to "stay humble," that "while you may appear to be unique, you're still simply doing what you're supposed to do, you're not really doing nothing grand. You're just simply doing what you're supposed to do."

Much of this sort of mentoring comes from women leaders, who are critically aware of the pitfalls of the pedestal effect. Several of them described their efforts to teach men both to be aware of the operation of male privilege in antiviolence work and to develop strategies to preempt, deflect, or use incidents of pedestaling as teachable moments. Janeen McGee says that when RAVEN's DV groups are co-facilitated by a woman and a man, the male partners are taught to "be intentional" in modeling how to listen and learn from women. When a woman facilitator has made a strong point, for instance, the man can say, "'That was a great point, I really appreciate you brought that up. That helps me think about my own behavior in this way'." A danger in male-female co-facilitated men's groups, McGee explained, is the tendency for men to "collude" with each other against the women. It is important, she explained, for a male facilitator to avoid collusion by actively rupturing an apparent taken-for-granted sexist consensus, even if it means taking a position that might put him in opposition to the men in the group. In effect, McGee wants the male facilitator to model the responsible bystander behavior they hope the men in the group will internalize.

> It is important that the male facilitator can set the example. Sometimes, you know, a lot of comments will come up—[men in the group will] say, "Well you know all women are like this," or "All women want this or that." It's particularly helpful for a male facilitator to say, "I don't agree with that," or "That hasn't been my experience," or when they say, "All men think this way," to say, "Well, I don't." If [male facilitators] aren't taking those opportunities to do that, then their silence, or their agreement or their politeness can even be taken as collusion or agreement.

Trina Greene says that to avoid such collusion, and to sidestep the tendency for men to be given greater credence and respect than women co-facilitators, one simple strategy she teaches in her program is what she calls "step up, step back": "If you're talking a lot, or you realize that you're receiving more privilege, you step back, right? And you let somebody else step up. 'Cause, you know you're a man and you're presenting and you realize you're getting too much praise and too much attention, acknowledge that, and go, 'OK I'm going to step back, because my voice is drowning out all these women's voices in this room, so let me step back and let some of the women step up because I'm not the only voice in here.'"

Patrick Donovan seems to have absorbed the spirit of this step-up, step-back strategy. "It's important," he said, "to stand *with* women doing the work and not stand in front of the women doing the work."

Although men in the antiviolence field tend to receive disproportionate praise, tangible rewards, and rapid career escalation, there is a flipside to the pedestal effect. Joe Samalin, for instance, says men in the field are sometimes elevated to "automatic rock star," but they are also subjected to skepticism and "mistrust." He finds this "understandable," he says, and has experienced "both extremes; I've found women who've given me accolades that were undeserved, just 'cause I'm a guy doing this work, on the other end really shut me down and shut me out and not wanted me in a space." Quentin Walcott explained that "men who do this work are put on a pedestal in a sense that you are perceived to be this perfect man . . . but then when you mess up—because the expectation is for you not to, and people hold you to a higher standard—it's going to resonate even much more." Similarly, Kevin Hawkins experiences male privilege and critical scrutiny in his work as a "double-edged sword . . . while it's really easy, I think, to sort of appreciate and coast on that automatic credibility that you get, the accolades you get, it's hard when you screw up, you know, when you're not who people perceive you to be . . . it does put a lot more scrutiny on it."

The women we interviewed told us that such critical scrutiny of men in the field should simply be expected. When she works with men in her position with the New York State Office of Domestic Violence Prevention, Gwen Wright said, "I certainly have an expectation that they have to be the best. . . . There is a level of scrutiny that kind of comes with the territory. It's expected and it's necessary." When asked if a man receives "extra scrutiny" compared with women in the field, Phyllis Frank replied, "True, 100 percent. And should. As I as a white woman should. Yup. Men are making many more errors. Because [of] the choreography to be entitled, and to define, and to stomp on, and to not respect leadership, and to not hear. So to have your ongoing way of being confronted feel like extra scrutiny, it's just scrutiny for the extra crap you do. It's not *extra* scrutiny. It's an appropriate response to the amount of errors you're making in comparison to women."

The younger generation of women, sometimes defining themselves as "third wave" feminists, appear to be more comfortable—and certainly less opposed ideologically—than were many of their 1970s sisters with the idea of partnering with men to stop gender-based violence.[15] But in the antiviolence field, a skeptical approach toward men is not simply the province of veteran feminist activists like Gwen Wright, Patti Giggans, or Phyllis Frank. Trina Greene, only twenty-eight years old when we interviewed her, said that when she first started working with Peace Over Violence, she was skeptical whenever she saw a man speak about violence against women, wondering how genuine and deep his commitment really ran: "I'm like, really what does that man know? I wonder, what does he do when he goes home? Does he really believe in this? Or is he just doing this for show? I was more skeptical of men when I first got into the movement. . . . I was like 100 percent skeptical, even if a man was presenting on violence against women, I was like, uh-huh, do I believe him? I wonder how he treats his own girlfriend. Is he teaching this, and is he really believing this?"

Both the women and the men we interviewed agree that women's skepticism and critical scrutiny of men in the field happens for good reasons. Men who work to prevent sexual assault and domestic violence are the public face of organizations that often define themselves as feminist; they are ultravisible exemplars of a different sort of man. Like it or not, this comes with a certain responsibility. For instance, Nina Alcaraz said that men's violence prevention with boys in public schools "is not a nine-to-five job—you don't just turn off when you leave the office or when you leave a classroom. And especially when you're working with young men, like you go out in public and you need to be able to walk the walk [and be] the example that you're trying to set. . . . When you're out there in the community, you don't just turn it off."

We heard a few stories that illustrated Alcaraz's point, stories of men who did not always "walk the walk" when they left the office. Patti Giggans' tone was incredulous as she told of a time when a group of men who run the batterer program for her at Peace Over Violence went out to dinner together. Giggans was "thunderstruck" when she learned the next day that some of them were "making comments about the body parts of the female server at the dinner table, sexualizing her," and that this was being "facilitated" by her co-supervisor, a social worker. Giggans saw this as an example of men reverting to how they had learned to bond together in groups, by sexualizing women, and she also saw this as a lesson in how "deep" sexist male privilege and entitlement ran, even among the good men she worked with: "This wasn't bad men, this was men doing what men do with entitlement and obliviousness to the connection between that and running a batterer program. Is that a story? That's the story. This is one that I remember because I was so thunderstruck that the men were interacting with me and doing body parts with a server. Just kept me thinking, 'This is deep'."

Men understand that women are subjecting them to critical scrutiny for these very reasons—that sexism and male privilege run deep, are still in play, even with men who identify as feminist allies. Michael Kaufman sees women's questions about the depth of men's commitment to feminist work as "healthy skepticism: 'Are you guys for real?'" And Jeffrey Buckholtz sees women's skepticism over the growing bonds within a "community of men" who are doing antiviolence work as understandable; "There's this hesitancy—I think for good reason–about like, are we [men] going to bond and all of a sudden we're like thumping our chests?" Keith Smith has observed that, "there's been some anger on the part of women around the fact that men are getting involved in this work." Given men's tendencies "to take over [and] to dominate," Smith understands women's fears that "suddenly men are the experts and women are sort of being pushed to the side."

This questioning of the depth of men's commitments has been amplified as the field has pulled away from its feminist movement roots. As we showed in Chapters 3 and 4, as successive cohorts of men entered antiviolence work from the late 1980s to the present, they did so in a context of increasing professionalization of the work, and medicalization of violence prevention. For longtime activists such as Janeen McGee, this creates challenges for feminist leaders in organizations like RAVEN, who see more and more men routing into domestic violence prevention work as part of professional training that lacks a feminist foundation: "[A] huge challenge is the men with social work or counseling backgrounds . . . there's a range of how important that feminist piece is. And there's a few that I still don't think they understand that's what we do [laughs]. You know, we'll talk about how this is about addressing male dominance. And occasionally I'll get that facilitator who says, 'No this is about your feelings!' [laughs] Well it's bigger than that!"

In addition to women's doubts about men's depth of commitment to feminist antiviolence work, and their fears about how male privilege might silence or displace women in the very field they have created, there is another even more visceral reason for the critical scrutiny of men. The rape and domestic violence prevention field exists, after all, because of women's collective responses to men's violence against women. Every day and for years on end, the women who work in the field talk with and assist survivors of domestic violence and sexual assault; indeed, many women in the field are themselves survivors of men's violence. It stands to reason that men who enter the field as allies—regardless of their stated intentions and commitments—will be seen *as men,* and feared as potential perpetrators of violence. Patrick Donovan was doing "100 percent prevention work" with men when we interviewed him, but previously he had done some hotline work at a rape crisis center, and he understood why some women who called in would ask to speak to a woman instead of him. "It's not anything personal, but it's this person has been victimized by a male and part of what they need to feel safe right now is working with a woman." But for some of the men we interviewed, it took some time to internalize the fact that, no matter how much good work they do, it still makes sense when women distrust them, even fear them. Marc Rich told a story that illustrated his own shock of recognition, when he was walking out to the parking lot one night after work.

> A woman was walking and she came around the corner and didn't see me, and she turned around and screamed, and I could have said, "Why are you scream-ing? I'm Dr. Mark Rich, I do sexual assault prevention work, you're safe." No, she fucking *should* scream, because men who look like me rape women. So I don't ever think that, "Oh these women shouldn't be resistant or shouldn't be suspicious." They've met men who look and act and talk like me—whether it's the president of their university or an employer or a significant other or a brother, whoever—that acted in hyper-masculine way that's oppressive. Would I be any different?

Patti Giggans agreed, saying that the doubts women have about men in the field are understandable as "a trust factor; I mean, when you have a rape crisis center or a DV shelter . . . you also have women who work in this field who have experienced male violence, and who have been edu-cated about and have resentment about male privilege." Similarly, when we told Shelley Serdahely that men in the field sometimes feel distrusted and scrutinized by women, she said "it makes sense to me that that would happen . . . if men perpetrate the violence and men are all somewhere on the spectrum of sexism or abuse of women, then why would women be comfortable working with them, particularly around this issue?" A few of the men we interviewed also said they were wary when new men got involved in the work, worrying they would get close to women in the group, and then commit violence against them. Brian Jara spoke of a time when exactly that happened in a group he advised, and said this is partly why it makes sense to skeptically scrutinize other men who claim feminist identification.

Leiana Kinnicutt pointed to an especially sticky question surrounding the fact that some of the men who are leaders in the domestic violence prevention field are themselves former perpetrators. Kinnicutt observed that these men are "some of the most powerful messengers around what it's like to go through that transformative process . . . and there's got to be a role for them in the movement as well." But she also acknowledged that these men's presence raised uneasy questions, especially among women co-workers: "Can you ever truly repent for bad behavior? . . . I mean, there's a lot of women survivors that are in the movement, and so there's I think a protective factor around not wanting to expose women who've been through traumatic experiences to men who've been violent. And that's really real. I mean you don't want to retraumatize."

Racialized Scrutiny

Even though increasing visibility and rapid pedestaling are professional benefits to a small number of men of color, it frequently comes with levels of suspicion and critical scrutiny that are amplified well beyond what most white male professionals face. Emiliano Diaz de Leon was twenty-one years old when he started working as the only man at a shelter for women and their children.

> From the very beginning, it was challenging being a Latino man and these kinds of expectations, not just the women that work [there], the women who are living at the shelter, but also their kids had of me, and really confronting that on a daily basis in terms of my behavior. The way I was around them was really difficult to kind of maneuver, like at first, I didn't know how to act, I didn't know what to say or do, like—there were a lot of questions about my sexual orientation, about my masculinity. The women challenged me, I think. And I didn't know, like at first I didn't know how to deal with those challenges, I wasn't sure I could do the work.

For Diaz de Leon, a good deal of his uncertainty and confusion likely had to do with his youth and inexperience; but even somewhat older men of color such as Jimmie Briggs described confronting a racialized ultravisibility he felt was due to "being a man, being a man of color, being a man of color with dreadlocks." Although some of the attention he gets on account of his appearance is positive, Briggs says, it also comes with an extra level of critical scrutiny that makes him hyperconscious of how he presents himself and what he says.

> I'm divorced, I'm single and you're working on an issue where you're surrounded by women all the time. So it's like, I almost feel like I have to somehow be the model man: hypercourteous, hypergentleman, you know I can't flirt, I can't ask anybody out, I can't, I can't. I feel like I can't be construed as being a player or anything like that. I would hate to do anything that would hurt

my credibility, like that's my fear, saying the wrong thing, saying something sexist or being perceived as a jerk. . . . I've had women feminists ask me, pretty high-level feminists ask me, am I doing this to meet women, you know, to hook up. My credibility, my authority rather, is constantly questioned.

Though all men in the violence prevention field felt the critical scrutiny of their women colleagues and supervisors, the particularly racialized constraint experienced by men like Diaz de Leon and Briggs is grounded in the historical legacy of Latino and African American men being stereotyped as both oversexed and violence-prone.[16] Men of color in the field navigate this stereotype daily. And sometimes, as in a story Don McPherson told us, they can draw from their own experiences of racism to build empathic bonds with women, and to develop intersectional discussions of oppression.

> There was one moment at a national domestic violence conference, and it was a panel of men, that this women stood up and berated us, cussed us *out*, angry, pissed off, screaming, and while she was doing that, I was like, "Give me the mic, I'm going to talk to her." (laughs) As she's screaming I'm grabbing the mic in front of me and I'm like, "I hear you," I said to her, "I agree with you, I wish that white people would address racism because it's the right thing to do, so I get your anger, that makes sense to me, and as someone whose eyes are open to this issue, if I were a woman I'd be pissed off a lot too, and I have the luxury, as a man, to walk in and out of that."

Shelley Serdahely is supportive of the growing number of men of color in the field, but she also warned of potentially regressive outcomes for antisexist work when men of color deploy the race card: "There are men of color in the violence-against-women's movement who are concerned about—and rightly concerned about—racism in the movement, but I think [they] feel entitled to bring it into the room in a way that stops their own looking at themselves around their own sexism. I've seen instances of almost bullying, men using tactics against white women and actually against women of color, because they sort of assume 'I can speak for women of color,' when maybe the women of color in the room haven't asked them to do that."

In this context of racialized scrutiny, Quentin Walcott has pondered over the years, "How are you going to be taken seriously as a man, a man of color, in a predominantly—and in terms of the leadership, it's still predominantly white female—how are you taken seriously in that environment?" Walcott has felt, he said, "a lot of pressure with that, like, 'Wow, I gotta be perfect'."

Not every man we interviewed said he felt pressured to be "perfect." But most were conscious of having to navigate the often perilously thin line between being put on a pedestal as a "rare man" and being the subject of critical scrutiny in their antiviolence work. Most of them built a sense of clarity about navigating this contradictory terrain by carefully thinking through—both individually and collectively—what it means for men to be "accountable" when doing violence prevention work. The recent case of Hugo Schwyzer is an extreme example of how a man who positions himself as a profeminist rock star can fail—in this case, massively and disastrously—to properly navigate this field. Public speaker, activist, community college professor, and blogger, Schwyzer was meteoric in the 2000s, becoming perhaps the most visible "male feminist" in the blogosphere—in the past decade a vibrant site for feminist thinking and debate, especially for younger feminists.[17] Schwyzer blogged, wrote articles, and tweeted tirelessly about men, feminism, violence, pornography, and sex for feminist and progressive online publications like *Jezebel*, *The Good Man Project*, and *Salon* and for more mainstream publications such as the *Atlantic*. He appeared on the Ricki Lake show and was a visible leader in a 2011 Slutwalk. And even though some feminists were openly skeptical about Schwyzer's apparent need to be the center of attention, many appreciated the contributions he was making to developing online conversations about men and feminism. In December 2011, Schwyzer was profiled in a glowing interview in *Feministe* as "a principled, passionate teacher who works hard to provide thoughtful feminist guidance for his students."[18]

In 2012–13, the roof fell in on Hugo Schwyzer. First, it came to light that years ago he had struggled with addiction and tried to murder his girlfriend, and to commit suicide. He admitted to having sexual relations with several of his women students.[19] Some of his writings—especially about teen sex and pornography—started to appear lurid and self-involved, especially in light of what was now evident of his past. Feminist women—even many who had previously supported Schwyzer—responded with outrage.

Following some months of his continuing to blog, crafting a public redemption narrative, Schwyzer melted down, telling the *LA Weekly* that he "had a mental breakdown," admitting to the *Pasadena Star News* that he had been sexting with a porn actress he had previously invited to speak to his class. He had started using drugs again, he admitted, and contrary to his redemption narrative, his extramarital affairs had also continued. The brutal online "takedown culture," he implied, had worn him down and he was retreating from public life. But soon, he was tweeting again, including admitting that he had basked in an accelerated and largely unearned ascent to male feminist rock-star status: "[I] built a career as a well-known online feminist on fraudulent pretenses," he wrote, adding, "I loved the attention and I was fucking awesome at getting it."

The feminist blogosphere, as might be expected, was afire for months. A Tumblr called "Fuck No, Hugo Schwyzer" was created, as was a Facebook page called "Feminists Against Hugo Schwyzer." A story about Schwyzer's rise and fall as a public male feminist appeared prominently in the *Atlantic*.[20] We had interviewed Schwyzer well before his public meltdown. And although we have decided not to use his interview material for this book, we outline the public aspects of his story here to illustrate how the pedestal effect can work in feminist online communities, and how a self-described feminist man can quickly come crashing down when it becomes clear that he has held himself accountable not to a feminist community or movement but rather mainly to his own aspirations to be seen, heard, and celebrated.[21]

In the wake of the Schwyzer meltdown, feminist activists expressed concern with the collateral damage, worrying especially how Schwyzer's actions might create or exacerbate problems for male allies—and the women they work with—and for violence prevention efforts with boys and men. Shira Tarrant told us that in ongoing conversations about male allies and feminism, Hugo Schwyzer has become "the elephant in the room; the lightning rod; case study number one." When Schwyzer imploded publicly, Tarrant said, "I was getting phone calls and emails from a lot of really distressed guys who were part of the movement, saying like, 'Oh my god, I'm afraid to say anything now, and I don't know what to make of this, and I had no idea', so it was really, really destructive . . . they were demoralized, distressed." Tarrant said this case raises another sticky issue that potentially undercuts the logic behind much of the violence prevention movement. In response to Schwyzer's revelations, she said, feminists who had always been skeptical of men's growing presence in the movement were now openly asserting that, " 'See, people don't change.' And I'm thinking, but then why go into the prisons and do work with incarcerated men who have been violent? You know? Why go talk to the military if it's an institution based on violence? I have to believe that somehow we're capable. And so this was undermining that perspective which [sighs] is always really dangerous."

Clearly, the Hugo Schwyzer story is an extreme case, but his spectacular crash-and-burn illustrates acutely the challenges that face all men in the field: navigating male privilege and feminist critical scrutiny. For the men we interviewed, as well as their women colleagues and mentors, the key to navigating the twin perils of the pedestal and scrutiny was how they define and enact accountability.

"Ask, Ask, Ask": The Politics of Men's Accountability

Men doing violence prevention work understand that they need to be strategically smart, assertive, and the sort of people who take creative initiative. However, most of them also understand that their everyday, close-up, and personal work—talking with high school boys about sexual consent; developing bystander intervention programs in the military, college athletic departments, or fraternities; facilitating workshops with domestic violence perpetrators—all takes place within a complicated political terrain that is fraught with pitfalls. Work that was originally shaped by and centered in a women's movement is increasingly stretching away from its politicized feminist roots as it is transformed into a professional field under the auspices of the state, foundations, nonprofits, and university administrations. In this shifting context, how do the men in this field define accountability? To whom are they accountable?

For the men of the Movement Cohort, being accountable initially meant keeping their work directly connected to the movement, and taking leadership from feminist women. As these men started to build violence prevention nonprofits like MOVE in the San Francisco Bay Area, being accountable to the women's movement meant structuring their incipient groups around a particular kind of feminist consciousness that prioritizes women's life experiences and leadership. This included things like, as Allan Creighton explained, building noncompetitive funding clauses into their nonprofits: "We're not going to compete [for funding] with anything identified as a shelter or rape crisis center or service; just not gonna happen." It also meant, according to Don Conway-Long, inviting women to train the first wave of RAVEN men working in St. Louis with domestic violence perpetrators: "We knew that we needed to seek women's leadership and seek women's supervision and eventually pay women to come in and supervise the peer counselors." It meant, according to Craig Norberg-Bohm, men's groups like RAVEN always seeking "advice and consent" from women, "and listening." When Michael Kaufman and his colleagues started the White Ribbon Campaign, he said, "[we] had a women's advisory board. When we started anything new we would phone women colleagues to get their advice, 'cause we *did*, you know, stumble and make mistakes, and we knew we weren't the experts on these issues. In those early years one of the pamphlets we put out, it was called something like, 'Ten Things That Men Can Do to End Violence Against Women,' and the first point of it was something like, you know, 'Listen to women, learn from women.' "

Over the years, some antiviolence efforts by men, however well intended, caused problems for local women's groups when the men did not ask for "advice and consent," did not "listen to women, learn from women." Ben Atherton-Zeman[22] told a story of a Texas man who "was very eager" to engage men in discussions about domestic violence. The man's strategy was

> to invite the Dallas Cowboy cheerleaders, with their outfits, to dance sexy for these men. He thought, that will bring men in, and then once they're there, I will talk to them about [how] men need to take responsibility for stopping domestic violence. And I was like, "Have you run this idea by your local domestic violence program?" And he was like "Yeah, and can you believe it? They don't like the idea! But I told them I know how to involve men, so I'm just going to do it anyway." I was like [incredulous voice] "You *can't* do it anyway if they don't approve!" And he's like, "Well, yeah, sure I can!" "Have you told the state coalition?" "Yeah, and can you believe it, they don't like it either." And I tried to convince him to be more accountable, to do something that they approved of. And he didn't, he went ahead and did it anyway. I do know it was a giant pain for the local advocate community. I called the executive director of that local shelter, and she was venting to me about how much time this was taking away from her other duties.

Several women and men in the field said that questions of accountability in men's work are more important today than ever, given the generally postfeminist cultural context, and how antiviolence work is increasingly grounded in nonfeminist organizations. The men of A Call to Men, Gwen Wright said approvingly, are aware that they "have worked primarily with criminal justice agencies, so they're in forums that are mostly men. I think that they have been very very cautious of the lack of authority that women have in those communities, and showed due diligence in changing that, in helping to bring women to the forefront, even in those professions. Whether it's law enforcement or probation or parole, but to really bring women's voices into the discourse. And they do that from an accountability perspective, that unless the work is informed by women's voices, it's for naught."

Tony Porter agrees with Wright, underlining that "we as ACTM are very clear that we're accountable to women," but Porter worries that as violence prevention work has become more professionalized, "We've lost touch with it. The more we become a field, the more . . . we've really shifted gears with accountability. We need the funding and the monies to help do the work, but the more you get the funding and the monies, the more you get tied into rules, regulations."

Movement Cohort veteran Paul Kivel also worries about depoliticization of men's antiviolence work. Though he agrees that today's popular bystander approach has a broad appeal, Kivel fears the approach lacks the "active component" needed to engage men as social change agents. The concept of being an ally—as opposed to that of a bystander—he says, helps "to develop a much more sophisticated [definition] of accountability" to a movement for social change, rather than simply to the idea of intervening to stop a potentially violent situation.

> We created a positive identity around being an ally that was somebody who actually had not only a responsibility, but a real opportunity to make a contribution, to be part of the community making change. So this became a way to really reframe the whole conversation for boys and men. Now the Men of Strength campaign kind of has that, but it doesn't have such an active component. And the bystander stuff, it's tricky because a bystander has a choice, right?—Which is good, but when you're an ally, you understand that you don't have a choice because you're part of this community.

Such a reframing of men's accountability not simply as responsible bystanders but as allies in feminist social change efforts makes particular sense, some men told us, in the current political context in which there are also men's organizations that are committed to antifeminist goals. Quentin Walcott is concerned that "a lot of men's organizations have an enemy consciousness, particularly father's rights organizations [have] this enemy consciousness between men and women. And getting feedback from women, I think, really eliminates most of that dynamic."

In this context of professionalization and antifeminist backlash, Patrick Donovan explained, part of being accountable is keeping the focus on violence against women, even as antiviolence activists acknowledge that boys and men too are sometimes victimized by gender-based violence. Donovan explained that he reaches out to teen males in his work in a way he hopes will appeal to them, focusing on "a bystander approach, making something they connect with." He is "trying as much as possible to be inclusive of male victims and LGBT victims, [but] in the end, the prevention work that we're doing is aimed at preventing violence against, by and large, women. And so if the women are telling us, 'What you're doing's not effective, [or] what you're doing is being done in a way that is disrespectful to the movement,' I think that we have an obligation to listen to that." Rob Buelow echoed this sentiment, asserting that accountability in his work means that he needs continually to "ask ask ask" the women he works with: "I just always wanted to make sure, like hey, is this OK that I'm doing this, or is this a good idea, or is that language all right?"

Most of the men we spoke with echoed this idea that accountability means checking with women, but they were also aware that this ask, ask, ask process is not as simple as it might seem. For one thing, if men are overly focused on whether or not feminist women approve of their violence prevention efforts, this can lead to a level of critical self-reflexivity that in the end impedes action. Jackson Katz is especially impatient with what he sees as too much hand wringing about accountability, and not enough action. Over the years, he says, he has been frustrated when profeminist men have "tied themselves in ideological knots" in their efforts to remain accountable to women. Some of this, he occasionally thinks, "comes from a reflexive self-loathing almost, or even maybe an internalization of a feminist critique of masculinity, such that they're disempowered by it." Katz told us several stories of men's groups he has worked with over the years who, in his mind, were "wildly ineffective because of their self-reflexivity to the nth degree about men doing this kind of work." Once, while working with a coalition of men's groups in Boston to organize Cease Fire: Ending Men's Violence Against Women, a weeklong series of events intended to draw media attention, a man in the coalition objected, saying, "We're men, why should we get coverage?" When the man suggested that the only legitimate action for male allies was "licking stamps or stuffing envelopes" for a women's organization, Katz was livid: "If that's what you think men can do is be the men's auxiliary to a women's organization, and you're gonna stuff envelopes, why be in a men's group? What's the point? I just think there's so much of that thinking in men's work; it's self-limiting. But I might have been afflicted with the opposite problem, which is I saw huge possibilities, I was like, oh my god there's so much we can do here."

Katz observed too that the recent development of online forums as public sites for feminist politics has created new opportunities for self-reflexive talk of the sort that feeds *inaction*. Once, he told us, following an online call from a United Nations agency for men to submit design proposals for an antiviolence t-shirt, a man on a profeminist listserv threw a monkey wrench into the discussion, objecting that the call was "clearly sexist because it excludes women." What to Katz had seemed "so noncontroversial—to me it was absolutely 100 percent a good thing"—then quickly devolved, in his view, to another instance of progressive men and women tying themselves in "ideological knots."

> And I'm like pulling whatever hair I have left out, you know what I mean? It's like this is so *stupid!* . . . It's almost like a right wing plot to prevent people on this listserv from doing anything productive. And it was all about being more progressive than the next person. In other words, "I'm more accountable"— "Oh yeah, hadn't thought of that, good point, good point, I hadn't thought that was sexist, now you make a really good point." I wanted to say, "STFU," which is, you know, Internet speak for "Shut the fuck up." And it all started from one guy, it was a man, who had pointed out that this is sexist.

Katz concluded that he is "sick and bored of this kind of conversation," but this does not mean that he is unaware, much less unwilling to make the sorts of preemptive accountability statements common to most men in the field. For instance, in an eloquent preamble to his online Ted Talk in 2013, Katz asserted to the crowd that he would not be standing there speaking about men's antiviolence efforts if it were not for what he had learned from feminist women.[23] Many veterans of men's ally work, like Katz, may find it wearying, but most believe it is crucial, especially for men new to the work, to engage in self-reflexive conversations about accountability. The men in the field also grapple with another complication to the matter of men's accountability: the question of *which women* to whom to be accountable.

Accountability to Whom?

The men of the Movement Cohort understood that their work was grounded in, and thus accountable to, the feminist movement. However, splits in the women's movement—especially the chasm that developed in the 1980s around the feminist sex wars—raised the question of "to *which* feminist women?" to be accountable. For most, this meant being accountable to the fragment of the women's movement to which they aligned themselves politically. Don Conway-Long explained that, for RAVEN, "the question of 'which feminist' is always a good one." Profeminist men should not seek to be told, "'Oh, you're so wonderful' by a more liberal feminist orientation," he explained. "That's not our purpose in being here. We want critical analysis of what we do, we want critical supervision to make sure we're not doing anything that would harm women's lives."

Although some Movement Cohort groups like MASV buckled under the tensions that came with the "to which feminists?" accountability question during the feminist sex wars, some of the male allies of the era found ways to avoid the perils of either-or choices. Paul Kivel explained that when he and Alan Creighton shaped the Oakland Men's Project as a multiracial nonprofit in the early 1980s, they had already learned from the MASV experience that "we had a very simple understanding of accountability in the early days, right? You do what you're told [laughs]. And then we stopped to think, 'Well what kind of ally are you if you're not creative and innovative and taking risks and making mistakes?' You know, what does it mean to be accountable?" For the OMP, accountability meant shaping an organization that would be, "multiracial in a conscious and intentional way, and then to learn from the men of color that we were working with. . . . We had all this knowledge about the women's movement and the right way to do things, and we paid a lot of attention to being accountable to that, but it was diverse. And it allowed for some space to really think about what works and what do people need and how do we build, you know, a broader base for this work."

For the next three decades, Kivel's feminist work with boys and men continued to be coupled with "a lot of racial justice work, from a white perspective," and this permitted, in his eyes, development of "a much more sophisticated level of thinking and talking about accountability."

Bridge Cohort member Alan Grieg also realized early on that he couldn't be accountable to "all women," and with the growing importance of foundations and nonprofits in the 1990s his and others' work was no longer grounded simply in a grassroots social movement. Instead, he said, "It's important for me that I'm accountable to groups working on feminist politics, feminist projects. It's not just kind of, 'You're a woman, you're running this foundation so I'm accountable to you.' Not necessarily, because I don't agree with everything you do." Accountability, Grieg has concluded, is "a relationship and a conversation, not just an event or a thing."

Jackson Katz, another key Bridge Cohort member, agrees that it's important for men to think of accountability not in terms of individual women but instead in terms of one's relationship to a movement. However, he concluded, "the devil's in the details . . . if there's a radical feminist who's saying that pornography is the central struggle, and then there's a liberal feminist who's saying, 'No, that's distracting us from these other structural issues that we want you to be working on', [do] I have to be accountable to the most radical person to be, you know, legitimate? Or is it OK to be accountable to the more liberal position?" When we asked Katz how he deals with this question, he responded with an admittedly controversial point of view: "Somebody could critique me for what I'm about to say, [that] it's coming from privilege, which is, I trust my own instincts better than anybody else's. Women or men . . . I think a lot of men are really tied up in knots around some of this stuff, and I think a lot of men retreat as a result of these sort of internal self-conscious kinds of conversations and they become more comfortable either doing nothing at all, which is a total shame, or thinking very small."

Katz's concern that profeminist men's self-reflexivity can lead to inaction or to "thinking very small" is the flip side of his inclination to think big and to act. But it is also the case that, at times, men who think big have gotten into very hot water when they have acted before carefully navigating the complicated nuances of the "which feminists?" accountability question. In 2013, for instance, longtime National Organization for Men Against Sexism leader Bob Brannon[24] was roundly criticized following a "Forging Justice" conference, co-hosted by NOMAS and HAVEN, a Michigan-based domestic violence and sexual assault agency. The conference presentations were all scheduled to be live-streamed on the Internet, but apparently Brannon, who currently heads the NOMAS Pornography, Prostitution, and Trafficking task group, and another leader independently decided at the last second to turn off the streaming for Emi Koyama, whose presentation criticized mainstream feminist and governmental perspectives on sex trafficking, reframing it as a transnational labor issue. Koyama, members of HAVEN, and some NOMAS members were furious with Brannon for what they perceived as a privileged white man's silencing of the voice of a feminist woman of color.[25] Brannon, who may have believed his action was a necessary act of accountability to the antitrafficking feminists he aligns himself with, was criticized not only for censoring a woman of color but also for silencing a powerfully emergent feminist perspective on trafficking, a standpoint that emerges from the experiences of sex workers and reflects a sophisticated transnational and intersectional feminist reframing of trafficking activism.[26]

Questions of accountability are still fraught with pitfalls for male allies, though younger men of the Professional Cohort seem to fret less about this issue than did their older brothers. Part of this shift may have to do with the influx of more men of color, who we have argued bring an organic intersectional lens to their violence prevention work, and thus also to their ways of thinking about accountability. Gilbert Salazar, as we have seen, routed to gender-based violence prevention through an initial engagement with male-on-male violence among poor Latino boys. And although he has come to learn how violence against women is linked to men's violence against other men, he is uncomfortable with what is implied when other men in his field say they need "to be accountable to women": "I think that's where my own sort of racial background comes in. And it's unfortunate but I think sometimes there's this idea of, you know, like who was oppressed first, or who was oppressed the most? . . . Being accountable to women, I personally, I don't sort of—doesn't quite strike me as something that seems very positive. Why should I be accountable to someone, anyone, not just women? I mean that's really where my independence really wants to come in and I just wanna fight and be like, 'Why can't we be accountable to each other?' "

Some other members of the Professional Cohort expressed similar sorts of discomfort with the idea of male accountability to women. When we asked Stephen Philp, twenty-five when we interviewed him, about accountability in his recent work as a program assistant for a university women's and men's center, he replied that it struck him as "such a weird question." His work, he said, was always done alongside women, so, "Am I accountable to women, like no? Yes? It's just an odd question. . . . I feel like I'm pretty confident that I know what a pro-gender-equality behavior is, you know, like I've been doing this long enough at this point and I'm firmly established enough in my feminist identity that I feel like I'm pretty capable on my own at figuring out what to do, and because of a lot of my involvement, even at this point, involves women, I don't feel like I need to explicitly get their approval."

John Erickson, twenty-seven years old when we interviewed him, echoed Philp's words, asserting that it is not necessary for women to be "overseers" of men's feminist work: "There are men's-based groups that work just with men and antiviolence work and it's just all men, I don't think they'd have to be held accountable to anyone, because if they're still working towards a positive feminist framework or outcome, then why are we micro-managing them?"

It is possible that these younger men's looser definitions of accountability have to do with their embeddedness in a broader, multiracial field of feminists who tend to view women and men as feminist partners, rather than seeing women as the feminists, and men as their supportive "pro-feminist" allies. Younger men's looser conceptions of accountability may also have to do with the depoliticized and increasingly professionalized context of antiviolence work. However, two other younger men we interviewed responded to questions about accountability with statements that sounded a lot more like those of Movement Cohort men in 1978, than like "third wave" feminists or professionalized violence preventionists. As college students, Dillon Thomson and Cameron Murphey both aligned themselves with a reemergent feminist antipornography coalition.[27] Thomson accepts radical feminist women's leadership and sees it as "men's responsibility first and foremost to end patriarchy." And Murphey says he gets along well and feels supported by "radical feminist groups" but does not feel comfortable with "liberal third-wave feminists, all these prosex feminists," who, he says, have a "really shitty analysis. And they're also the least supportive of men as well." When he and other men wanted to do a speak-out in support of a showing of *The Vagina Monologues*, he said, some women opposed them and some supported them. The men realized that they could not be accountable to all women; they had to decide to align themselves with "certain women, and particularly women who . . . really understand a radical analysis, what I consider to be 'true feminism'. And at some point it boils down to that: I've checked in with myself as a feminist, I've checked in with other women who are feminist, you can't please everyone."

Though likely everyone we interviewed would agree that differences among feminists mean that a male ally "can't please everyone," most men we interviewed took seriously the question of what it means to be an accountable ally. A common theme in discussing this issue was the acknowledgment that being an ally is an ongoing process, not the outcome of a single action or public proclamation. Ben Atherton-Zeman said he learned long ago that being an ally is "a concept and a goal, certainly rather than something I can achieve, like 'OK, now I'm accountable'." Atherton-Zeman was one of two men—Joe Samalin being the other— who said he learned a powerful lesson from an ally statement put out some years ago by the Women of Color Caucus of the National Sexual Violence Resource Center.

> Basically it says, "Your ally badge, as whites, as men, you gotta give it back at the end of every day. You give it back, and you earn it the next day." So it's not like I have the badge and I'm done. It's the same with accountability. For me accountability means that if I have this great idea, the local program and the state coalition don't like it, I don't do it. It means that, for most decisions, I run them by someone like a Phyllis Frank or a Suzanne Pharr or a Rose Geary before I actually do it.

For a longtime movement veteran like Atherton-Zeman, the idea that one never fully and finally earns his "ally badge," that you have to "earn it [again] the next day," serves as a powerful reminder of what it means to be an accountable ally.

It means, in the words of Gwen Wright, that when male allies run a program, "women have the first word and women have the last word," because in the end "they want women to introduce them to the community, but they also want women at the end of the day to be the endorsers of their work." But what does this idea of accountability mean? And how does it play out when, as is increasingly the case today, "the community" is large-scale organizations like organized sports and the military—still largely male-run hierarchical institutions whose purpose is to train young men to deploy valorized forms of violence?

CHAPTER 6

Conclusion: Men, Feminism, and Social Justice

When Air Force Lt. Colonel Jeffrey Kusinski was arrested for sexual battery in May 2013, it was a lowlight of what had already been a very bad year for the U.S. military. After all, Kusinski was then serving as the officer in charge of overseeing the Air Force's Sexual Assault and Prevention Program, and his arrest occurred amid a steady flow of damning reports of continuing failures by all branches of the military to deal with a wide-ranging wave of sexual assault against women within its ranks.[1] A 2012 *New York Times* editorial sounded the alarm over "the military's dirty secret": record high rates of sexual harassment and assault in its three military academies[2]; stunning levels of sexual assault and harassment among recently deployed service women and men[3]; and escalating levels of family violence perpetrated by returning soldiers, especially those suffering from PTSD after multiple deployments to the wars in Iraq and Afghanistan.[4]

When confronted in congressional hearings or in the mass media on their problem with gender-based violence, the military has frequently noted that it is being proactive with sexual assault prevention programs such as the Army's "I. A. M. STRONG" program, a bystander campaign that encourages soldiers to "intervene, act, and motivate" in order to "change army culture." In the award-winning 2011 documentary *The Invisible War*, about sexual assault in the military, the filmmakers ask a cadet about these prevention programs, which included posters adapted for the military from the "My Strength" campaign (depicted in Figures 6.1 and 6.2). Her response: they are "a joke."[5]

Figure 6.1
"MY STRENGTH IS FOR DEFENDING" poster.
"My strength is for defending" poster copyright © 2014 by John Stoltenberg, reprinted by permission (contact media2change@gmail.com.) Photography by Lotte Hansen.

Figure 6.2
"MY STRENGTH IS FOR DEFENDING" poster.

"My strength is for defending" poster copyright © 2014 by John Stoltenberg, reprinted by permission (contact media2change@gmail.com.) Photography by Lotte Hansen.

The military was not the only institution that had problems with sexual assault blow up in their faces during the time we were writing this book. Several college campuses, among them Occidental College and the University of Southern California, faced legal challenges that the institutions had not taken seriously, or had in some cases covered up, reports of sexual assaults. In May 2014, the U.S. Department of Education's Office of Civil Rights announced it was investigating Occidental, USC, and fifty-three other colleges "for possible violations of federal law over the handling of sexual violence and harassment complaints."[6] Meanwhile, high school football players in various places—the 2012 Steubenville, Ohio, case the most notorious among them—perpetrated horrendous sexual assaults that were rendered visible through social networking and by radical whistleblowers like the group "Anonymous." Male college athletes accused of sexual assault, athletic department cover-ups, and university administration failures to hold perpetrators accountable also continued to make news headlines.[7] Likely the most egregious case in recent years—and an example of the absolute failure by high-profile university coaches and administrators to model the sorts of responsible bystander behavior that they say their young athletes should engage in—was the years of silence surrounding Penn State University football coach Jerry Sandusky's serial sexual assaults of children.

Many of these institutions—including the U.S. military and many university campuses and athletic departments—have had sexual violence prevention programs up and running for years. As we have seen, Jackson Katz launched both the MVP program, which is a model for bystander prevention in college sports, and the U.S. military's prevention programs. Katz sees the "hierarchical leadership and pressure from the top" as the reason the "The Air Force is way ahead of college campuses" and other civilian institutions in putting into place violence prevention programs. Katz imagines a scenario where, "some admiral, for example, in the Navy gets a directive from the secretary of the Navy that says, 'Make this happen dude,' you know, 'Make this happen. This is embarrassing, what are we doing about this? When we go to Congress in the next year to testify to what we're doing about sexual assault in the Navy, what are we gonna tell them?' So I as admiral have just heard from the secretary of the Navy that I need to do something, and when an admiral speaks in the Navy, [snaps finger] people just jump."

Clearly it is in the interest of the military to visibly "do something" about the "embarrassing" problem of sexual assault. And it is also evident that in a relatively short period of time, such snapping of fingers by admirals sparked a rapid growth and development of violence prevention programs in the military. But news stories and government research reports on the deep and enduring problem of sexual assault and other forms of gender-based violence in the military raise questions about what sort of impact such prevention programs are having, if any. Do the continuing sexual assaults perpetrated by men in the military or in big-time sports programs support the conclusion that such prevention programs are "a joke?" Or worse, that they serve as public relations window dressing through which these institutions create an impression that they are addressing a problem, while they continue with business as usual? After all, the military, college football, and college fraternities are institutions historically constituted by hierarchical male-dominant gender regimes within which violence and interpersonal domination are valorized. The interactional "glue" that bonds men in such groups flows from a tradition of eroticized misogyny and homophobia that polices the boundaries of narrow (and often violent) conceptions of masculinity, while putting at risk women and not-conventionally-masculine boys and men (both inside and outside the group).[8]

How, or to what extent, can prevention programs within institutions like the military, football, or fraternities actually succeed in mitigating gender-based violence, much less ending it? A number of years ago, Michael Messner assisted Mark Stevens in an intervention with a college football program after members of the team were accused of sexually assaulting a woman at an off-campus party. Before the first of what would be two workshops with the team, Messner wondered if such a brief intervention might be effective mostly in allowing the college to claim it had done something about the problem. Worried, Messner asked Stevens if he really thought that a few hours of talk could change a football team's values system, could challenge the erotic of heterosexual dominance bonding that so commonly cements team members' loyalties while simultaneously putting women and vulnerable men at risk. Stevens answered no, he did not think a workshop or two could so quickly transform the culture of a football team. "But," he added, "if we can empower one or two guys who, down the road, might intervene in a situation to stop a sexual assault, then our work will have made the world safer for at least one woman." Messner and Stevens agreed that, to them, this made the effort worthwhile, and they conducted the workshops.[9] But they also shared a view with many of the men we interviewed for this book, that the goal of individual change embedded in such a bystander approach to violence prevention, though worth the effort, is a far cry from the sorts of radical social change needed to prevent sexual violence on a broad scale.

Mark Stevens' words also illustrate a larger pattern that we have described in earlier chapters: for violence prevention workers to believe that the work they are doing with boys and men is effective involves something akin to the faith that teachers must have about the ultimate and long-term impact of their work in the classroom. In fact, though each man we interviewed had a handful of anecdotes of positive change in boys and men he had worked with, and despite organizational attempts to develop evidence-based research on the impact of violence prevention efforts, we really don't know whether or to what extent bystander intervention programs will prevent future acts of gender-based violence.

But we can ask two critical questions about these programs. First, to what extent do violence prevention programs, once in place, become available to host institutions as valuable public relations that can be used to gloss over, rather than directly confront, the root causes of gender-based violence? This is particularly troubling in cases where—as we have seen in some of the recent military and college football stories—survivors of sexual assault are silenced, or blamed and punished by the institution, rather than being supported. As we showed in Figure 1.1, prevention programs developed historically following feminist social movement actions that first focused on putting into place progressive *responses* to violence—both supporting survivors and making perpetrators accountable for their actions. In the absence of such systems of support for survivors and accountability for perpetrators following violence, it is very unlikely that people will take seriously such institutions' violence prevention campaigns—like the Air Force Sexual Assault Prevention Program, or MVP-style bystander programs in college football programs. In short, these programs risk being dismissed as "a joke."

Many of the violence prevention workers we interviewed, of course, work in schools with kids and do not confront the same sorts of institutional constraints and vested interests faced by those who work within masculinist institutions such as the military or football programs. And most of the men we interviewed who did work with such institutions— notably Jackson Katz and Don McPherson—believed they could create enough elbow room to have a positive impact within these contexts. One man, however, told us that he had been hired by a big-time college sports program to institute a violence prevention program, only to find it "incredibly disappointing" when he learned that his employers had hired him not to make any changes but mostly to work with male athletes of color to keep them eligible to play sports.

What drew me here and what I was promised . . . I thought that they were genuinely ready to do something, you know, make some changes. And it was more like they were just paying me to kind of, you know, be quiet [laughs]. I got kind of duped. The athletics department . . . needed people of color. You know, because obviously the athletes of color are the ones that fund this whole thing, you know what I'm saying? And also I had this particular background [in violence prevention] so that was really enticing for them, and they had no intention of actually letting me do any of that work. So once I got here, it was—it's been a real struggle. It's been a real struggle.

A second critical question we raise about many of today's violence prevention programs—largely severed as they are from their politicized feminist movement roots—is, to what extent are these programs geared to engage boys and men as critical thinkers, probing deeply the roots of violence within institutions like the military, sport, fraternities, or even high schools, and then acting as agents of institutional change? On the one hand, we can safely say that if prevention programs did have this radically transformative orientation, they would probably not be allowed by the military brass, or by those with a stake in perpetuating multimillion-dollar industries like college football. Longtime profeminist activist Craig Norberg-Bohm sees bystander violence prevention programs as useful, but he also wonders whether mounting such campaigns in the context of the military, an institution that recruits young men by "marketing for toughness," might be "the ultimate in contradiction." The original domestic violence prevention program for the military, Norberg-Bohm said, "was called 'the domestic violence *containment* program.' Think about the words. How do you tell someone whose job it is to beat someone up, to be willing to kill or to hit and be violent, that [being] violent is ultimately wrong?" The thought that violence prevention programs in the military might, at most, aim to "contain" violence in ways that increase the efficiency of an institution whose raison d'être is the efficient and ruthless projection of violence, gives pause to longtime movement activists. Others, though, find unacceptable the alternative, which is simply to leave those institutions untouched by efforts to stop sexual assault, harassment, and domestic violence.

The National Football League's response to the recent head injury crisis is also instructive as an institutional strategy of violence "containment."[10] The medical field has for years supplied evidence that repeated concussions can lead to long-term cognitive decline, including early-onset dementia; but only in recent years has the NFL been forced—by their players' association and by media muckrakers—to acknowledge that routine football collisions are a source of such injuries.[11] The devastating effect of head injuries on the lives of former football players is finally coming to light; less known or discussed is evidence that men's head injuries are also linked with other forms of violence, including violence against women. Sociologist Todd Crosset, drawing from medical research, pointed out more than a decade ago that men who have experienced repeated head injuries are several times more likely to commit acts of violence in their personal lives, including intimate partner violence[12] (an issue that exploded into public awareness in late 2014 following reports of several high-profile NFL players' violence against their girlfriends, wives or children).

Responding to the mounting awareness of the head injury problem, the NFL instituted some minimal rules that penalize helmet-to-helmet collisions and hold concussed players out of games, and they continue to explore the development of improved protective equipment. College football has instituted some similar protective rules. But let's be clear: nobody has advocated for the sorts of rule changes that would make it truly safe to play the game of football. To do so would be to render the game no longer football-as-we-know-it. There are huge stakes—vested interests in a multibillion-dollar high school, college, and professional sports-media-commercial complex that make such fundamental changes unlikely to happen. Meanwhile, boys and men who play the game will continue to accumulate injuries large and small, including head injuries; they will continue to be cheered for dishing out "big hits" to opposing players, and rewarded for their willingness to absorb hits, take pain, and play hurt. And this celebratory joining of men's violence against other men with violence against their own bodies, will also likely remain connected to a third part of the triad of men's violence: sexual and domestic violence against women.[13] What can we expect bystander violence prevention programs to accomplish, in such a context of celebratory violence?

PARADIGMATIC SHIFTS IN ANTIVIOLENCE WORK

It appears that violence-prevention programs, including men's growing roles in these efforts, are here to stay. But the impact of these endeavors is as yet unclear and will likely be determined by what sorts of strategies people develop on the ground. Although this book has charted an historical perspective on shifting cohorts' experiences with antiviolence work, it is crucial to see this history as a continuing and always unfinished process, characterized over time by emergent and opposing paradigms on gender-based violence, each of which implies new strategies. In Table 6.1, we summarize in broad brushstrokes three large paradigmatic shifts, the final one, we will argue, now in its germinal state. First, responding to a prefeminist view of rape and domestic violence as a problem perpetrated by a small number of deviant, bad men (often imagined in the United States as black men), the women's movement in the 1970s introduced a radical paradigmatic shift. As we outlined in Chapter 2, feminists of the 1970s and early 1980s argued that violence against women was foundational to men's systemic domination of women. Men who raped or hit women were not deviants, feminists asserted; they were overconformists with dominant conceptions of masculinity. The first Movement Cohort of antiviolence men developed strategies premised on this feminist assumption that ending violence against women required radical changes in power relations in society, including men's rejection of culturally honored forms of violent and dominating masculinity.

From the early 1990s and stretching into the 2000s, this feminist movement position was largely eclipsed by an emergent public health model of violence prevention. As "violence against women" was recast as "gender-based violence," we showed in Chapters 3 and 4, a configuration of government and foundation initiatives, community nonprofits, professional associations,

Table 6.1 PARADIGMATIC SHIFTS IN VIEWS ON GENDER AND VIOLENCE.

Paradigm	Naming Problem	Theory/Cause	View of Perpetrators	Strategies
Prefeminist (before 1970s)	A few bad men	Deviance/bad men	Individual deviants (racialized "others")	Weed out bad apples; protect women
Feminist (1970s–1980s)	Violence against women	Patriarchy: men's domination of women's bodies	Overconformists with masculinity	Gender equality: "stop being a man"
Public Health (Early 1990s–Present)	Gender-based violence; intimate partner violence	Disease model: unhealthy relationships bad information	Poorly socialized individuals	Prevention education; social marketing; bystander approach: "be a good man"
Social Justice (emergent)	Violence connected with social injustice	Violence as linking process in matrixes of domination	Interpersonal and institutional violence linked	Relinking personal and political: multiracial, transnational feminism; restorative justice

and individual contractors introduced violence prevention curricula and programs in schools, universities, sports programs, and the military. A central strategic shift in this process was the development of a good-men/bystander approach to violence prevention with boys and men, an approach that, while broadly appealing, also risked jettisoning a feminist analysis that pointed to links between gender-based violence and institutional relations of gender, race, and class inequalities and injustices.

As antiviolence work shifted from a social movement base to a professional base in paid occupations, we have shown, the work broadened its scope, while pulling away from its more politicized feminist roots, creating strains and tensions for practitioners in the field, many of whom retained feminist views and goals. Today's violence preventionists develop strategies within a social space that is *broadening,* with expanding numbers of state and foundation-funded programs, professional occupations, and curricula, but that is also simultaneously *thinning,* as gender-based violence is understood and confronted increasingly as a discrete health-oriented problem, rather than as a link and part of a larger system of social inequalities.

Violence preventionists today are further constrained when they work within institutions that seek to contain gender-based violence as a public relations problem. However, we observed many of these same preventionists actively seeking to retain or deepen the progressive movement-based visions of fundamental social change that originally germinated antiviolence efforts. We call this loosely configured array of progressive strategies an emergent "social justice" paradigm. In what follows, we will outline some indicators of this emergent paradigm. And we will suggest that how social justice strategies are theorized, coordinated, and played out— most importantly, how they make connections between gender-based violence and structured injustice—will determine the extent to which future violence prevention efforts will contribute to progressive changes, rather than simply containing the problem of violence so as to stabilize an emergent helping profession as part of the apparatus of institutional hierarchical control. Creating progressive strategies in antiviolence work is crucially important for everyone in the field, most of whom still today are women. But we think it is especially crucial for male allies to carefully think through these dilemmas, given how, as we discussed in Chapter 5, some male antiviolence professionals in this expanding field enjoy access to accolades, material rewards, and star status as rare men. Put simply, given the higher rewards available to a few men in the field, these men risk being more susceptible to being co-opted as instruments of institutional violence containment strategies.

Movement Cohort member Chris Anderegg compared today's professionalized antiviolence field with that of the 1970s and early 1980s and
lamented, "All of the rage is gone." Janeen McGee also worried that
younger people today enter a professional field that limits their understandings of the sources of violence, and thus the range of actions needed
to confront it. This is not young people's fault, McGee concludes; it's just
that today "there is no movement there." Another Movement Cohort veteran, Paul Kivel, also worries that "within this increasingly professionalized, conservative nonprofit sector," it has become more difficult for
activists to do antiviolence work so as to build progressive communities
working for fundamental social change. Within this context, Kivel says,
"there's no political framework for doing more than having pretty limited
goals. Male violence is still defined pretty narrowly, it's not—people aren't
talking about our wars in Iraq and Afghanistan when they're talking male
violence generally. . . . You're not building the long-term capacity of individuals and communities to work together over time for significant social
change, social justice work."

We, too, lament the decline of a mass social movement base for antiviolence work, and we have pointed to the limits of professionalized antiviolence work in this book. But we do in fact see a good deal of passion—even
sometimes rage—fueling the antiviolence engagements of the younger
activists whom we interviewed. And we also see in many of the members of the Professional Cohort a growing political sophistication that
runs much deeper than a superficial view of gender-based violence as just
another "public health problem" to be dealt with through short-term and
superficial efforts of the sort that sociologist Nina Eliasoph criticizes as
depoliticized "empowerment projects" that change little, while allowing
middle-class volunteers to feel better about themselves.[14]

At the heart of this dilemma, we think, is a limited and perhaps out-
dated idea of what a feminist social movement is or should be. Though
it is true that some of the women and men we interviewed are nostalgic
for the mass feminist movement of the 1970s, most of them still identify
the work they do as "feminist," and they often refer to their professional
networks as "the movement." What they are expressing, in other words,
is not the end of feminism but rather the institutionalization and professionalization of feminism.[15] Such social movement institutionalization
does commonly raise what sociologist James Jasper calls "the organization dilemma," the question of "the extent to which bureaucratization
helps or hurts movements."[16] Sociologist Patricia Yancey Martin sees the

institutionalization of feminist organizations since the 1980s not as a co-optation of the movement but as a movement accomplishment that, for instance, allows rape crisis centers to engage with "helping victims" while also "changing society."[17] In other words, professionalized feminist organizations can connect the helping professions' goal of victim services with feminist movement goals of social transformation. This makes good sense. After all, institutionalized antiviolence work—from the passage of the federal Violence Against Women Act, to the funding of statewide and local rape and domestic crisis centers, to the sustained presence of campus-based women's centers and gender studies programs—exists as an historic accomplishment of the feminist movement. It is true, as we argued earlier, that movement feminism has indeed been "eclipsed" by professionalization and by the health model of violence prevention, but it is also the case that feminism is clearly still an active element of the political terrain of antiviolence work.

This idea—that feminism is not gone but rather has permeated and reformed institutions while largely morphing from an on-the-streets movement to one embedded in organizations—reveals a second limitation to either-or thinking about today's violence prevention efforts. A corollary to updating our conceptions of social movements is recognizing that there is too often a false dichotomy drawn between liberal reform and radical action. Liberal antiviolence reforms like those enacted by the feminist movement can broaden the field of action in concrete and important ways. But such institutionalized changes also always create new strains and tensions to be navigated with further progressive action.

Clearly, the antirape and anti–domestic violence activists we interviewed feel both enabled and constrained by the professionalization and institutionalization of antiviolence work that feminists helped to create. They understand the constraints imposed by the conservatism of many of the institutions with whom they work, but rarely do they see opting out of the work as an option. Nor do they imagine their actions helping to spark a sudden revolutionary transformation in the foreseeable future. Rather, they engage gender-based violence pragmatically and strategically, while sustaining themselves over the long haul through communities and networks (increasingly via the Internet) of like-minded colleagues and allies who share a vision of social justice.

The emergent social justice approach to antiviolence work aims to bring about changes that create a space between the limitations of band-aid liberal reforms and currently unreachable visions of radical transformation, pragmatically forging what we call "radical reforms" that reflect three elements: (1) an analysis of gender-based violence that illuminates the structural roots of violence as a patterned social issue, rather than viewing it superficially as an individual act of deviance against members of a specific identity group[18]; (2) on-the-ground strategies that confront the connections between intimate gender-based violence and institutionalized violence and social injustice—that, to revive an older feminist slogan, link "the personal and the political"; and (3) working with communities to bring about changes that, even if likely falling short of absolute radical transformation, will alter institutions so as to increase equality, amplify the possibilities for democratic action, and elevate peace over violence. We see this pursuit of radical reform as the strategic arm of an emergent social justice paradigm in violence prevention, a paradigm that works within the constraints of the hegemonic marketized public health paradigm, while seeking to push beyond its limits.

We see elements of this emergent social justice paradigm in the creative, stealth-feminist, antiracist, on-the-ground strategies of antiviolence activists. We saw it, for instance, in Gilbert Salazar's work with Latino high school boys, as he melded theater of the oppressed methods with the standard My Strength curriculum. We saw it in the many ways in which men and women creatively turned moments of unearned praise for men into teachable moments about how privilege works. We saw it in the innovative ways younger activists are using social media to build feminist and social justice communities that move beyond the limits of institutionalized antiviolence work. In what follows, we outline three general sources of this emergent social justice paradigm: feminist professional networks in various areas of antiviolence work, the rise of what we have called "organic intersectionality" in the violence prevention field, and emergent transnational networks of gender-based violence prevention work, especially in the Global South.

Professional Feminists

One of the most substantial accomplishments of feminist activism has been the creation of organizations and professional occupational niches now occupied by feminists, mostly women. We have noted throughout this book that these developments created "paradoxes of professionalization" that do limit the depth of feminist activism, but we also see feminist professionals as a resilient source of activism, critique, and potential change. Academia is one of the most substantial sites of such feminist professionalization, and if anything, it has become more important over time. The mass women's liberation movement was the main source that sparked the activism of the Movement Cohort in the 1970s and early 1980s. Many younger men of subsequent cohorts reported that their awareness and understanding of violence against women was first sparked in women's and gender studies courses, and it blossomed through activist connections with campus-based women's centers and antiviolence groups. If university-based feminists need a reason today to fight for the continued existence of women's and gender studies programs, they need look no further than our research, which so clearly illustrates their central importance in helping to launch a new generation of antiviolence activists.

Feminist professionals are also thriving in the helping professions of social work and counseling psychology, especially in specialized subfields created by feminists, focusing on domestic violence, sexual violence, and child abuse. Since the early 1990s, "feminist therapy" has deepened a "family systems" approach to traditional family and couples therapy, confronting traditional gender assumptions about men's and women's "proper roles" and challenging socially contextualized power inequities between men and women.[19] Feminist therapy's roots in the women's movement positions it to serve as a counterforce against the conservative individualizing tendencies of psychotherapeutic approaches to such issues as sexual violence, child abuse, and domestic violence, instead connecting individual solutions with efforts to change unequal and oppressive social relations in families, organizations, and communities.

Some professional activists we interviewed are also creatively building communities, including online networks of antiviolence and social justice groups. Robbie Samuels, for instance, noticed in 2006 that there was a large array of mostly disconnected social justice groups in Boston, including men's profeminist groups like NOMAS, of which he was a part. Samuels built SoJust.Org, an online meet-up site that within four years had "fourteen hundred members online and an active calendar" and was "about building a cross-issue progressive community, network, and movement in Boston." On a broader geographic scale, Ramesh Kathanadhi lauded the mostly online Building Movement Project for helping those working in nonprofits and human services professions to network and "reconnect them to the social justice roots of their work." Activist-intellectual Rob Okun joins his longtime work with men's antiviolence organizations in Massachusetts by editing *Voice Male,* a magazine that provides a forum for profeminist men and facilitates links between disparate local, national and international organizations.[20]

Progressive professionals are also fighting within federal, state, and local governments to protect or deepen hard-won state policies that support antiviolence work. Professionals are also working to infuse the dominant public health model of violence prevention with a social justice orientation. Jackson Katz and his colleagues wrote a thoughtful essay on the "social justice roots" of high school–based bystander intervention programs like his MVP program.[21] And it's not just antiviolence veterans like Katz who are thinking this way; so are some of the youngest men we interviewed. After working in a university violence prevention program, Rob Buelow returned to Harvard University to study public health, which he intends to help shape into a field where he "can still do socially progressive work." Another member of the Professional Cohort, Daniel Healy, had just completed his studies in public health at UCLA when we interviewed him. Healy recognizes that "the issue of dealing with violence is a political one," but he sees the field of public health strategically, as "almost a political, [where] people can come around violence as a public health issue because health is important to all. Like, everyone cares about health to some degree; they're not anti-health!" When we interviewed him, Healy was working with a Centers for Disease Control (CDC)–funded violence prevention project that linked the Los Angeles Unified School District and the Los Angeles Police Department. Healy and his colleagues were attempting to stitch this government project together with three community-based organizations that work to empower race- and class-marginalized youths around violence and related issues. In short, Healy was working with and through the dominant public health antiviolence model, strategizing to make the sorts of connections implied in a social justice approach.

There is one more social justice dimension operating in the professional antiviolence field: intergenerational mentoring. As we have shown in previous chapters, women and men of the Movement and Bridge cohorts continue to teach younger antiviolence recruits about the history of the movement, working to keep alive feminist values, analysis, and practices in the work itself. In a study of women's policy organizations in Washington, DC, Suzanne Beechy found that younger women valued the opportunity to get paid for being a "professional feminist." Beechy observed that these younger women appreciated the mentoring they received from older feminist women, but they also sometimes reported instances of "intergeneration tensions" with feminist bosses. Beechy's young interviewees echoed many of those we interviewed who worked in the entry levels of the antiviolence profession in identifying a problem built into such work, that the "generally low pay and inadequate benefits serve to close out feminists who otherwise would like to work for women's policy organizations but cannot afford to do so, thus reinforcing the middle-class status quo within women's organizations."[22]

Organic Intersectionality

One of the more striking elements in our comparison of the age cohorts of male allies doing antiviolence work was the shift from the 1970s field being made up mostly of white men to (beginning mostly in the 1990s and continuing today) a more racially diverse field of work. Men of color enter the field through pathways generally different from those of their white counterparts—less often through campus women's and gender studies courses that illuminate the problem of violence against women; more often through a combination of life experiences with violence, college and community encounters with race- and class-based antiviolence work and often by being recruited into entry-level professional positions to work with at-risk boys in schools or in the criminal justice system.

The diverse pathways into antiviolence work among men of color—and we would also add the visible presence of gay, queer, and transgender men such as Robbie Samuels as well[23]—tend to fuel more complicated orientations to the work itself, introducing what we call "organic intersectionality." We label this sort of intersectionality "organic" for two reasons. First, it springs from activists' understandings of violence as embedded in everyday experiences of race, class, gender, and sexual relations, contrasting with the tendency of most white men in the field to have absorbed intersectional theory in the classroom, which they then tack onto a violence-against-women perspective that still assumes gender inequality always to be foundational.[24] Second, organically intersectional understandings of violence fuel more sophisticated intervention strategies that draw links between racialized violence, class-based violence, and homophobic and transphobic violence, with violence against women.

An organically intersectional approach to antiviolence work often starts from a standpoint of boys' and men's vulnerabilities and experiences with violence, both as survivors and as potential perpetrators of family, dating, school, and street violence. "Gender-based violence," in this regard, includes a focus on boy-on-boy and man-on-man violence— from school-based bullying to gang street violence—and illuminates links to men's sexual and domestic violence against women and children. It also sheds light on how violence against girls and women is linked with violence against gay, queer, and transgender people.

Organic intersectionality has had a profound impact on how longstanding feminist antiviolence organizations define themselves. We saw in Chapter 4 how the name change of Los Angeles Commission on Assaults Against Women (LACAAW) to Peace Over Violence (POV) in part reflected a shift in the larger antiviolence field to less overtly political nonprofits and foundation-funded professional organizations. But this sort of shift was more than a simple rebranding for marketing purposes. It also reflected an understanding that the old-school language of feminism, for many, no longer captured the range of work that such organizations were doing. "We always say we were founded by feminists," Patti Giggans explained of POV. "Foundationally, we were a feminist organization when we started [but] we also have an oppression perspective—other oppressions, not just the sexism and misogyny, but [also] race, and homophobia." Though many would argue that a properly intersectional understanding of feminism does in fact capture the sorts of connections that Giggans wants POV to make, her words likely reflect a strategic reframing, setting aside the feminist label and situating the work within a broader language of social justice, providing a suitable umbrella under which various sorts of progressive violence-prevention efforts can join.

Organic intersectionality, in other words, is at the heart of antiviolence activists' and organizations' attempts to make the sorts of connections that risk being lost in a depoliticized public health model of violence prevention. Organic intersectionality illuminates a greater sensitivity in boys' and men's lives to the triad of men's violence—the connections between violence against women, violence against other men, and violence against one's self. And organic intersectionality pushes organizations to build sophisticated strategies based on an expansive understanding of institutionally interconnected violences, rather than viewing various manifestations of violence as discrete phenomena.[25] This kind of analytic connective tissue is at the heart of social justice orientations to antiviolence work. Indeed, sociologist Patricia Hill Collins has eloquently defined violence as "a saturated site of intersectionality . . . a form of conceptual glue that enables racism, sexism, class exploitation, and heterosexism to function as they do." Collins concludes that "the beginnings of a comprehensive antiviolence project must go hand in hand with a commitment to social justice, broadly defined."[26] It is these sorts of connections and commitments that we see many in the field today working together to make.

Transnational Antiviolence Connections

Although this book has focused almost entirely on antiviolence efforts in the United States (and to a smaller extent, in Canada), it became evident to us in some of our interviews that there are growing transnational networks of antiviolence efforts. Many of these efforts address local violences, often in poor and developing nations of the Global South, but they also point to expanded ways to view and confront gender-based violence, beyond the common first-world limitations we have outlined in this book. In particular, we suggest, activists in wealthy nations like the United States can learn from colleagues in the Global South how to redraw connections between gender-based violence with broader efforts at social transformations that confront institutionalized poverty and the effects of militarism and war.[27]

A 2013 World Health Organization (WHO) analysis of 141 studies in eighty-one countries estimated that more than one-third of women worldwide have been raped or physically abused. Both the global extent and depth of violence against women, as well as the particulars of local expressions of violence, are being documented in a growing scholarly field of research.[28] And although a full review of this literature is not possible here, this growing body of work links rape, domestic violence, feminicide, and other forms of violence against women with the denial of educational, economic, and political rights to women, institutionalized poverty, inadequate public healthcare, racism, colonialism, and the devastating effects of war. Indeed, when asked how the WHO will tackle the shockingly high rates of violence against women found in their recent report, WHO spokesperson and physician Claudia Garcia Moreno veered decidedly away from the language of a simplistic health model, warning that even though "there is no magic bullet, no vaccine or pill" for rape and abuse, the problem can begin to be addressed by educating women, and by empowering women economically.[29]

Social conditions are of course very different in nations of the Global North, but activists in places like the United States can nevertheless learn from these sorts of connections, possibly taking lessons that will help to counter the conservatizing tendencies that occur when first-world feminists have collaborated with the neoliberal state to institutionalize antiviolence efforts.[30] Researchers in the Global South have found, for instance, that increasing women's access to reproductive health services also helps them begin to confront sexual and domestic violence.[31] Feminist scholar Cynthia Enloe has shown for decades how wars, and the aftermath of wars, tend to make women and children more vulnerable to rape and other forms of gender-based violence.[32] And researchers in poor regions of southern India and in South Africa have illuminated the links between women's and men's employment status, socioeconomic vulnerabilities, and community HIV crises with levels and types of violence against women.[33] These connective analyses of gender-based violence in the poor nations of the Global South are being coupled with efforts to economically empower women, while developing programs with boys and men to build respect for women, expand their views and practices as fathers, and develop orienta-tions to sexual relations that decrease risk of HIV transmission.[34] Efforts that link violence prevention with economic, health, labor, or racial justice hold the potential, in the words of sociologist Raewyn Connell, to create situations in which men become more likely "to support a project of gen-der justice, especially where there is explicit solidarity with women in the same situation."[35]

Antiviolence efforts in India and South Africa are spearheaded by local feminist organizing—in some cases including support from devel-oping networks of male allies—and often coordinated and funded through transnational feminist networks and antiviolence NGOs.[36] To be sure, these efforts at violence reduction in poor nations of the Global South are constrained by the health model orientations of interna-tional nonprofits, by funding levels that fall far short of what it might take to even begin to tackle foundational issues like rural poverty, and by resistance to change by powers-that-be, both local and national. But for our purposes here, we simply note that it is precisely the sorts of connections being forged in many such efforts in the Global South that can fuel expansive gender-based violence interventions grounded in social justice–oriented strategies. Indeed, some of the men we inter-viewed are developing transnational antiviolence efforts with boys and men. Following fifteen years as a journalist, often in such war zones as Rwanda and the Congo, where he constantly witnessed "violence against women [and] increasingly those stories came into my view-finder," Jimmie Briggs decided to become a violence prevention activ-ist: "I met a lot of refugees, I met a lot of rape survivors, I met a lot of people affected by conflicts and disaster who not only endured but overcame through faith. It would amaze me, going to these displace-ment camps or going to hospitals in Africa or Afghanistan and talking to women who have been assaulted or mutilated or had acid thrown on them because they were women, or because they were pawns in war."

In 2010 Briggs founded Man Up, "a youth-led, youth-focused move-ment to stop violence against women," through which he strategized to use "sports, specifically soccer, and music, specifically hip-hop, to start working with young people, but especially reaching young men." Similarly, In 1999 Gary Barker formed Promundo in Brazil, an NGO that aimed to work with boys and men in Mexico, Latin America, and the Caribbean, conducting research that would help organizations like the United Nations and the WHO develop programs with boys and men in the Global South, developing "HIV work, gender-based violence preven-tion, engaging men as fathers."

Men like Jimmie Briggs, Gary Barker, and others in recent years have begun to build networks that connect antiviolence work in war-torn nations, poor nations of the Global South, and transnational organizations like the United Nations. In 2009, nineteen men from seventeen countries spanning Africa, Europe, the Americas, Asia, the Middle East, and the Pacific met in the Netherlands to share strategies for developing antiviolence programs for boys and men. Sponsored by the Women Peacemakers Program of the International Fellowship of Reconciliation, the group drafted a statement entitled "Together for Transformation: A Call to Men and Boys." Signed first collectively as "Gender Sensitive Active Non Violent Men," and then individually, the document outlines the basic principles of a program for boys and men "to join hands" with women as allies, with the goal of promoting "transformative change" of peace, "gender equality and social justice."[37]

Such transnational feminist coalitions to stop violence against women inevitably push activists toward a broad peace and social justice program. In a powerful analysis of violence against women in Guatemala, for instance, sociologist Cecilia Menjívar draws from the United Nations Declaration on the Elimination of Violence against Women to develop such an expansive understanding of violence. Essentially, Menjívar defines all forms of social injustice against women as violence against women.[38] Although some activists might worry that this expansive definition of violence deflects attention from the particularities of rape and domestic violence against women, we believe it is precisely this understanding of violence-as-embedded, violence as both cause and effect of broadly structured social injustices, that risks being lost when violence prevention is defined as a discrete issue to be "prevented" through a conventional health model. It was, after all, rape and domestic violence's systemic embeddedness in patriarchy that was at the heart of 1970s women's movement's confrontation with violence against women. Today we see a redrawing and deepening of such connections, emerging as a social justice paradigm within networks of feminist professionals, within organically intersectional antiviolence work, and within transnational feminist antiviolence efforts.

ALLIES UPSTREAM

We opened this book with a story about a river, a tale that allegorizes the history of the movement to stop rape and domestic violence. In this story, women heroically rescue babies that they find floating downstream in baskets. Eventually, some men are inspired by the women's actions and head upstream to stop those who are putting the babies at risk. The women in the story, of course, represent the thousands of women who started the feminist antiviolence movement, tirelessly working downstream to help survivors of sexual assault and domestic violence. The men represent those who later joined the movement as allies, committing themselves to working "upstream" with boys and men to prevent future acts of violence. This book has been about their work.

The life histories we have drawn from here have illustrated much of the promise as well as the challenges and limitations of men's upstream work as feminist allies. And our analysis of their stories suggests that the upstream-downstream river allegory is a bit simplistic. To symbolize the antiviolence field as comprising a solitary river may falsely imply singular causes and thus singular solutions to gender-based violence. Rather, we have come to see the antiviolence field as a system of tributaries, each with its own historical and social coursings, but still ultimately interconnected with other streams and rivers. There is the domestic violence tributary and the sexual assault tributary, both pushed along by the powerful current of male domination so familiar to feminist activists of the past forty years. But there are also the raging tributaries of war and militarism, flooding the rivers of institutionalized poverty, racism, and colonial domination. There are the virtual tributaries of mass media and the Internet, and the homophobia, heteronormativity, and transphobia tributaries. And even though no individual or small organization can hope to intervene within every tributary that flows into larger rivers and pools of violence, social justice activists develop local antiviolence strategies with an understanding of these systemic interconnections. And they build alliances and cultivate connections with communities of other social justice activists who are working in other tributaries.

Activists today who are immersed in a feminist and social justice orientation to antiviolence work understand that these tributaries, seemingly separate, are in fact interconnected. Whether one works downstream or upstream, in this tributary or that one, ultimately we all share the same waters.

These proverbial waters are, after all, our shared and lived history. Pick a spot; join hands, wade in.

APPENDIX 1

List of Interviewees with Demographic Descriptors

Birth Year	Name	Self-Reported Race/Ethnicity	Self-Reported Gender Identity	Self-Reported Sexual Identity	Highest Level of Education Completed	Occupation at Time of Interview (Position, Organization, City, State)	Interviewer
1941	Santiago Casal	LCH (Latino)	Male	Heterosexual	MA	Retired, Kaiser Permanente Employee Diversity Program, Berkeley, CA	MM
1942	**Phyllis B. Frank**	**White**	**Female**	**Queer**	**MA++**	**Associate Executive Director, Volunteer Counseling Services, New York City, NY**	TP
1946	Allan Creighton	White	Male	Heterosexual	BA (4–5 years of graduate work)	Social Justice and Violence Prevention Health Educator, UC Berkeley, CA	MM
1947	Greg Ross	White (Caucasian)	[male symbol]	Straight	Acupuncture license	Retired, Detox and HIV/AIDS Acupuncturist, Highland General Hospital, Oakland, CA	MM
1948	Paul Kivel	White/Jewish (Ashkenazi)	Male	Heterosexual	BA	Independent Social Justice Activist, Educator and Author, Oakland, CA	MM

(Continued)

Appendix 1 (Continued)

Birth Year	Name	Self-Reported Race/Ethnicity	Self-Reported Gender Identity	Self-Reported Sexual Identity	Highest Level of Education Completed	Occupation at Time of Interview (Position, Organization, City, State)	Interviewer
1949	Larry Mandella	White (Caucasian: Italian American)	Male	Heterosexual	MA	Self employed Contractor and Carpenter, Berkeley, CA	MM
1949	**Patti Giggans**	**Italian**	**Female**	**Lesbian**	**MA**	**Executive Director, Peace Over Violence, Los Angeles, CA**	MG
1950	Chris Norton	White	Male	Straight	BA	Carpenter (on disability), Sebastopol, CA	MM
1950	Timothy Beneke	White	Male	Straight	BA	Independent Software Writer, Oakland, CA	MM
1950	**Shelley Serdahely**	**White**	**Female**	**Open**	**BA**	**Director of Development, Men Stopping Violence, Decatur, GA**	TP
1951	Chris Anderegg	White	Male	Hetero	MA	Acting Director, Information Technology Dept., Sonoma County, CA	MM
1951	Craig Norberg-Bohm	White (Caucasian)	Male	Heterosexual	BS	Coordinator, Men's Initiative, Jane Doe Inc., Boston, MA	MG
1951	Don Conway-Long	White (Irish)	Male (60% masc; 40% fem)	Bisexual	PhD	Associate Professor, Social Science, Webster University, Webster Groves, MO	MM

1951	Michael Kaufman	White/Jewish	Male	Heterosexual	PhD	Independent Speaker, Writer, and White Ribbon Campaign Cofounder, Toronto, Canada	MM
1952	**Phyllis Miller**	**African American (Multiracial)**	**(Left blank)**	**Heterosexual**	**MSW**	**Executive Director, Dekalb Rape Crisis Center, Decatur, GA**	**TP**
1954	Mark Stevens	White (Caucasian)	(Left blank)	Heterosexual	PhD	Director of University Counseling Services, CSU Northridge, Los Angeles, CA	MM
1955	**Gwen Wright**	**African American**	**Female**	**Lesbian**	**BFA**	**Bureau Director, New York State Office for the Prevention of Domestic Violence, Albany, NY**	**TP**
1957	Tony Porter	African American	Male	Straight (heterosexual)	BA; certifications in mental health and substance abuse	Cofounder and Co-director of A Call to Men, Charlotte, NC	TP
1958	Robert Jensen	White	Male	married to a woman; with bisexual past	PhD	Professor of Journalism, University of Texas, Austin, TX	MM

(Continued)

Birth Year	Name	Self-Reported Race/Ethnicity	Self-Reported Gender Identity	Self-Reported Sexual Identity	Highest Level of Education Completed	Occupation at Time of Interview (Position, Organization, City, State)	Interviewer
1960	Jackson Katz	White/Jewish	Male	Hetero	PhD	Independent Activist, Speaker, Author, Film Maker, Long Beach, CA	MM
1961	Alan Greig	White	Male	Straight	MA	Technical Assistance, Partners in Prevention, New York City, NY	MG
1961	David Lee	White	Male	Heterosexual	MPH	Director of Prevention Services, California Coalition Against Sexual Assault, Sacramento, CA	MM
1961	Gary Barker	White	Male	Straight (heterosexual)	PhD	International Director of PromundoDC, Washington, DC	TP
1961	Juan Carlos Areán	LCH (Latino)	Male	Heterosexual	MA	Senior Program Director, Futures Without Violence, Amherst, MA	MG
1962	Allen Corben	White	Male	Heterosexual	MA	Assistant Registrar, Fuller Theological Seminary, Pasadena, CA	MM
1962	Frank Blaney	White (Irish-American)	Male	Straight	MA	Director of Youth Leadership Development, Peace Over Violence, Los Angeles, CA	MG

1963	**Shira Tarrant**	**White**	**Female**	**Heterosexual**	**PhD**	**Associate Professor, CSU Long Beach, CA**	MM
1965	Donald McPherson	Jamaican	Male	Straight (heterosexual)	BA	College Football Commentator, Social Educator, Public Speaker, New York, NY	TP
1965	Keith Smith	African American	Male	Straight/ bisexual	MA	Clinical Counselor, University of Vermont, Burlington, VT	MM
1966	Ben Atherton Zeman	Mostly white, some Native (Shawnee),	(Left blank)	Bisexual	BA (some graduate work)	Public Speaker/Actor Comedian, Voices of Men, Maynard, MA	TP
1967	Hugo Schwyzer	White	Male Cis	Straight (hetero)	PhD	Professor, Pasadena City College, Pasadena, CA	TP
1968	Marc Rich	White/Jewish	Male	Straight (heterosexual)	PhD	Professor, CSU Long Beach, Long Beach, CA	TP
1969	Charles More	White (Caucasian)	Male	Straight	Current PhD student	Graduate Student; Founder, Teaching Equality, Boston, MA	MG
1969	Jimmie Briggs	African American	Male	Straight	BA	Executive Director, Man Up Campaign, New York, NY	MG
1969	**Janeen McGee**	**Caucasian**	**Female**	**Heterosexual**	**BS**	**Executive Director, RAVEN, St. Louis, MO**	MM

(Continued)

Appendix 1 (Continued)

Birth Year	Name	Self-Reported Race/Ethnicity	Self-Reported Gender Identity	Self-Reported Sexual Identity	Highest Level of Education Completed	Occupation at Time of Interview (Position, Organization, City, State)	Interviewer
1970	Quentin Walcott	African American (Black)	(Left blank)	Straight (heterosexual)	MS	Project Director, CONNECT, New York, NY	TP
1971	Todd Henneman	White	Male	Gay	MBA	Assistant Director, Center for Women and Men, University of Southern California, Los Angeles, CA	MM
1973	Kevin Hawkins	African American	(Left blank)	Gay	MA	Manager, Volunteer Program, RAVEN, St. Louis, MO	MM
1974	Robbie Samuels	White	Transgender man	Queer	MSW	Special Events Manager, Gay and Lesbian Advocates and Defenders, Boston, MA	TP
1974	Timothy Love	White (Caucasian)	Male	Heterosexual	BA	Primary Prevention Specialist, Texas Association Against Sexual Assault, Austin, TX	MM
1976	Brian Jara	Bi/multiracial (white + Asian/Filipino)	Male	Gay	PhD educ + women's studies	Instructor and Adviser, Pennsylvania State University, State College, PA	TP

1976	Emiliano Diaz de Leon	LCH (Chicano)	Male	Straight	AA	Primary Prevention Specialist, Texas Association Against Sexual Assault, Austin, TX	MM
1976	Joe Samalin	White/Jewish (Russian Jewish heritage)	(Left blank)	Straight/ heterosexual	MA	Coordinator of Training and Technical Assistance, Men Can Stop Rape, New York, NY	TP
1976	Ramesh Kathanadhi	South Asian	Male	Hetero	JD	Transforming Communities, Center for Domestic Peace, Marin County, CA	MG
1977	Seth Avakian	White	(Left blank)	Straight	MA	Prevention Specialist, Office of Sexual Assault Prevention and Response, Harvard University, Cambridge, MA	MG
1978	Eli Crawford	White/Jewish	Male	Heterosexual	MSW	Program Director, Northwest Men's Project, Seattle, WA	MG
1978	Jeffrey Bucholtz	White	Disappointed	Bisexual	MA	Director, We End Violence, Boston, MA	MG
1978	**Danielle Lancon**	**Caucasian**	**Female**	**Gay**	**MSW**	**Director, Center for Women and Men, University of Southern California, Los Angeles, CA**	**MM**

(Continued)

Appendix 1 (Continued)

Birth Year	Name	Self-Reported Race/Ethnicity	Self-Reported Gender Identity	Self-Reported Sexual Identity	Highest Level of Education Completed	Occupation at Time of Interview (Position, Organization, City, State)	Interviewer
1979	Patrick Donovan	White/Caucasian	(Left blank)	Bisexual	BA	School-based Youth Violence Prevention Coordinator, Healing Abuse Working for Change, Salem, MA	MG
1980	**Nicole Daley**	**Caribbean American**	**Female**	**Straight**	**MPH**	**Director of Teen Dating Violence Prevention Program, Boston Public Health Commission, Boston, MA**	MG
1980	**Nina Alcaraz**	**Pacific Islander/ Filipina**	**Female**	**(Left blank)**	**BA**	**Deputy Director, Monterey County Rape Crisis Center, Salinas, CA**	MM
1981	Sean Tate	Black/African American	Male	Straighter side of the continuum	BA	Academic Counselor, Intercollegiate Athletics Dept., University of Texas, Austin, TX	MM
1981	**Leiana Kinnicutt**	**Caucasian, Native Kinnicutt**	**Female**	**Lesbian**	**MSW**	**Senior Program Specialist, Futures Without Violence, Boston, MA**	MG
1982	Brandon Molina	White	Male	Straight	MBA	LegalZoom, Glendale, CA	MG

Year	Name	Race/Ethnicity	Gender	Sexuality	Degree	Status	Description	
1982	Gilbert Salazar	LCH (Chicano, Latino)	Male	Bisexual	BA		Rape Prevention Education Manager, Monterey County Rape Crisis Center, Salinas, CA	MM
1983	Daniel Healy	White (Caucasian)	Male	Heterosexual	MPH		Community Liaison and Training Coordinator, Violence Prevention Coalition of Greater Los Angeles, CA	MG
1984	**Trina Greene**	**African American**	**Female**	**Heterosexual**	**MA**		**Start Strong Program Manager, Peace Over Violence, Los Angeles, CA**	MG
1985	John Erickson	White	Male	Gay		Current PhD student	Graduate Student, Claremont Graduate University, Claremont, CA	TP
1985	Rob Buelow	White	Male	Straight (heterosexual)		Current MS student	Graduate Student, Harvard University, Cambridge, MA	TP
1987	Steven Philp	White	Male	Gay		Current Mdiv/MSW student	Graduate Student, University of Chicago, Chicago, IL	TP
1988	Cameron Murphey	White	(Left blank)	Straight		Current undergraduate student	Undergraduate Student, Western Washington University, Bellingham, WA	TP

(Continued)

Appendix 1 (Continued)

Birth Year	Name	Self-Reported Race/Ethnicity	Self-Reported Gender Identity	Self-Reported Sexual Identity	Highest Level of Education Completed	Occupation at Time of Interview (Position, Organization, City, State)	Interviewer
1988	Dillon Thomson	Caucasian/white	(Left blank)	Straight (heterosexual)	Current undergraduate student	Undergraduate Student, Western Washington University, Bellingham, WA	TP
1990	Jamonte Pitts	African American	Male	Het	HS	Youth Educator, Peace Over Violence, Los Angeles, CA	MG
1991	James Campos	LCH (Hispanic)	Male	Heterosexual	HS	Youth Educator, Peace Over Violence, Los Angeles, CA	MG

APPENDIX 2
The Authors' Moments of Engagement

In this book, we have examined how historical moments of engagement with feminism and antiviolence work have differently enabled and constrained how three age cohorts of men viewed and attempted to stop or mitigate sexual assault and domestic violence. Here, we three coauthors briefly describe our own "moments of engagement" with these issues and reflect on how this may have shaped our approach to the research.

MICHAEL A. MESSNER

When I started college in 1970, there was little sign of women's studies in the curriculum, but feminism was already exploding to life all around me, from the radical personal transformations taking place with the women in my life, to an increasingly visible national women's movement. By the time I started a Ph.D. program in 1978 at UC Berkeley, women's studies was growing rapidly as a field and feminist scholarship was creatively disrupting my discipline of sociology. I found all of this exciting, and I got in on the ground floor in contributing to the development of a feminist analysis of men and masculinities. Simultaneously, I was drawn to East Bay activists such as Chris Norton, and profeminist men in grassroots groups like MASV, who were trying to bring feminist ideas and politics to life in the community, particularly with boys and men.

In the terms we have deployed in this book, my moment of engagement with feminism is fully congruent with the men and women of the Movement Cohort. I shared a vision of radical social transformation with feminist women I was meeting and reading in the 1970s and 1980s, with Berkeley men such as Chris Norton, Tim Beneke, and Allan Creighton, and with men I was connecting with in organizations I was joining, like the National Organization for Changing Men and the California Anti-Sexist Men's Political Caucus (CAMP). I admired these feminist activists and imagined myself to be on their team. But even in grad school, I was never much of an activist. I hated meetings, for one thing; I preferred reading, research, and the classroom. So when I met Chris Norton and learned about MASV in the late 1970s, I was drawn to them and wanted to contribute something to the cause, but I never joined up. Instead, I studied them, and that's pretty much what I still do today.

A few years ago, I attended a public lecture by a well-known feminist scholar. In reflecting on her career, she stated that everything she had done, whether in the classroom or in her published writings, had been motivated by her commitment to social justice. This of course drew nods of approval and hearty applause. I joined in. But I also thought, "Honestly? Aren't our motivations way more multilayered, and a bit more contradictory than that?" After all, this scholar's important progressive work has been well rewarded: with a secure position as a tenured professor, with a salary that presumably puts her in the top 5 percent of earners in the world, and of course with our public applause and adulation. Might it be that some of these substantial rewards served as additional motivating factors for the years of hard work through which she had built and sustained such a successful career?

As I worked on this project, I have tried to remain cognizant of this tension between doing research that I hope contributes to progressive social change (with the reality of my own privileged position as a salaried tenured professor), how this book might further enhance my professional status (if not my pay), and of course how I hope it will help to launch long and successful careers for my coauthors, Tal and Max. That this is a contradiction built into my work should come as no surprise. Some of our interviewees even alluded to this. When I interviewed Allan Creighton, a man who labored many years working for social justice for very little pay, he recounted a poignant memory of a sociology graduate student who in the mid-1980s joined Creighton's MOVE (Men Overcoming Violence) collective to study it. The student eventually published an article, Creighton said, arguing that the men of MOVE were "all kind of lost about what they're doing in their lives, they're all white guys of a certain class background. And their actual decisions about how to continue are actually class-based. That they're all beginning careers and are gonna get paid for their careers and this is a way to move on up." This article, Creighton said, made him "so mad . . . I want to tear it up." Well, Creighton and many other men in MOVE *did* in fact build careers in antiviolence work. But, I hasten to add, the sociology grad student who conducted the critical class analysis of the MOVE men's professional aspirations and motivations likely also gained professional status by publishing this article. I'd guess he eventually earned a higher salary, too, than did many of the MOVE men.

As we did the research for this book, we tried to keep in mind that doing this sort of work is inherently contradictory, yes, but this does not mean it should not be done. It is crucial, I think, to keep in mind how one might err: on the one hand, if we simply and uncritically applauded the courageous work of our interviewees—and let's be clear, I *do* admire the work these women and men are doing; I often left an interview feeling upbeat and hopeful just knowing that this person is in the world—we would not only contribute to putting them on a pedestal; we also would not be doing our jobs as critical sociologists. On the other hand, if we lambasted our interviewees for their professional careerism, for not being radical or "political" enough, we would not only be ignoring the good that some of them are doing in the world; we would also be engaging in the worst sort of holier-than-thou political correctness—after which we would then go on to collect our own professional kudos for doing a great piece of critical research, and then of course collect our salaries, too.

Rather than seeing this as an either-or choice—critique versus celebration of one's research subjects—I see it as a task of critical sociology to analyze how our interview subjects themselves make sense of and creatively navigate the tensions and contradictions in their field. For me this is also a self-reflexive task, a self-navigation of tensions that are grounded in my own privileged position as a white, heterosexually identified man with a secure professional class career that largely insulates me from many of the problems I study. One way to navigate this tension, for me, is to try to listen and learn from my interviewees. Here's an example from this study, and it's a bit embarrassing to admit that this was something I did not already know. When we asked the men in our interviews how they navigated the "pedestal effect"—the tendency for men doing feminist work to be elevated, listened to, and rewarded more readily than women doing the same work—several of them said that when they are invited to another community to speak or to lead a workshop, they always try in advance of the visit to connect with women's shelters or rape crisis centers in that community. Instead of simply parachuting in and soaking up applause and cash for being an "expert" on sexual assault or domestic violence, these men ask how they can use their visit to support or make visible the local work that's being done on the ground, most likely by women activists. I have taken this advice to heart, and I now do this when I am invited to talk about this research.

This project has been a great deal of fun for me. I loved doing the interviews, and I must acknowledge that part of the ease of this process lies in my being twice removed from the actual topic: gender-based violence. I am fortunate never to have experienced violence in my own families, and I have been relatively insulated from male-on-male violence throughout my life. And interviews with prevention activists and professionals, for the most part, will not usually have the sort of devastating emotional impact as, say, interviewing those who have been directly traumatized by sexual assault or domestic violence. The interviews were also pleasurable thanks to the identification I felt with the interviewees. Many of the older individuals in the study are people whom I have known, or at least knew of, for a very long time. I have long admired these older men's and women's commitment to social change, and it was an inspiration to meet a younger generation of men who have taken up the work in recent years. Tal Peretz and Max Greenberg have also inspired me. In fact, I got the idea for doing this project from Tal and Max, who, a few years ago as new Ph.D. students, started to educate me on the new and growing proliferation of antiviolence work on campuses and in communities, to which they were both committed as scholar-activists. I have learned a great deal from each of these young men and look forward to seeing their careers develop.

At the end of all interviews, we asked individuals if there was anything they would like to add, anything that we have failed to ask them that they feel is important. When Tal asked Tony Porter this question, he paused and then said, "I just want you do the right thing, with the information you got from me and the information you got from everybody else, and to know that we're all trusting you to do the right thing. That's the nature of the work, there's a lot of weight on your shoulders; there's a lot on mine, too."

The men and women we interviewed are out in the trenches every day, many of them for years, decades, working with individuals, families, schools, sports teams, workplaces, the military, trying to make a difference. They are not perfect in their work; nor are we perfect sociologists. But I know that in conducting the research, in analyzing and making sense of our interviews, we have tried our best to do the right thing.

MAX A. GREENBERG

When I left the suburbs of Boston for the School of Management at the University of Massachusetts in 2002, I didn't think much of the movements of the 1960s and 1970s beyond the vague sense that they had done their job. Two years later—and a full two decades after Jackson Katz was the first man to choose a women's studies minor at UMass—I was signing the tricolor carbon slip to minor in women's studies. What happened in between, my "moment of engagement," aligns with the at-once-more-intimate debates around violence and the more-structured world of feminism running throughout our stories in this book of the "professional generation."

As a sophomore management major looking for blow-off credits, I stumbled into one of the pockets of institutionalized feminism in the academy: sociology of sport, taught by Todd Crosset, a sociologist marooned in a sport management program. What I remember most of this introduction to social justice and feminist thinking was that it felt sturdy and vast but distant from my daily life. While my friends fetched coffee as summer interns or burnt out as activists, I dug into books.

At the same time, a feminist, my first college girlfriend, urged me to a Take Back the Night speak-out. At dusk, crumpled at the back of the crowd, I remember waves of anger, fear, guilt, and loneliness, but what has most endured is a sensation, primed in classrooms, that the wires in my brain were being stripped and clipped and twisted. This was not a feeling of epiphany, but the sense that a seed deep in my brain had sprung to life. When the time came to yell and chant, I felt awkward, not sure where to stand or how to carry myself. The march felt like a relic of an old battle.

Shaken from my path and searching for something to hold on to, I became increasingly involved with Take Back the Night in the years that followed. As a senior, I coasted on privilege into a leadership position, eager to put on a massive event—to fix everything. Those months were the most spirited of my young life as I debated, consulted, and argued about what it meant to be a man doing antisexist work. I remember hearing the feminist mantra "the personal is political" and wondering why they had ever needed to say that out loud. Eventually I stopped believing that it would be a surrender of my personal integrity to step down. I focused on a men's engagement initiative and supported the women who stepped up to take on the major organizing.

My experience, like those of many men in the professional cohort, is that antiviolence work is in large part mundane, as much about arguments on long car rides over *Maxim* magazine, navigating politics at family holidays, and job openings with good benefits as it is about protest and patriarchy. The wider structures that framed my triumphs and struggles were course credits and meetings and dinner dates; my turmoil was at turns beautiful and crushing, but just as often plodding.

After college, I was drawn to the world of nonprofits, which tend to be the landing pad for activist types when loans come due, and I enjoyed the work: organizing conferences, launching national campaigns, providing services. After a stint working with a marketing watchdog, in part challenging the sexualization of children's toys, I returned to my mentors, Naomi Gerstel and Todd Crosset, to ask for advice on graduate school. They steered me to Mike Messner, and I have been a strand in the network of feminist professionalism since. During my second year of graduate school, I searched for a fieldsite that could help me understand what was happening with antiviolence activism and found Peace Over Violence. Struggling for a foot in the door, I asked Mike for help and he put me in touch with Jackson Katz, who made a call to Abby Simms at POV, who welcomed me with open arms and thick stacks of paperwork.

I came into POV at a moment of transition, a suite stacked with moving boxes on their way to a new office. The changes have kept coming for the last four years, with increasing funding for programs aimed at men. In my volunteer work and eventually in my role as a board member at POV, I have gotten to know the world of institutionalized antiviolence—at turns hopeful, invigorating, bureaucratic, and alienating. In seemingly endless trainings and small moments, the driven women and men have taught me so much about what it means to do antiviolence as a job, propelled by the strange twin engines of feminism and funding.

Time and again, during hundreds of conversations, both casual and tape-recorded, I heard a similar sentiment, one that I often recognize in myself: longing for the "old days of the movement." In this moment of institutionalized feminism, we miss the streets, the protests, the emotion, and the connection. I hope this book gives context to that nostalgia. The days "in the streets" are gone, a particular set of strategies from a particular moment in time. But there is a new moment just over the horizon, the outlines of which I hope we can bring into view.

In a culture where men's friendships are portrayed often through their sexism, feminist men can have trouble finding male friends. I know I have pushed away my fair share. To sit across from these men over the course of weeks and months as they told their stories, their lives in feminism and antiviolence, I was in awe, but I also wondered why it took a research project to get us to sit down and talk. And in one way or another, most of the men we spoke with seemed to echo this disconnection between their work and the work of others, a sentiment that rings emotionally true and empirically false to me. There are today more conferences, organizations, websites, and resources than ever before dedicated to men engaged in antiviolence work.

And still, even as the movement is more vibrant than ever, many of us feel tired and distant.

Like so many of the men I spoke with, I have learned the lessons of professional antiviolence: how to perform for a crowd, run a meeting, fill out paperwork. But I feel myself hedge when it comes to the hard work of talking. And this is trouble for the long haul, because the emotional weight of professional antiviolence work requires a different kind of balancing than was called for during the Movement or Bridge years, yet we remain tethered to a paradigm of inner versus outer work. Professionalization, for all its concrete benefits, still feels thin. When confronted with this, we too often check the rearview for answers, wishing for a return to an idealized movement past instead of working to build a more just future.

TAL PERETZ

Looking back on my entry into feminism through the lens of this book, it is very clear to me that I grew up during a period of movement abeyance. I don't remember ever hearing the word *feminism* until taking my first women's studies class, in my second year of college in 2002. On the one hand, I'm glad I managed to avoid the stereotypes that circulate about feminism and feminists; on the other, I also had very little knowledge or awareness about gender inequality or gender-based violence. I had experienced more than my share of what James Messerschmidt calls "masculinity challenges," including some male-on-male violence that was clearly about gender policing, but my privilege had also shielded me from knowing about structural oppression.

That first women's studies class, while opening my eyes to structural inequalities and the oppression of women, also helped me better understand my own experiences. I began seeing my own life through a feminist lens, and the feminist maxim "the personal is political" helped me also to develop a sociological analysis. I saw that my own experiences of marginalization and violence were linked to larger structures of oppression and began to see others who suffered from those structures as my comrades. I also started seeing how those same structures benefited me, through male privilege, white privilege, and straight and cis-gendered privilege, and began thinking about how to be an effective ally while navigating between my own experiences of privilege and marginalization.

The lessons I learned about institutionalized forms of feminism in that women's studies class led me to more activism and grassroots organizing.

My involvement pathway moved through many groups and institutions and was facilitated by some very dear mentors. Marla Jaksch, the teacher of that first women's studies class, invited me to be her teaching assistant the next semester, helping me to see feminism as a space where I was welcome and could make a contribution. I attended Take Back the Night, *Vagina Monologues*, and the March for Women's Lives in Washington, DC, and got involved in student activist groups for racial, sexual, and gender equality and in a men's antiviolence group. I took a feminist theory course with Brian Jara, who began to teach me about accountability and continues to mentor me today, and a class on African American women with Dr. Aaronette White, who invited me to work with her on a study of black men's feminist activism.

About this same time I began volunteering at the local sexual assault and domestic violence center, where I continued to benefit from the guidance of women and from male privilege. As my postcollegiate activism and volunteering continued, I met and became friends with more male feminists. We would talk, and often found that we shared some experiences as men in the movement, such as receiving profuse praise that felt unearned or unequal, or being asked how we got involved and why we cared about "women's" equality. I did a small, informal study among my friends and began coming up with questions and concepts (such as the "pedestal effect") that have continued to interest me.

When I asked how to best continue working for social justice, Dr. White sent me to graduate school with the advice that, given my skills, my privilege, and my interest in getting more men involved in what our society troublingly views as "women's work," academia would allow me to be the most beneficial ally. In my doctoral program, I have benefited from Mike's mentorship, which continues through the production and publication of this book. The availability of both men and women as mentors and the fact that my entry pathway moved through multiple institutionalized feminist spaces are both consistent with my moment of engagement as part of what we refer to in this book as the Professional Cohort.

This mentorship served me well throughout graduate school, as did the clear sense that my reason for being there was to become the best ally I could be. I continued my research with male antiviolence activists, studying a campus-based men's group and discovering many tensions and contradictions in their work, some of which appear in this book as well. During this research, however, I began to notice that the literature on men's antisexist work frequently overlooks the experiences of men of color, queer men, and other members of marginalized groups. I returned to the research on black men that I had done with Dr. White and decided to do a broader intersectional project for my dissertation. I found that in Atlanta there were groups of men doing gender justice work but also organizing around their own marginalized identities. I moved there and spent a year working with and interviewing the members of Muslim Men Against Domestic Violence and the Sweet Tea Southern Queer Men's Collective, both majority-black groups. I found out a good deal about intersectionality and men's feminist organizing, such as the more organic ways in which marginalized men understand gender oppression, and the different pathways they frequently take to engagement.

How did the historical moment and my pathway to engagement influence my part in the research for the book you are holding in your hands? They definitely shaped who I thought of as potential interviewees: student activists, academics, employees at domestic violence shelters, and national men's antiviolence organizations. Many of the men I interviewed were men I had met or worked alongside in activist groups, nonprofits, or academic settings. Moreover, my own pathway shaped who I felt accountable to in the research process: feminist academics in both sociology and women's studies, activists and service professionals working on the ground, and queer communities and communities of color. I think they also enhanced my ability to relate to and understand interviewees, since I have had experience in many of the same types of groups and organizations where they do their work.

The historical moment clearly shapes some of my own viewpoints: I am concerned about the blunted radicalism that comes with institutionalization and worry about losing the centrality of women in women's studies. Much of my thinking is influenced by the Internet, feminist blogs, and articles shared over social networks. This is definitely the "fluoride" feminism that Jo Reger writes about, where feminist consciousness can easily become an everyday, constant presence—but it can just as easily be glossed over in favor of pictures of animals with pithy captions. Feminism is everywhere and nowhere, and since leaving undergrad I've had to make conscious efforts to keep a connection to movement-based feminism.

I am definitely still figuring out how to be useful and accountable to feminism, while also using my own skill set to the best advantage and creating a life that can sustain me through future years of engagement. I struggle to maintain a close and accountable connection to the feminist movement, and I'm still learning and developing strategies to do so while also meeting the demands of academic life. Although I'm sure I'll get better at it in the future, I don't think this struggle is a symptom of being early in my career. I think it's part of a constant process of learning and navigation required of men doing feminism, and it will be for as long as being a man brings unearned privilege. As our research has shown, this learning and navigation has some common strands over time, but it also changes along with the historical moment. I'm sure I will continue learning and navigating as the field shifts and we see what the next historical moment of men's engagements looks like.

NOTES

PREFACE

1. See David Lee. 2012. "Moving Upstream 2.0." *Prevention*, May 15, 2012. http://calcasa.org/prevention/moving-upstream-2-0/. A much earlier use of this metaphor appeared in a 1974 presentation at a medical conference on the prevention of heart disease. John B. McKinlay. 1974. "A case for re-focusing upstream: The political economy of illness." In *Applying behavioral science to cardiovascular risk: Proceedings of the American Heart Association Conference*, pp. 7–17, Seattle, WA, June 17–19. American Heart Association.

CHAPTER 1

1. The National College Women Sexual Victimization (NCWSV) Survey also noted that if projected to a full calendar year, rather than a nine-month academic year, 5 percent of all college women experience rape during a five-year college career. B. S. Fisher, F. T. Cullen, and M. G. Turner. 1999. "Extent and nature of the sexual victimization of college women: A national level analysis." National Institute of Justice (December) NCJ 179977: 1–2.

2. Christopher P. Krebs, Christine H. Lindquist, Tara D. Warner, Bonnie S. Fisher, and Sandra L. Martin. 2007. "The campus sexual assault (CSA) study." National Institute of Justice (January). NIJ 2004-WG-BX-0010.

3. The bystander approach to violence prevention focuses not on men as perpetrators but instead on men's responsibilities to step up and act to prevent violence—for instance, at a fraternity party—when they see signs of danger that a sexual assault might be about to occur. For recent research on the bystander approach, see Christine A. Gidycz, Lindsay M. Orchowski, and Alan Berkowitz. 2011. "Preventing sexual aggression among college men: An evaluation of a social norms and bystander intervention program." *Violence Against Women* 17: 720–742; Jennifer Langhinrichsen-Rohling, John D. Foubert, Hope M. Brasfield, Brent Hill, and Shannon Shelley-Tremblay. 2011. "The men's program: Does it impact college men's self-reported bystander efficacy and willingness to intervene?" *Violence Against Women* 17: 743–759.

4. National surveys of campus police and judicial affairs offices revealed that male athletes—especially those who play in high-status aggressive team sports—are more likely than other male students to sexually assault women. Todd W. Crosset, Jeffrey R. Benedict, and Mark McDonald. 1995. "Male student athletes reported for sexual assault: A survey of campus police departments and judicial affairs offices." *Journal of Sport and Social Issues* 19: 126–140; Todd Crosset, J. Ptacek,

M. MacDonald, and Jeffrey Benedict. 1996. "Male student athletes and violence against women: A survey of campus judicial affairs offices." *Violence Against Women* 2: 163–179. Sociologist Timothy Curry's analyses of male athletes' interactional dynamics in college locker rooms and sports bars revealed the social basis of athletes' off-field violence against women and assaults against other men. Timothy Curry. 1991. "Fraternal bonding in the locker room: Pro-feminist analysis of talk about competition and women." *Sociology of Sport Journal* 8: 119–135; Timothy Curry. 2000. "Booze and bar fights: A journey to the dark side of college athletics." In Jim McKay, Donald F. Sabo, and Michael A. Messner, eds. *Masculinities, gender relations, and sport*, pp. 162–175. Thousand Oaks, CA: Sage. And a more recent study traces a strong relationship for high school boys between participation in contact sports like football and off-field violence. Derek A. Kreager. 2007. "Unnecessary roughness? School sports, peer networks, and male adolescent violence." *American Sociological Review* 72: 705–724.

5. Over the years, the work of Cynthia Enloe has documented the links between masculinized militarism—both at home and abroad—and the devaluation and exploitation of women's labor and sexual assaults perpetrated against women. See Cynthia Enloe. 1988. *Bananas, beaches and bases: Making feminist sense of international politics.* Berkeley: University of California Press; Cynthia Enloe. 2000. *Maneuvers: The international politics of militarizing women's lives.* Berkeley: University of California Press; Cynthia Enloe. 2004. *The curious feminist: Searching for women in a new age of empire.* Berkeley: University of California Press.

6. In addition to being a frequent public speaker on campuses, Katz has helped to produce and narrate several educational films with the Media Education Foundation, including *Tough Guise,* a widely praised film about boys, men, and violence that is popular in college courses. He has written two books, including his 2006 work *The Macho Paradox,* and he pens a regular blog that appears on his own website, http://www.jacksonkatz.com. His op-eds appear frequently on the *Huffington Post* and elsewhere.

7. The 2010 and 2011 U.S. Census numbers show that of the 153,000 people in Salinas, California, 31.4 percent are eighteen or younger (compared with 25 percent statewide), 75 percent report Hispanic or Latino origin (vs. 37.6 percent statewide), 67 percent are foreign-born (vs. 27.2 percent statewide), and 18.1 percent lived below the poverty line (13.7 percent statewide). http://quickfacts.census.gov/qfd/states/06/0664224.html

8. In 2010, the violent crime rate in Salinas was 99 percent higher than the national rate and 83 percent higher than California's statewide rate. http://www.cityrating.com/crime-statistics/california/salinas.html#.UHmTphikCJo

9. In 2012, the *New York Times* reported that efforts to reduce gang-related violent crime in Salinas had apparently yielded some modest declines in violence. http://www.nytimes.com/2012/01/30/us/in-salinas-fighting-gang-violence-on-a-shoestring.html?pagewanted=all&_r=0

10. Of course, viewers could see that Gleason's character Ralph Kramden's threats to Alice were empty ones, never carried out, and largely functioned as face-saving strategies to cover his own ineptitude as a man. But our point here is simply to underline the normalization of violence against women as "humor" in pre–feminist era popular culture.

11. What Angela Davis called "the myth of the black male rapist" served as a key ideological construct in the continued race and class subordination of black males

in the post–Civil War years. When men who had been slaves attempted to move into the paid labor force, many white men viewed them as a threat and used terror tactics such as lynchings to enforce a color bar in the workforce. Some people, including many northern whites, responded to this terror with outrage. So instead of simply lynching black men, the white terrorists invoked the image of an aggressively sexualized black male who threatened white womanhood: now black men were lynched *and* castrated. The imposition of an animalistic, sexualized image onto black men served as a means of control within a system of race and class stratification that had been destabilized by the legal emancipation of slaves. See Angela Davis. 1981. *Woman, race and class.* New York: Vintage Books. Concerning the white men's projection of dangerous and violent masculinity on to black men, see Paul Hoch. 1979. *White hero, black beast: Racism, sexism and the mask of masculinity.* London: Pluto Press.

12. Pamela Allen. 1970. *Free space: A perspective on the small group in women's liberation.* New York: Times Change Press.

13. See Patricia Yancey Martin (with F. E. Schmitt). 2007. "The history of the anti-rape and rape crisis center movements." In Claire M. Renezetti and Jeffery Edleson, eds., *Encyclopedia of interpersonal violence.* Thousand Oaks, CA: Sage; Patricia Yancey Martin. 2009. "Rape crisis centers: Helping victims, changing society." In Y. Hasenfeld, ed., *Human service organizations.* 2nd ed. Thousand Oaks, CA: Sage; Kathleen J. Tierney. 1982. "The battered women's movement and the creation of the wife beating problem." *Social Problems* 29: 207–220.

14. For a recent example of such public contestation of rape jokes—both direct and on the Internet—in 2012 comedian Daniel Tosh was interrupted and contradicted by a woman in the audience when he made a series of jokes about how funny rape is. He reportedly responded to her from the stage by saying, "Wouldn't it be funny if that girl got raped by like, five guys right now? Like right now? What if a bunch of guys just raped her. . . ." In the days following this live show, Tosh was widely lambasted for his "jokes" and issued an apology, albeit a weak one. Michael Sebastian. 2012. "Comedian Daniel Tosh tweets 'sincere' apology for rape joke." *Ragan's PR Daily* (July 11). http://www.prdaily.com/Main/Articles/12119.aspx

15. Susan Brownmiller. 1975. *Against our will: Men, women and rape.* New York: Simon & Schuster.

16. This conceptual framework was first introduced in Max A. Greenberg and Michael A. Messner. 2014. "Before prevention: The trajectory and tensions of feminist antiviolence." In Marcia Texler Segal and Vasilikie Demos, eds. *Gendered perspectives on conflict and violence (Part B),* pp. 225–250. Bingley, West Yorkshire, England: Emerald.

17. Women's self-defense classes have for decades been part of a broader feminist antiviolence strategy. Though some feminists have feared that an emphasis on self-defense might shift emphasis away from a prevention focus on potential perpetrators of violence, Jocelyn Hollander's research has shown how women's self-defense, if embedded in larger feminist forms of organization, can both empower individual women and enhance other antiviolence efforts. Jocelyn A. Hollander. 2009. "The roots of resistance to women's self-defense." *Violence Against Women* 15: 574–594; Jocelyn A. Hollander. 2014. "Does self-defense training prevent sexual violence against women?" *Violence Against Women* 20: 252–269.

18. As early as 1971, a few men were writing about their experiences in men's consciousness-raising groups, e.g., Men's Consciousness-Raising Group. 1971.

Unbecoming men. Washington, NJ: Times Change Press. By mid-decade, some men's CR groups expanded to men's centers and local newsletters (mostly in college towns), and few scholars (most initially were psychologists) had begun to write feminist-inspired essays on men and masculinity. Perhaps the first published collection of these works was Joseph H. Pleck and Jack Sawyer, eds. 1974. *Men and masculinity.* Englewood Cliffs, NJ: Prentice-Hall. More politically oriented profeminist writings were collected in Jon Snodgrass, ed. 1977. *For men against sexism.* Albion, CA: Times Change Press.

19. Susan Faludi. 1991. *Backlash: The undeclared war against American women.* New York: Crown.

20. We will discuss the feminist sex wars in Chapters 2 and 3, especially in terms of how they had an impact on the work of men who were doing violence prevention work in the 1980s and beyond.

21. For discussions of women's movement abeyance, see Verta Taylor. 1989. "Social movement continuity: The women's movement in abeyance." *American Sociological Review* 54: 761–775; Suzanne Staggenborg and Verta Taylor. 2005. "What ever happened to the women's movement?" *Mobilization: An International Journal* 10: 37–52. For further discussions of social movement abeyance, see Laurel L. Holland and Sherry Cable. 2002. "Reconceptualizing social movement abeyance: The role of internal process and culture in cycles of movement abeyance and resurgence." *Sociological Focus* 35: 297–314; Paul Bagguley. 2002. "Contemporary British feminism: A social movement in abeyance?" *Social Movement Studies* 1: 169–185.

22. Suzanne Franzway, Dianne Court, and R. W. Connell. 1989. *Staking a claim: Feminism, bureaucracy and the state.* Sydney: Allyn and Unwin.

23. Stoltenberg's political work and writings were foundational to the development of men's ally work in the 1980s, particularly with the more radical wing of the feminist antipornography movement. John Stoltenberg. 1989. *Refusing to be a man: Essays on sex and justice.* Portland, OR: Breitenbush Books. As we will discuss in Chapter 4, Stoltenberg's antiviolence work has spanned the three historical moments this book will analyze, including his having a hand in creating today's "My Strength" curricula.

24. Michael S. Kimmel and Thomas E. Mosmiller. 1992. *Against the tide: Pro-feminist men in the United States, a documentary history.* Boston: Beacon Press.

25. For a critical overview of "men's movements" of this era, see Michael A. Messner. 1997. *Politics of masculinities: Men in movements.* AltaMira Press.

26. For instance, Pamela Allen wrote in 1971: "We do not allow men in our movement because in a male supremacist society men can and do act as the agents of our oppression. This takes not only obvious forms, such as physical and psychological brutality, but subtle forms as well, such as intellectual manipulation and maintaining concrete economic privileges. Even the most well intentioned man exists in a world which presumes his superiority; this clouds and colors his thinking to our detriment. It is not in our self interest to have men help us to define our needs; they cannot understand them. But this does not mean that we do not welcome their help. We do, but we wish to define that help." Pamela Allen. 1970. *Free space: A perspective on the small group in women's liberation.* New York: Times Change Press, p. 40.

27. For recent insightful analyses of younger men's relationships with feminism, see Shira Tarrant, ed. 2008. *Men speak out: Views on gender, sex, and power.* New York and London: Routledge; Shira Tarrant. 2009. *Men and feminism.* Berkeley, CA: Seal Press.

28. In an early attempt to understand this ally phenomenon in social movements, McCarthy and Zald argued that "conscience constituents" are members of privileged groups who ground their participation in social justice movements primarily on moral grounds, while "beneficiary constituents" belong to oppressed groups and base their participation more on instrumental grounds. John D. McCarthy and Mayer N. Zald. 1977. "Resource mobilization and social movements: A partial theory." *American Journal of Sociology* 82: 1212–1241. While offering a good starting point that recognizes how group interests tie in to social justice movements, this view seems overly dichotomized and simplistic, especially when taking into account cross-cutting (e.g., race, class, gender) identities and complex, multilayered motivations and definitions of "interests." See, for instance, Messner and Solomon's discussion of the complexities of men's interests in supporting Title IX, a law that benefits girls and women in sports: Michael A. Messner and Nancy M. Solomon. 2007. "Social justice and men's interests: The case of Title IX." *Journal of Sport and Social Issues* 31: 162–178.

29. Becky Thompson. 2001. *A promise and a way of life: White antiracist activism.* Minneapolis: University of Minnesota Press; Cooper Thompson, Emmett Schaeffer, and Harry Brod, eds. 2003. *White men challenging racism: 35 personal stories.* Durham, NC: Duke University Press; Mark R. Warren. 2010. *Fire in the heart: How white activists embrace racial justice.* New York: Oxford University Press.

30. Daniel J. Myers. 2008. "Ally identity: The politically gay." In Jo Reger, Daniel J. Myers, and Rachel L. Einwohner, eds. *Identity work in social movements,* pp. 167–187. Minneapolis: University of Minnesota Press.

31. Chandra Russo. 2014. "Allies forging collective identity: Embodiment and emotions on the migrant trail." *Mobilization: An International Quarterly* 19: 489–505.

32. There is a growing social scientific literature on men's pathways into feminist ally work. See Erin Casey. 2010. "Strategies for engaging men as antiviolence allies: Implications for ally movements." *Advances in Social Work* 11: 267–282; Erin Casey and Tyler Smith. 2010. "'How can I not?' Men's pathways to involvement in antiviolence against women work." *Violence Against Women* 16: 953–973; Patricia M. Fabiano, H. Wesley Perkins, Alan Berkowitz, Jeff Linkenbach, and Christopher Stark. 2003. "Engaging men as social justice allies in ending violence against women: Evidence for a social norms approach." *Journal of American College Health* 52: 105–112; Michael Flood. 2011. "Involving men in efforts to end violence against women." *Men and Masculinities* 14: 358–377; Jacqueline R. Piccigallo, Terry G. Lilley, and Susan L. Miller. 2012. "'It's cool to care about sexual violence': Men's experiences with sexual assault prevention." *Men and Masculinities* 15: 507–525.

33. See Ben Atherton-Zeman. 2009. "Minimizing the damage—Male accountability in stopping men's violence against women." *The Voice: The Journal of the Battered Women's Movement* (Spring): 8–13.

34. James M. Jasper. 2004. "A strategic approach to collective action: Looking for agency in social movement choices." *Mobilization: An International Journal* 9: 1–16; Aidan McGarry and James Jasper, forthcoming. "Introduction: The identity dilemma, social movements and contested identity." In Aidan McGarry and James Jasper, eds., *The identity dilemma: Social movements and collective identity.* Philadelphia, PA: Temple University Press.

35. Raewyn Connell. 1995. *Masculinities.* Berkeley: University of California Press, p. 89. Connell also elaborates the uses and limits of theorized life histories in

Raewyn Connell. 2010. "Lives of the businessmen: Reflections on life-history method and contemporary hegemonic masculinity." Österreichische Zeitschrift für Soziologie, 35: 54–71.

36. C. Wright Mills. 1959. *The sociological imagination.* New York: Oxford University Press.

37. See Harry Brod. 1988. *A mensch among men: Explorations in Jewish masculinity.* Freedom, CA: Crossing Press; Harry Brod and Shawn Zevit. 2010. *Brother keepers: New perspectives on Jewish masculinity.* Harriman, TN: Men's Studies Press; Michael S. Kimmel. 1987. "Judaism, masculinity and feminism." *Changing Men* (Summer/Fall).

38. See Jackson Katz. 2010. "Not-so-nice Jewish boys: Notes on violence and the construction of Jewish-American masculinity in the late 20th and early 21st century." In Harry Brod and Shawn Zevit, eds. *Brother keepers: New perspectives on Jewish masculinity,* pp. 57–75. Harriman, TN: Men's Studies Press; Dan Lainer-Vos. 2014. "Masculinities in interaction: The co-production of Israeli and American Jewish men in philanthropic fundraising events," *Men and Masculinities* 17: 43–66.

39. All of the interviewees granted us permission to use their real names in this book.

CHAPTER 2

1. Carolyn Bronstein. 2011. *Battling pornography: The American feminist anti-pornography movement, 1976–1986.* New York: Cambridge University Press, quote from p. 158.

2. A version of Dworkin's speech was published two years later in an edited collection about the growing feminist antipornography movement. See Andrea Dworkin. 1980. "Pornography and grief." In Laura Lederer, ed. *Take back the night: Women on pornography,* pp. 286–291. New York: William Morrow, quote from p. 288.

3. There are differing stories on where and when "Take Back the Night" rallies and marches began. Laura Lederer's 1980 book credits the 1978 San Francisco event as the first-ever TBTN event. Laura Lederer, ed. 1980. *Take back the night: Women on pornography.* New York: William Morrow. Wikipedia notes an antiviolence memorial held in Pittsburgh in 1977 that took the name "Take Back the Night" but denotes the 1978 event in San Francisco as the first TBTN public march. http://en.wikipedia.org/wiki/Take_back_the_night

4. Susan Brownmiller. 2000. *In our time: Memoir of a revolution.* New York: Dial Press. pp. 301–302.

5. Even the most exhaustive rendering of the event, chronicled by historian Carolyn Bronstein, describes Andrea Dworkin and others on that night speaking to "a packed auditorium of women" with no mention of the small group of men in the auditorium. Bronstein 2011, p. 165.

6. Some of this thumbnail sketch of MASV history is gleaned from interviews with former members of the organization, and from Robert Feinglass's fine M.A. thesis on MASV. Feinglass states that the MASV membership list reached a high of fifty-six, but most meetings were attended by ten to twenty men. Robert Allen Feinglass, 1981. *Male adjusted feminism: A history of an anti-sexist men's organization.* Master's thesis, San Francisco State University.

7. It is estimated that WAVPM had about one thousand members in the Bay Area in 1978. The group disbanded in 1983. Carolyn Bronstein devotes an entire chapter to the growth and actions of WAVPM, arguing that the group

"functioned as a swing group during a transition period (1978–80)" that facilitated a transformation of feminist activism from a more general critique of sexism in mass media to "the rise of the antipornography movement." Bronstein 2011, p. 134.

8. In particular, feminists objected to scenes in the film when then-twelve-year-old actress Brooke Shields appeared nude. Protestors argued that the film was an example of the general trend of the mainstreaming of pornography, and in particular of child pornography.

9. Christine Stansell's sweeping history of the feminist movement includes a strong overview of the feminist sex wars. Christine Stansell. 2010. *The feminist promise: 1792 to the present*. New York: Random House.

10. In a recent study, sociologist Nancy Whittier analyzes the social movement dynamics of the 1980s convergence of antipornography feminists and antipornography conservatives. Nancy Whittier. 2014. "Rethinking coalitions: Antipornography feminists, conservatives, and relationships between collaborative adversarial movements." *Social Problems* 61: 175–193.

11. NOCM characterized itself as a men's movement organization that embodied "pro-feminism, gay affirmation, and enhancing men's lives." By 1990, largely to distinguish itself from more conservative men's organizations that had begun to spring up, the organization changed its name to the National Organization for Men Against Sexism (NOMAS).

12. This was the previously mentioned first national conference on men and masculinity.

13. Raewyn Connell. 1987. *Gender and power*. Stanford, CA: Stanford University Press; Raewyn Connell. 1995. *Masculinities*. Berkeley: University of California Press.

14. James W. Messerschmidt. 2000. *Nine Lives: Adolescent masculinities, the body, and violence*. Boulder, CO: Westview Press. For a more recent elaboration of these ideas, see also James W. Messerschmidt. 2010. "The struggle for recognition: Embodied masculinity and the victim-violence cycle of bullying in secondary schools." In Michael Kehler and Michael Atkinson, eds. *Boys' bodies: Speaking the unspoken*, pp. 113–131. New York: Peter Lang.

15. Messerschmidt points to other family dynamics as well, including traditional versus egalitarian gender divisions of labor between parents, and the quality of communication—especially about violence—from parents to children.

16. In his informative master's thesis on MASV, Feinglass states that "in the period just before joining, members had participated politically in labor union organizing and reform, ecology and anti-nuke movements, and cooperative food store, residence collectives, and a variety of social welfare work." Feinglass 1981, quote from p. 25.

17. Morgan's often-reprinted article was originally written as part of a feminist action to take over the male-dominated left magazine *Rat*. Robin Morgan. 1970. "Goodbye to all that." *Rat*. (January). Though the thrust of this feminist critique of sexism in the New Left was focused on the white (and mostly college-educated) "revolutionary" male leadership, similar angry charges were echoed later in the decade in Michele Wallace's blistering critique of the sexism of many male leaders of the Black Power Movement. See Michelle Wallace. 1979. *Black macho and the myth of the super-woman*. New York: Warner Books.

18. As it turned out, the VVAW had become a site of some of the worst sectarian left factionalism of the era, including a partly successful takeover of the organization by the Stalinist-oriented Revolutionary Communist Party. Greg

Ross was experiencing this in Buffalo, New York, as a recently discharged war veteran: "Every meeting was totally disruptive and full of shit and then I quit and shortly after I quit, some of the people that were disrupting the meeting got busted as COINTELPRO [an FBI undercover counterintelligence operation that infiltrated and attempted to disrupt and delegitimize left groups]. You know, and when I came out here [to the Bay Area] I got involved again and that time I looked around and it wasn't COINTELPRO, it was the RCP, the Royal Communist Party as we liked to call them, you know [laughs]. They had infiltrated."

19. Beneke's interviews with both convicted rapists and "men on the street" yielded deep and often disturbing insights into men's anger toward women, their insecurities, and their views about rape. The book became a text for many of the first rape-prevention activists, and parts of the book are still reprinted in anthologies on rape, gender, and men. Timothy Beneke. 1982. *Men on rape.* St. Martin's Press.

20. The community "radical therapy movement" blossomed in the 1970s and early 1980s in progressive areas like the Bay Area as part of a radical antipsychiatry movement that included feminist critiques of male-dominated medicine, especially Freudian psychoanalysis. With a strong emphasis on face-to-face democratic, and antiprofessional processes, radical therapy included efforts to develop "co-counseling" networks (MASV member Larry Mandella was a part of this) and "transactional analysis" (which Santiago Casal was affiliated with). Transactional analysis included a feminist-inspired radical therapy approach created by renegade psychotherapist Claude Steiner that aimed to help men rethink and purge their internalized toxic masculinity. See Claude Steiner. 1977/1978. "Feminism for men, part I." *Issues in Radical Therapy* 20 (Fall); "Feminism for men, part II." *Issues in Radical Therapy* (Spring). Casal, Mandella, and others brought these radical therapeutic viewpoints and skills to MASV.

21. As part of a 1980 research project on men's groups, Mike Messner interviewed Chris Norton about his involvement in the then-vibrant MASV group. We also interviewed him thirty years later, along with other former members of the group. We use pieces of the 1980 interview sparingly here, to illustrate shifts in perspective over time, when it is useful to do so.

22. It would be an oversimplification to think of this as a simple linear sequence, as for many of these men these events or engagements happened with some simultaneity.

23. Social movements scholar James Jasper would see this as a "Janus dilemma," the common tension for movement activists between "'reaching in' to attend to the needs of their own members rather than 'reaching out' to fix the world." James M. Jasper 2011. "Emotions and social movements: Twenty years of theory and research. *Annual Review of Sociology* 37: 1–14, quote from p. 6.

24. McGarry and Jasper call this "the identity dilemma," faced generally by social movements who seek to benefit from developing a strong and coherent collective identity but must grapple simultaneously with differences and inequalities among their members. Aidan McGarry and James Jasper, forthcoming. "Introduction: The identity dilemma, social movements and contested identity." In Aidan McGarry and James Jasper, eds., *The identity dilemma: Social movements and collective identity.* Philadelphia: Temple University Press.

25. Maxine Baca Zinn, Lynn Weber Cannon, Elizabeth Higgenbotham, and Bonnie Thornton Dill. 1986. "The costs of exclusionary practices in women's studies." *Signs: Journal of Women in Culture and Society* 11: 290–303.

26. See Harry Brod. 1983–84. "Work clothes and leisure suits: The class basis and bias of the men's movement." *M: Gentle Men for Gender Justice* 11: 10–12, 38–40; Andrew Tolson. 1977. *The limits of masculinity: Male identity and women's liberation*. New York: Harper & Row; Robert Staples. 1982. *Black masculinity: The black male's role in American society*. San Francisco: Black Scholar Press.

27. Collins argued, for instance, that African American women tend to have an "outsider within" standpoint—as black, in the predominantly white women's movement; as women in the male-dominated civil rights and Black Power movements—which gave them a uniquely important and powerful perspective on the limits and possibilities of these movements. Patricia Hill Collins. 1990. *Black feminist thought: Knowledge, consciousness, and the politics of empowerment*. Boston: Unwin Hyman. We are suggesting here that Greg Ross and Santiago Casal had similarly unique standpoints concerning their work with MASV.

28. Feminist writer Ann Koedt's 1968 essay was read and discussed in many women's consciousness-raising groups. Ann Koedt. 1968. "The myth of the vaginal orgasm." In *Notes from the first year*. New York: Radical Women.

29. A widely discussed idea in Jong's popular novel was the assertion that like men, women should assert their right to enjoy the pleasures of a "zipless fuck"—a one-night stand that required no emotional commitments and resulted in no stigma. Erica Jong. 1973. *Fear of flying*. New York: Holt, Rinehart & Winston.

30. Susan Griffin. 1971. "Rape: The all-American crime." *Ramparts*. September, pp. 26–35.

31. Susan Brownmiller. 1975. *Against our will: Men, women and rape*. New York: Simon & Schuster, quote from p. 6.

32. Robin Morgan. 1978. "Theory and practice: Pornography and rape." In her *Going too far: The personal chronicle of a feminist*, pp. 163–169. New York: Vintage. Quotes from pp. 164–165, 168–169.

33. COYOTE (Call Off Your Old Tired Ethics), founded in 1973 in California by Margo St. James, pushed for the next three decades for decriminalization of sex work.

34. Some of the most important feminist essays on sexuality at this time were collected in Ann Snitow, Christine Stansell, and Sharon Thompson, eds. 1983. *Powers of desire: The politics of sexuality*. New York: Monthly Review Press; and Carol S. Vance. 1993. *Pleasure and danger: Exploring female sexuality*. London: Pandora Press.

35. In 1984, feminist cultural critic Alice Echols criticized the often-repeated slogan "Pornography is the theory; rape is the practice," dubbing it "the domino theory of sexuality. It identifies pornography as the scourge which leads directly to violence against women." Although many radical feminists at the time, according to Echols, continued to embrace "a dualistic approach to sexuality—one which acknowledged both the danger and the pleasure associated with sexual exploration for women," antipornography feminists "tried to silence their intra-movement critics," essentially positioning themselves as the true feminists. Alice Echols (1984) 2002. "The taming of the id: Feminist sexual politics, 1968–1983." In Alice Echols. *Shaky ground: The sixties and its aftershocks*, pp. 108–128. New York: Columbia University Press. Quotes from pp. 113–114, 116.

36. Gayle Rubin. (1993) 2011. "Misguided, dangerous and wrong: An analysis of anti-pornography politics." In Gayle Rubin, *Deviations: A Gayle Rubin reader*, pp. 254–275. Durham and London: Duke University Press. Quotes from pp. 256–257.

37. Echols, ibid., p. 126.

38. Andrea Dworkin. (1983) 1993. "I want a twenty-four hour truce during which there is no rape." In Andrea Dworkin. *Letters from a war zone*, pp. 162–171. Chicago: Lawrence Hill Books. Quote from p. 163.
39. Dworkin. ibid., quote from p. 167.
40. For a more detailed discussion of this development, see Michael A. Messner 1997. *Politics of masculinities: Men in movements*. Lanham, MD: Alta Mira Press; Michael A. Messner 1998. "The limits of 'the male sex role': The discourse of the men's liberation and men's rights movements." *Gender & Society* 12: 255–276.
41. James Jasper discusses the central importance as well as the limits and dangers of emotions in social movements. See James M. Jasper. 2011. "Emotions and social movements: Twenty years of theory and research." *Annual Review of Sociology* 37: 1–14.
42. Feinglass 1981, quote from pp. 76–77.
43. Andrea Dworkin. 1977. "Why so-called radical men love and need pornography." Palo Alto, CA: Frog in the Well.
44. Feinglass 1981, quote from p. 79.

CHAPTER 3
1. A decade later, cultural studies scholar Wendy Chun wrote, "This move to mourn the murders in Montreal in the context of other violent acts, this move to make the act of mourning the link between disparate violent events, enabled many women to respond to the Montreal massacre." Wendy Hui Kyong Chun. 1999. "Unbearable witness: Towards a politics of listening." *Differences: Journal of Feminist Cultural Studies* 11: 112–149 (quote from p. 134).
2. Kaufman edited one of the first scholarly collections of feminist essays on men and masculinity in 1987, including his essay introducing a conceptual framework that is still foundational to scholars of gender-based violence today. Michael Kaufman 1987. "The construction of masculinity and the triad of men's violence." In Michael Kaufman, ed. *Beyond patriarchy: Essays by men on pleasure, power and change*, pp. 1–29. Toronto and New York: Oxford University Press.
3. See http://www.whiteribbon.ca/.
4. Or perhaps, as we will suggest in subsequent chapters, Kaufman's strategic decision marks the start of a transformation in how "social movements" are defined and operate.
5. The "Transitional Period" on Figure 1.2 actually contains twenty-one interviews with men. However, four of these men engaged with antiviolence work later in life, in the 2000s, so although they are a part of this middle age cohort, their "moments of engagement" with feminist antiviolence work occurred in the period we are calling "Professionally Institutionalized Feminism," so their stories fit in Chapters 4 and 5.
6. For a discussion of how the women's movement grappled with these issues more generally during the eighties and nineties, see Nancy Whittier. 1995. *Feminist generations: The persistence of the radical women's movement*. Philadelphia: Temple University Press.
7. Maxine Baca Zinn, Lynn Weber Cannon, Elizabeth Higgenbotham, and Bonnie Thornton Dill, 1986. "The costs of exclusionary practices in women's studies." *Signs: Journal of Women in Culture and Society* 11: 290–303. This influential article was part of a larger mid-1980s burst of powerful multiracial feminist critique of the white and middle-class basis and bias of the feminist movement, and of the incipient women's studies. bell hooks, for instance, argued in 1984 that

second-wave feminism's "emphasis on Sisterhood was often seen as emotional appeal masking the opportunism of bourgeois white women." bell hooks. 1984. *Feminist theory: From margin to center.* Boston: South End Press, quote from p. 44.

8. Susan Faludi. 1991. *Backlash: The undeclared war against American women.* New York: Crown.

9. Overtly antifeminist (some of them openly misogynist) men's rights writings were collected in Francis Baumli, ed. 1985. *Men freeing men: Exploding the myth of the traditional male.* Jersey City: New Atlantis Press.

10. For an overview of the research on violence against men in families, see Jack C. Straton. 1994. "The myth of the 'battered husband syndrome'." *Masculinities* 2: 79–82.

11. Herb Goldberg's and Warren Farrell's writings were more typical of those that asserted a symmetry between women's and men's sufferings as a result of what they viewed as traditional sex roles. See Herb Goldberg. 1976. *The hazards of being male: Surviving the myth of masculine privilege.* New York: Signet; Warren Farrell. 1974. *The liberated man;* New York: Random House. Warren Farrell. 1993. *The myth of male power: Why men are the disposable sex.* New York: Simon & Schuster. For critical analyses of men's rights movements from the 1970s to the 1980s, see Messner, *Politics of masculinities.*

12. For a recent case-study analysis of a legal contestation of battered women's shelters and services by men's rights organizations, see Molly Dragiewicz. 2011. *Equality with a vengeance: Men's rights groups, battered women, and antifeminist backlash.* Boston: Northeastern University Press.

13. Phyllis Schlafly. 1981. "How to clean up America by stopping the Equal Rights Amendment." In Jerry Falwell, ed. 1981. *How you can help clean up America*, pp. 23–29. Washington, DC: Moral Majority.

14. Jo Reger. 2012. *Everywhere and nowhere: Contemporary feminism in the United States.* New York and Oxford: Oxford University Press.

15. See Janice McCabe. 2005 "What's in a label? The relationship between feminist self-identification and 'feminist' attitudes among U.S. women and men." *Gender & Society* 19: 480–505.

16. Lisa Markowitz and Karen W. Tice. 2002. "Paradoxes of professionalization: Parallel dilemmas in women's organizations in the Americas." *Gender & Society* 16: 941–958; See also Ruth Wilson Gilmore. 2007. "In the shadow of the shadow state." In INCITE! Women of Color Against Violence, ed., *The revolution will not be funded: Beyond the nonprofit industrial complex*, pp. 41–52. Cambridge, MA: South End Press; Paul Kivel. 2007. Social service or social change? In ibid. (pp. 129–149).

17. Lois Ahrens. 1980. "Battered women's refuges: Feminist cooperatives vs. social service institutions." *Radical America* 14(3): 41–48. See also Judy Andler and Gail Sullivan. 1989. "The price of government funding." *Aegis: Magazine on ending violence against women* (Winter/Spring): 10–15; John M. Johnson. 1981. "Program Enterprise and official cooptation in the battered women's shelter movement." *American Behavioral Scientist* 24: 827–842.

18. Suzanne Staggenborg. 1988. "The consequences of professionalization and formalization in the pro-choice movement." *American Sociological Review* 53: 585–605, quotation from p. 585.

19. Patricia Yancey Martin. 1990. "Rethinking feminist organizations." *Gender and Society* 4: 182–206, quote from p. 183. See also Amy Fried. 1994. "It's hard to change what we want to change: Rape crisis centers as organizations." *Gender & Society* 8: 562–583.

20. Legal scholar Rose Corrigan argues that the conservative climate of the Reagan years of the early 1980s, coupled with a general climate of "silence and aversion" about "the relationship of rape to sex and sexuality [, made] it a particularly tense issue to address through political or legal mobilization. To deal with these unavoidable and uncomfortable realities, rape is often obscured by a broader focus on domestic violence, trafficking, or other 'stand-ins' which obscure some of the unique problems associated with sexual assault." Rose Corrigan. 2013. *Up against the wall: Rape reform and the failure of success.* New York and London: New York University Press, quote from p. 14.

21. For a brief history and outline of the principles of the Oakland Men's Project, see http://www.paulkivel.com/resources/articles/23-article/70-the-oaklands-men-p roject.

22. A simple one-page handout or poster, the "Act Like a Man Box" provides a useful foundation for group discussions about how narrow definitions of masculinity "box men in," limit their range of socially acceptable emotional expressions, and encourage destructive and self-destructive behaviors. http://paulkivel.com/ component/jdownloads/finish/2/58/0. See also Allan Creighton and Paul Kivel. 2011. *Helping teens stop violence, build community and stand for justice* (Second ed.). Alameda, CA: Hunter House.

23. Following several years of national "men and masculinity conferences," NOCM was formed in 1982–83 as an organization self-defined as "profeminist, gay-affirmative, antiracist, enhancing men's lives." By the end of the decade, in an increasingly conservative climate that included the emergence of antifeminist men's organizations, NOCM changed its name to "National Organization for Men Against Sexism" (NOMAS), the name it retains today.

24. Michael S. Kimmel, ed. 1985. "Men confronting pornography." Special issue. *Changing Men: Issues in Gender, Sex and Politics* 15 (fall). Kimmel eventually used this special issue as a springboard for the development of a longer edited volume that provided a forum for debate about men and pornography among scholars and activists: Michael S. Kimmel, ed. 1990. *Men confront pornography.* New York: Crown.

25. The issue of *Changing Men* that likely spelled the magazine's end was one in 1992 that included an ad from NAMBLA, the North American Man-Boy Love Association, and a personal essay by one of the magazine's editors about one of his first sexual experiences having been with a younger boy who was a minor. A firestorm of feminist criticism of the magazine erupted, focusing on pedophilia in particular, and more generally questioning the editors' commitment to stopping violence against women and children.

26. There is a long history of feminist activism and influence in peace movements. See, for instance, Linda Gordon. 1990. "The peaceful sex?: On feminism and the peace movement." *NWSA Journal* 2: 624–634.

27. Sociologists Barrie Thorne and Barbara Laslett collected thirteen personal essays of scholars who fought, and often paid a high personal price, for establishing women's studies in academia. See Barrie Thorne and Barbara Laslett, eds. 1997. *Feminist sociology: Life histories of a movement.* New Brunswick, NJ: Rutgers University Press.

28. A scattering of women's studies courses were offered in the late 1960s, but San Diego State College and SUNY Buffalo are often credited as housing the first women's studies programs in the United States in 1970, and the Universities of Toronto and Waterloo were the first in Canada, also around 1970.

29. Michael Reynolds, Shobha Shagle, and Lekha Venkataraman. 2007. *A national census of women's and gender studies programs in U.S. institutions of higher education.* National Women's Studies Association (NORC Project 6433.01.62).

30. Judith Stacey and Barrie Thorne. 1986. "The missing feminist revolution in sociology." *Social Problems* 32: 301–316.

31. In Chapter 4, we discuss the implications of the bystander approach having become the most popular approach to violence prevention work with boys and men.

32. Zinn et al. 1986, 290–303.

33. Of course, our identification of these major hubs of antiviolence work is in part a function of our intentional sampling mainly in these areas. In doing this, we risk rendering invisible the fact that, as early as the mid-1980s, men's profeminist activism and antiviolence work had begun to spring up in many smaller, medium-sized, and large cities—such as Portland, Oregon; Chicago; Washington, DC; and Atlanta—and also especially in college towns all over the United States and Canada.

34. Markowitz and Tice 2002.

35. Lichterman observed that in 1986, during the time of his study, fourteen of the seventeen male volunteers in MOVE were "counselors, M.A.-level psychotherapists, social service or public health workers." Paul Lichterman. 1989. "Making a politics of masculinity." *Comparative Social Research* 11: 185–208, quotes from pp. 188–189.

36. Lichterman 1989, 199.

37. The VAWA was not the first effort to create national legislation to address violence against women. There were unsuccessful national domestic violence bills introduced in 1977 and 1978, and in 1979 President Jimmy Carter created the Office of Domestic Violence, which was later eliminated by President Ronald Reagan. Molly Dragiewicz. 2011. *Equality with a vengeance: Men's rights groups, battered women, and antifeminist backlash.* Boston: Northeastern University Press.

38. Molly Dragiewicz. 2008. "Patriarchy reasserted: Fathers' rights and anti-VAWA activism." *Feminist Criminology* 3: 121–144.

39. Carol McClurg Mueller and John D. McCarthy. 2003. "Cultural continuity and structural change: The logic of adaptation by radical, liberal, and socialist feminists to state reconfiguration." in Lee Ann Banaszak, Karen Beckwith, and Dieter Rucht, eds., *Women's movements facing the reconfigured state*, pp. 219–241 Cambridge: Cambridge University Press, quote from p. 237.

40. Rose Corrigan 2013, quote from p. 262.

CHAPTER 4

1. Part of this brief organizational history is assembled from our interviews with LACAAW and POV employees, and part of it is from the organization's website: http://peaceoverviolence.org/organization/about-us/history/1971-1980/.

2. David Lee 2011. "What are we working for? New names of sexual violence and domestic violence organizations." *PreventConnect*, April 25, 2011. http://www.preventconnect.org/2011/04/new-names-of-sexual-violence-domestic-violence-organizations/.

3. Ms. Foundation for Women. 2010. *Efforts to address gender-based violence: A look at foundation funding.* Ms. Foundation for Women, quotes from p. 6.

4. Jennifer Wolch. 1990. *The shadow state: The government and the voluntary sector in transition.* New York: Foundation Center.

5. Gilmore concludes that "the work that people set out to accomplish is vulnerable to becoming mission impossible under the sternly specific funding rubrics and structural prohibitions that situate grassroots groups . . . in the shadow of the shadow state." Ruth Wilson Gilmore, 2007. "In the shadow of the shadow state." In INCITE! Women of Color Against Violence, ed., *The revolution will not be funded: Beyond the nonprofit industrial complex*, pp. 41–52. Cambridge, MA: South End Press, quotes from pp. 46, 47.

6. Suzanne Beechy. 2005. "When feminism is your job: Age and power in women's policy organizations." In Jo Reger, ed. *Different wavelengths: Studies of the contemporary women's movement*, pp. 117–136. New York: Routledge.

7. See Kristin Bumiller. 2013. "Feminist collaboration with the state in response to sexual violence: Lessons from the American experience." In Alli Mari Tripp, Myra Marx Ferree, and Christina Ewing, eds. *Gender, violence, and human security: Critical feminist perspectives*, pp. 191–213. New York: New York University Press.

8. Gilmore 2007 argued that the nonprofit industrial complex—the institutional linkages between the state, foundations, and nonprofits—leaves progressive activists limited options to confront only certain problems, such that they are precluded from addressing systemic roots of problems, requiring "grassroots organizations to act like secure suburbanites who have only a last corner of the yard to plant." Quote from p. 47.

9. Linda L. Dahlberg and James A. Mercy. 2009. *The history of violence as a public health issue*. Centers for Disease Control Division of Violence Prevention (DVP) Annual Report; Sarah DeGue, Thomas R. Simon, et al. 2012. "Moving forward by looking back: Reflecting on a decade of CDC's work in sexual violence prevention, 2000–2010." *Journal of Women's Health*, 21: 1211–1218.

10. Kristin D'Agostino. 2009. "HAWC embraces new name, new mission." *Wicked Local Salem*, March 26. http://www.wickedlocal.com/salem/news/x1672264504/HAWC-embraces-new-name-new-mission

11. One in Six is an organization that works with men who are recovering from childhood sexual abuse. https://1in6.org/ The "one in six" number comes from research conducted for the U.S. CDC that states 16 percent of all males have suffered some form of sexual abuse by the time they are eighteen years of age. S. R. Dube, R. F. Anda, C. L. Whitfield, et al. 2005. "Long-term consequences of childhood sexual abuse by gender of victim." *American Journal of Preventive Medicine* 28: 430–438.

12. Jensen's perspective—that cosmetic surgery is a bodily manifestation of women's oppression and is thus antithetical to feminist antiviolence efforts—is in line with common second-wave perspectives on gender and power. However, a few feminists—for instance, Kathy Davis—view women's choices to alter their bodies through surgery as potentially empowering. Kathy Davis. 1994. *Reshaping the female body: The dilemma of cosmetic surgery*. New York: Routledge.

13. Danielle M. Giffort. 2011. "Feminist dilemmas and implicit feminism at girls' rock camp." *Gender & Society* 25: 569–588.

14. There is one exception: Jimmie Briggs was born in 1969, but we include him in the Professional Cohort because his moment of engagement with antiviolence work was a bit later in life, during the current time period we refer to as the era of professionally institutionalized feminism.

15. Despite its current abeyance as a visible grassroots national movement, Reger notes how feminism manifests in local campus- and community-based activism. Many of our interviewees in recent years were involved in such local organizing.

See Jo Reger. 2012. *Everywhere and nowhere: Contemporary feminism in the United States*. New York and Oxford: Oxford University Press.

16. Sociologist Jess Butler, in her study of contemporary college "hook-up culture," defines postfeminism as a shared belief system that sees feminist political action as no longer necessary, promotes an ethic of female empowerment that is closely linked to desirability and heterosexual "hotness," celebrates women's sexual "liberation," conceptualizes men and women as biologically different but socially equal, and draws on a vocabulary of individual choice and personal responsibility. Jess Butler. 2013. "For white girls only? Postfeminism and the politics of inclusion." *Feminist Formations* 25: 35–58.

17. As early as the start of the 1980s some college courses, often taught by men, were also being offered on "men and masculinity." And by the late 1980s, what Harry Brod called "the new men's studies" had begun to take shape as an adjunct field of women's studies. Harry Brod. 1987. *The making of masculinities: The new men's studies*. Sydney: Allen & Unwin. By the 2000s, many women's studies programs had changed their names to "gender studies," or "women's and gender studies," partly to incorporate the study of boys and men as gendered people, and to address the field's increasingly fluid and multivalent (as opposed to binary) conception of gender. For discussions of men teaching about feminism and gender, see William Breeze. 2007. "Constructing a male feminist pedagogy: Authority, practice, and authenticity in the composition classroom." *Feminist Teacher* 18: 59–73; Wade Edwards. 2008. "Teaching women with a Y-chromosome: Do men make better feminists?" *Feminist Teacher* 18: 145–159; Michael Flood. 2011. "Men as students and teachers of feminist scholarship." *Men & Masculinities* 14: 135–154; Michael A. Messner. 2011. "The privilege of teaching about privilege." *Sociological Perspectives* 54: 3–13.

18. Erin Casey and Tyler Smith. 2010. "'How can I not?' Men's pathways to involvement in antiviolence against women work." *Violence Against Women* 16: 953–973. See also Erin Casey. 2010. "Strategies for engaging men as antiviolence allies: Implications for ally movements." *Advances in Social Work* 11: 267–282.

19. Tal Peretz. (Under review). "Engaging diverse men: An intersectional analysis of men's pathways to antiviolence activism."

20. For an examination of how Latino men's structural vulnerability and sense of declining power vis-à-vis women connects to violence against women, see M. Cristina Alcalde. 2011. "Masculinities in motion: Latino men and violence in Kentucky." *Men & Masculinities* 14: 450–469.

21. Adia Harvey Wingfield. 2012. *No more invisible man: Race and gender in men's work*. Philadelphia: Temple University Press.

22. My Strength, which we will discuss more at length later, became the dominant men's violence-prevention curriculum in the 2000s.

23. An earlier iteration of MenCARE existed at USC in the late 1980s and early 1990s, overseen by Mark Stevens, who then worked in the campus counseling center. MenCARE disappeared for several years. Its revival and survival since 2000, partly with funds from a DOE grant, is due largely to the university's having dedicated a paid staff position (since held by Todd Henneman) to running MenCARE.

24. Peretz. ibid., p. 30 (emphasis in the original).

25. Kristen Schilt. 2011. *Just one of the guys? Transgender men and the persistence of gender inequality*. Chicago: University of Chicago Press.

26. Gloria T. Hull, Patricia Bell Scott, and Barbara Smith, eds. 1993. *All the women are white, all the blacks are men, but some of us are brave.* CUNY: Feminist Press. The essays in this influential volume amplify and deepen black and multiracial feminist criticism of the 1980s that argued that the women's movement tended to reflect white black women's interests and issues, while the civil rights and black power movements reflected black men's interests, with both movements therefore rendering black women marginal and less visible.

27. Michael A. Messner and Mark A. Stevens. "Scoring without consent: Confronting male athletes' violence against women." In Margaret Gatz, Michael A. Messner, and Sandra J. Ball-Rokeach, eds. *Paradoxes of youth and sport*, pp. 225–240. Albany: State University of New York Press.

28. See Michael J. Murphy. 2009. "Can 'men' stop rape? Visualizing gender in the 'My Strength is Not for Hurting' rape prevention campaign." *Men and Masculinities* 12: 113–130. For a rejoinder to Murphy, see Patrick McGann. 2009. "A letter to Michael Murphy in response to 'Can "men" stop rape? Visualizing gender in the "My strength is not for hurting" rape prevention campaign'." *Men and Masculinities* 12: 131–134.

29. A year after we interviewed Gilbert Salazar, he left his job with the Monterey County Rape Crisis Center and enrolled in a graduate program in USC's School of Theatre, where he developed a theater of the oppressed–inspired approach to doing antiviolence work with youths. Grounded in the work of Brazilian educator Paulo Freire, theater of the oppressed was developed first by Brazilian playwright Augusto Boal. See Augusto Boal, 1993. *Theatre of the oppressed.* Theatre Communications Group.

30. See Marc D. Rich. 2010. "The interACT model: Considering rape prevention from a performance activism and social justice perspective." *Feminism and Psychology* 20: 511–528.

31. Tristan S. Bridges. 2010. "Men just weren't made to do this: Performances of drag at 'Walk a Mile in Her Shoes' marches." *Gender & Society* 24: 5–30. For an analysis of the extent to which drag may subvert gender dichotomies or stereotypes, see Leila J. Rupp and Verta Taylor. 2003. *Drag queens at the 801 Cabaret.* Chicago: University of Chicago Press.

32. The embracing of the term *slut* is an example of what sociologist Jo Reger calls "gender reclamation," a process through which activists take a stigmatizing term and publicly valorize it. Reger 2012, p. 111.

33. Kristen Barber and Kelsey Kretchmer. 2013. "Walking like a man?" *Contexts* 12: 40–45. In fact, following the University of Southern California's 2013 "Walk a Mile" event, some members of the transgender community criticized the meanings of men wearing high heels; in response, organizers of the 2014 WAM event decided not to encourage men to wear heels.

34. See, for instance, recent studies that attempt to measure change among college men and high schoolers exposed to antiviolence curricula: Sarah DeGue et al. 2012. "Moving forward by looking back: Reflecting on a decade of CDC's work in sexual violence prevention, 2000–2010." *Journal of Women's Health*, 21: 1211–1218; Patricia M. Fabiano, H. Wesley Perkins, Alan Berkowitz, Jeff Linkenbach, and Christopher Stark. 2003. "Engaging men as social justice allies in ending violence against women: Evidence for a social norms approach." *Journal of American College Health* 52: 105–112; J. D. Foubert, J. T. Newberry, and J. L. Tatum. 2007. "Behavior differences seven months later: Effects of a rape prevention program on first-year men who join fraternities." *Journal of Student Affairs Research and*

Practice, 44: 728–749; Christine A. Gidycz, Lindsay M. Orchowski, and Alan Berkowitz. 2011. "Preventing sexual aggression among college men: An evaluation of a social norms and bystander intervention program." *Violence Against Women* 17: 720–742; Lisa H. Jaycox et al. 2006. "Impact of a school-based dating violence prevention program among Latino teens: Randomized controlled effectiveness trial." *Journal of Adolescent Health*, 39(5), 694–704; Jennifer Langhinrichsen-Rohling, John D. Foubert, Hope M. Brasfield, Brent Hill, and Shannon Shelley-Tremblay. 2011. "The men's program: Does it impact college men's self-reported bystander efficacy and willingness to intervene?" *Violence Against Women* 17: 743–759; Elizabeth Miller et al. 2011. "'Coaching boys into men': A cluster-randomized controlled trial of a dating violence prevention program." *Journal of Adolescent Health* 48: S85-S86. Although most of these studies report generally positive findings concerning the impact of antiviolence interventions, Michael Flood evaluates a range of such studies, offering a nuanced view, breaking them down into those deemed as "effective, promising, and potentially promising." Michael Flood. 2011. "Involving men in efforts to end violence against women." *Men and Masculinities* 14: 358–377.

35. MenCARE was rejuvenated following a dormant period of several years after the demise of the Men C.A.R.E. group started previously by Mark Stevens.

36. See http://sait.usc.edu/mencare/.

37. Douglas Schrock and Irene Padavic. 2007. "Negotiating hegemonic masculinity in a batterer intervention program." *Gender & Society* 21: 625–649. Quotes from pp. 643–644. For other works that raise critical questions about evaluations of violence prevention efforts, see Piper Fogg. 2009. "Rape-prevention programs proliferate, but 'It's hard to know' whether they work." *Chronicle of Higher Education*. (November 15). Retrieved from http://chronicle.com/article/Rape-Prevention-Programs/49151/. Elizabeth Reed, Anita Raj, Elizabeth Miller, and Jay G. Silverman. 2010. "Losing the 'gender' in gender-based violence: The missteps of research on dating and intimate partner violence." *Violence Against Women*, 16: 348–354.

38. See Jackson Katz, H. Alan Heisterkamp, and W. Michael Fleming. 2011. "The social justice roots of the Mentors in Violence Prevention model and its application in a high school setting." *Violence Against Women* 17: 684–702.

CHAPTER 5

1. This is Webster's definition for *ally* when used as a noun. The term also can be a verb, which Webster defines as "to join (yourself) with another person, group, etc., in order to get or give support." http://www.merriam-webster.com/dictionary/ally.

2. Daniel J. Myers. 2008. "Ally identity: The politically gay." In Jo Reger, Daniel J. Myers, and Rachel L. Einwohner, eds. *Identity work in social movements*, pp. 167–187. Minneapolis: University of Minnesota Press, quotes from pp. 167–168.

3. For a discussion of how privilege works in men's antiviolence activism, see Michael Flood. 2003. "Men's collective struggles for gender justice: The case of antiviolence activism." In Michael Kimmel, Jeff Hearn, and R. W. Connell, eds. *The handbook of studies on men and masculinities*. Thousand Oaks, CA: Sage.

4. Matthew W. Hughey. 2012. "Stigma allure and white antiracist identity management." *Social Psychology Quarterly* 75: 219–241, quote from p. 220. See also Jennifer L. Eichstedt. 2001. "Problematic white identities and a search for racial justice." *Sociological Forum* 16: 445–470.

5. Tal Peretz (under review). "Seeing the invisible knapsack: Feminist men's responses to the continuation of male privilege in feminist spaces."

6. This idea is developed more fully in Michael A. Messner. 2011. "The privilege of teaching about privilege." *Sociological Perspectives* 54: 3–13.

7. Tarrant is a scholar-activist whose work focuses on younger men's engagements with feminism. See Shira Tarrant. ed. 2008. *Men speak out: Views on gender, sex, and power.* New York: Routledge; Shira Tarrant. 2009. *Men and feminism.* Berkeley, CA: Seal Press.

8. Arlie Russell Hochschild (with Anne Machung). 1989. *The second shift: Working parents and the revolution at home.* New York: Viking.

9. Christine Williams. 1992. "The glass escalator: Hidden advantages for men in the 'female' professions." *Social Problems* 39: 253–267; see also Michelle J. Budig. 2002. "Male advantage and the gender composition of jobs: Who rides the glass escalator?" *Social Problems* 49: 258–277; Christine Williams. 2013. "The glass escalator, revisited: Gender inequality in neoliberal times." *Gender & Society* 27: 609–629.

10. Wingfield finds that black male nurses have very different interactions with the patients, doctors, and other nurses than do the mostly white male nurses that Christine Williams had studied. As a result, racism all but cancels out the sorts of male privileges that serve to escalate white male nurses. Adia Harvey Wingfield. 2009. "Racializing the glass escalator: Reconsidering men's experiences with women's work." *Gender & Society* 23: 5–26.

11. Deniz Kandiyoti. 1988. "Bargaining with patriarchy." *Gender & Society* 2: 274–290.

12. A "social business" uses the principles of capitalism—marketing, profit generation, etc.—but instead of accumulating profits to enrich investors, revenues are reinvested in communities and progressive social change organizations.

13. Katz's position reflects what sociologist James Jasper describes as a "bridge-builder's dilemma" common to social movements, wherein "individuals who can mediate between groups . . . often lose the trust of their own groups by doing so." James M. Jasper. 2004. "A strategic approach to collective action: Looking for agency in social movement choices." *Mobilization: An International Journal* 9: 1–16, quote from p. 13.

14. Audre Lorde. 1984. "The master's tools will never dismantle the master's house." *Sister outsider: Essays and speeches.* Berkeley, CA: Crossing Press.

15. Blossoming in the 1990s, a younger generation of "third wave" feminists defined themselves, in part, in opposition to "second-wave" feminists of the 1970s, who the younger feminists perceived as separatists who viewed men as "the enemy" and thus would not work with them. See Leslie Heywood and Jennifer Drake, eds. 1997. *Third wave agenda: Being feminist, doing feminism.* Minneapolis: University of Minnesota Press. Indeed, several older men we interviewed said that they experienced in recent years more openness among younger women to working alongside men. However, these same men all had stories of feminist women who had encouraged, mentored, and worked with them in the past, thus puncturing any simplistic image of second wave feminists as separatists. And though we are not sure what to make of it here, Shira Tarrant—who has her fingers on the pulse of younger generations of feminists—told us that she sees a renewed tendency toward female-only separatist politics among a strand of today's younger radical feminists.

16. See Geoffrey Canada. 1995. *Fist, stick, knife, gun: A personal history of violence in America.* Boston: Beacon Press; Victor Rios. 2011. *Punished: Policing the lives*

of black and Latino boys. New York: New York University Press; Robert Staples. 1982. *Black masculinity: The black male's role in American society*. San Francisco: Black Scholar Press.

17. Debates and conflicts that take place in the feminist blogosphere have real-world repercussions in how people connect, talk about issues, and strategize for change. In fact, during the latter stages of doing this research, we were asked for our thoughts on Hugo Schwyzer by several people who had been following his unfolding drama online, some of whom wondered aloud about what it meant to include men in antiviolence work. Feminist scholarship on the Internet as a site of politics has begun to flourish in recent years. See, for instance, Sonia Nuñez Puente. 2011. "Feminist cyberactivism: Violence against women, Internet politics, and Spanish feminist praxis online." *Continuum: Journal of Media and Cultural Studies*, 25: 333–346; Laura Rapp, Deeana M. Button, Benjamin Fleury-Steiner, and Ruth Fleury-Steiner. 2012. "The Internet as a tool for black feminist activism: Lessons from an online antirape protest." *Feminist Criminology* 5: 244–262; Jessie Daniels. 2009. "Rethinking cyberfeminism(s): Race, gender and embodiment." *Women's Studies Quarterly* 37: 101–124.

18. Clarisse Thorn. 2011. "Sex, drugs, theology, men and feminism: Interview with Hugo Schwyzer." *Feministe* (December 17). http://www.feministe.us/blog/archives/2011/12/17/sex-drugs-theology-men-feminism-interview-with-hugo-schwyzer/.

19. In fact, Schwyzer had previously publicly admitted to these past troubles; however, many in the feminist blogosphere learned this information only in 2012 and 2013, and for them, including many of Schwyzer's admirers in the violence-against-women community, these were shocking revelations that undermined his credibility.

20. See, for instance, Susan Elizabeth Shepherd. 2013. "Man quits Internet: Goodbye, Hugo Schwyzer." *Hairpin* (August 1), http://thehairpin.com/2013/08/man-quits-internet-goodbye-hugo-schwyzer; Raphael Magarik. 2012. "Exile in gal-ville: How a male feminist alienated his supporters." *Atlantic* (February 13) http://www.theatlantic.com/national/archive/2012/02/exile-in-gal-ville-how-a-male-feminist-alienated-his-supporters/252915/?single_page=true.

21. We decided not to use Schwyzer's interview material for this book largely because, in our view, the issues that emerged about his personal struggles with addiction and mental illness clouded the broader social patterns and issues we hope to illuminate in this book. However, the public outline of Schwyzer's saga we see as indicative—albeit of course, in an extreme way—of the everyday patterns of male privilege and scrutiny faced by men in the field.

22. For an expanded discussion of men and accountability, see Ben Atherton-Zeman. 2009. "Minimizing the damage—Male accountability in stopping men's violence against women." *The Voice: The Journal of the Battered Women's Movement* (Spring): 8–13.

23. Jackson Katz. 2013. "Violence against women: It's a men's issue." TED talk. http://www.ted.com/talks/jackson_katz_violence_against_women_it_s_a_men_s_issue.html.

24. A psychologist and co-founder of NOMAS, Brannon is perhaps best known among gender studies scholars as coauthor of one of the first texts on men and masculinity. Deborah Sarah David and Robert Brannon. 1976. *The forty-nine percent majority: The male sex role*. New York: Addison-Wesley.

25. See Emi Koyama. 2013. "Silencing and intimidation of women of color at 'Men against sexism' conference." *Shakesville* (August 14). http://www.shakesville. com/2013/08/silencing-and-intimidation-of-women-of.html.

26. For a scholarly presentation of this transnational feminist reframing of trafficking as a labor issue, see Rhacel Salazar Parrenas. 2011. *Illicit flirtations: Labor, migration, and sex trafficking in Tokyo.* Stanford, CA: Stanford University Press.

27. A feminist antipornography coalition has revived in recent years, largely around the writings and organizational work of Gail Dines and Robert Jensen. See Gail Dines 2011. *Pornland: How pornography has hijacked our sexuality.* Boston: Beacon Press; Robert Jensen. 2007. *Getting off: Pornography and the end of masculinity.* Cambridge, MA: South End Press.

CHAPTER 6

1. Pearce, Matt. 2013. "Air Force sex-assault chief arrested on sexual battery charges." *Los Angeles Times,* May 6.

2. The *New York Times* article references a Defense Department survey of the three U.S. military academies that found 51 percent of academy women and 10 percent of men reported having been sexually harassed during the previous year. Twelve percent of women and 2 percent of men reported experiencing "unwanted sexual contact." "The military's dirty secret." 2012. Editorial. *New York Times,* December 30. http://www.nytimes.com/2012/12/31/opinion/ the-militarys-dirty-secret.html?emc=eta1and_r=0. For the original report, see U.S. Department of Defense. 2012. *Annual report on sexual harassment and violence at the military service academies: Academic program year 2011–2012.* Department of Defense, generated on 2012 Dec 06 RefID: D-4399D8B.

3. The 2012 *New York Times* references "an unpublished report by the Veterans Affairs Department" that surveyed recently returned veterans of the Afghanistan and Iraq wars and found that "nearly half of the women and 10 percent of the men said they had been sexually harassed at least once while they were deployed, and 23 percent of women reported at least one sexual assault." "The military's dirty secret." 2012. Editorial. *New York Times,* December 30. http://www.nytimes.com/2012/12/31/opinion/the-militarys-dirty-secret. html?emc=eta1and_r=0.

4. In 2009, the *New York Times* reported escalating rates of rape, sexual assault, domestic violence, and homicide committed by Army men who had returned from multiple deployments to the war in Iraq. Lizette Alvarez and Dan Frosch. 2009. "A focus on violence by returning G.I.'s." *New York Times* (January 1). The Veterans Administration now targets domestic violence as a major problem on its website, pointing especially to the finding that returning veterans with PTSD are two to three times more likely than other veterans to engage in intimate partner violence. See U.S. Department of Veterans Affairs. 2013. "Intimate partner violence." http://www.ptsd.va.gov/public/pages/ domestic-violence.asp.

5. The 2012 Academy Award– and Emmy-nominated documentary *The Invisible War* received a great deal of critical praise, helping to raise critical awareness that fueled congressional hearings on sexual violence in the military.

6. U.S. Department of Education. 2014. "U.S. department of education releases list of higher education institutions with open Title IX sexual violence investigations." (May 1). http://www.ed.gov/news/press-releases/

us-department-education-releases-list-higher-education-institutions-open-title-i.

7. Controversy erupted in 2013 when news broke that Florida State University officials may have quashed a woman student's accusation that star quarterback Jameis Winston sexually assaulted her. Journalist Tim Murphey put this case into the context of a history of such assaults, attempts at institutional cover-ups, and dearth of holding perpetrators accountable. Tim Murphey. 2013. "Forty Years of College Football's Sexual Assault Problem." *Mother Jones* (December 5). http://www.motherjones.com/media/2013/12/college-football-sexual-assualt-jameis-winston

8. See Michael A. Messner. 2005. "The triad of violence in men's sports." In E. Buchwald, P. R. Fletcher, and M. Roth, eds. *Transforming a rape culture.* Minneapolis, MN: Milkweed Editions; Peggy Sanday. 1990. *Fraternity gang rape: Sex, brotherhood and privilege on campus.* New York: New York University Press; C. J. Pascoe 2011. *Dude, you're a fag: Masculinity and sexuality in high school.* Berkeley: University of California Press.

9. See Michael A. Messner and Mark A. Stevens. 2002. "Scoring without consent: Confronting male athletes' violence against women." In Margaret Gatz, Michael A. Messner, and Sandra J. Ball-Rokeach, eds. *Paradoxes of youth and sport,* pp. 225–240. Albany: State University of New York Press.

10. Sociologist Jeffrey Montez de Oca has discussed the history of college football in the United States as reflecting a Cold War policy of "containment"—not just of communism, but of a feared softening of American masculinity. Jeffrey Montez de Oca. 2013. *Discipline and indulgence: College football, media, and the American way of life during the Cold War.* New Brunswick, NJ: Rutgers University Press.

11. Eric Anderson and Edward M. Kian. 2012. "Examining media contestation of masculinity and head trauma in the National Football League." *Men and Masculinities* 15: 152–173.

12. Drawing from medical research, Crosset notes that men who have experienced head injuries—including sports-related head injuries—are six times more likely to engage in battery and other forms of marital violence. Todd Crosset. 2000. "Athletic affiliation and violence against women: Toward a structural prevention project." In Jim McKay, Michael A. Messner and Don Sabo, eds. *Masculinities, gender relations, and sport,* pp. 147–161. Thousand Oaks, CA: Sage.

13. Michael Kaufman. 1987. "The construction of masculinity and the triad of men's violence." In Michael Kaufman, ed. *Beyond patriarchy: Essays by men on pleasure, power and change.* Toronto and New York: Oxford University Press; Messner 2005.

14. Though Eliasoph was not studying antiviolence activists or professionals, her cautionary analysis of the limits of volunteerism is useful for raising questions about some public antiviolence events today, such as for instance the "walk a mile in her shoes" events discussed in Chapter 5. Eliasoph examines "empowerment projects" that are "morally magnetic . . . most Americans, including myself, find them to be simply and almost irresistibly good, for reasons that we assume don't need much further explanation." But she observes that youth empowerment projects that aim, for instance, to help feed the poor operate by "severing any connection between civic volunteering and political engagement," thus breeding "hopelessness about finding any solutions." These programs, she concludes, amount to "civic and political engagement disconnected." Nina Eliasoph.

2011. *Making volunteers: Civic life after welfare's end*. Princeton, NJ: Princeton University Press (quotes from pp. x, 12, and 114).

15. See Suzanne Staggenborg. 1988. "The consequences of professionalization and formalization in the pro-choice movement." *American Sociological Review* 53: 585–605; Suzanne Staggenborg and Verta Taylor. 2005. "What ever happened to the women's movement?" *Mobilization: An International Journal* 10: 37–52.

16. James M. Jasper. 2004. "A strategic approach to collective action: Looking for agency in social movement choices." *Mobilization: An International Journal* 9: 1–16, quote from p. 7.

17. Patricia Yancey Martin. 2009. "Rape crisis centers: helping victims, changing society." In Y. Hasenfeld, ed. *Human service organizations*. Second ed. Thousand Oaks, CA: Sage.

18. Laurel Westbrook. 2014. "Interchangeable victims? How identity-based antiviolence activism can obscure patterns of violence." *Sex and Gender News: Newsletter for the Sex and Gender Section of the American Sociological Association* (spring), pp. 2–3.

19. For a foundational work in feminist therapy, see Lenore E. A. Walker. 1990. "A feminist therapist views the case." In Dorothy W. Cantor, ed. *Women as therapists*, pp. 78–79. New York: Spring.

20. Also see Rob A. Okun 2014. *Voice male: The untold story of the pro-feminist men's movement*. Northampton, MA: Interlink Publication Group.

21. Jackson Katz, H. Alan Heisterkamp, and Wm. Michael Fleming. 2011. "The social justice roots of the Mentors in Violence Prevention model and its application in a high school setting." *Violence Against Women* 17: 684–702.

22. Suzanne Beechy. 2005. "When feminism is your job: Age and power in women's policy organizations." In Jo Reger, ed. *Different wavelengths: Studies of the contemporary women's movement*, pp. 117–136. New York: Routledge, quote from p. 124.

23. See Doug Meyer. 2012. "An intersectional analysis of lesbian, gay, bisexual, and transgender (LGBT) people's evaluations of anti-queer violence." *Gender & Society* 26: 849–873.

24. In an introduction to a special issue of *Signs* devoted to intersectionality, Sumi Cho, Kimberlé Crenshaw, and Leslie McCall argue that although intersectionality has had a powerful impact across various fields of academic inquiry, it is not simply an academic endeavor. Rather, they argue, "praxis"—the joining of theory and action seen in on-the-ground progressive movements for social justice—"has been a key site of intersectional critique and intervention." One such field of praxis, we are suggesting, is antiviolence work. Sumi Cho, Kimberlé Williams Crenshaw, and Leslie McCall. 2013. "Toward a field of intersectionality studies: theory, applications, and praxis." *Signs* 38: 785–810, quote from p. 786.

25. Medical anthropologist Arthur Kleinman argues for an expansive definition of violence, including "The hidden injuries of class, the wounding of the self under racialism, the spoiling of identity due to stigmatizing social conditions, the variety of forms of violence toward women: all are salient." Such an approach, he argues, will illuminate the limits of "standard approaches of policies and intervention programs." Arthur Kleinman. 2000. "The violences of every day life." In Venna Das, Arthur Kleinman, Mamphela Ramphele, and Pamela Reynolds, eds. *Violence and subjectivity*, pp. 226–241. Berkeley: University of California Press, quote from p. 227.

26. Patricia Hill Collins. 2013. "The ethos of violence.", In Patricia Hill Collins. *On intellectual activism*, pp. 187–197. Philadelphia: Temple University Press, quotes from pp. 190, 197.

27. For a recent example, a study of violence in India that sheds light on violence in the United States, see Bandana Purkayastha and Kathryn Strother Ratcliff. 2014. "Routine violence: Intersectionality at the interstices." In Marcia Texler Segal and Vasilikie Demos, eds. *Gendered perspectives on conflict and violence (Part B)*, pp. 19–44. Bingley, UK: Emerald.

28. See, for instance, Rosa-Linda Fregoso and Cynthia Bejarano, eds., 2010. *Terrorizing women: Feminicide in the Americas*. Durham and London: Duke University Press; Aili Tripp, Myra Marx Ferree, and Christina Ewig. 2013. *Gender, violence and human security: Critical feminist perspectives*. New York: New York University Press.

29. Michealeen Doucleff and Rhitu Chatterjee. 2013. "WHO finds violence against women is 'shockingly' common." *NPR News*, June 20. http://www.npr.org/blogs/health/2013/06/20/193475321/who-finds-violence-against-wo men-is-shockingly-common.

30. Kristin Bumiller argues, for instance, that feminist collaboration with the neoliberal state has gutted the feminism from antiviolence work. Our research suggests that this view is too extreme, that in fact feminism has changed but is still present in various forms in antiviolence work. However, we do note throughout this book the strains and limitations, including the danger of movement cooptation, placed on feminist antiviolence efforts through such collaborations. See Kristin Bumiller. 2013. "Feminist collaboration with the state in response to sexual violence: Lessons from the American experience." In Alli Mari Tripp, Myra Marx Ferree, and Christina Ewing, eds. *Gender, violence, and human security: Critical feminist perspectives*, pp. 191–213. New York: New York University Press.

31. See K. S. Chibber and S. Krishan. 2011. "Confronting intimate partner violence: A global health priority." *Mt. Sinai Journal of Medicine* 78: 449–457.

32. Feminist international relations scholar Cynthia Enloe has spent a career making women visible as both objects and subjects of militarization and war, including discussing militarized rape and sexual exploitation of women. See, for example, her chapter "When soldiers rape," Cynthia Eloe. 2000. *Maneuvers: The international politics of militarizing women's lives*, pp. 108–152. Berkeley: University of California Press.

33. See S. Krishnan, C. H. Rocca, A. E. Hubbard, K. Subbiah, J. Edmeades, and N. S. Padian. 2010. "Do changes in spousal employment status lead to domestic violence? Insights from a prospective study in Bangalore, India." *Social Science and Medicine*, 70: 136–143; Shari L. Dworkin, Christopher Colvin, Abbey Hatcher, and Dean Peacock. 2012. "Men's perceptions of women's rights and changing gender relations in South Africa: Lessons for working with men and boys in HIV and antiviolence programs." *Gender & Society* 26: 97–120.

34. Shari L. Dworkin, Abbey Hatcher, Chris Colvin, and Dean Peacock. 2013. "Impact of a gender-transformative HIV and antiviolence program on gender ideologies and masculinities in two rural, South African communities." In *Men and masculinities* 16: 181-202; Shari L. Dworkin, Megan S. Dunbar, Suneeta Krishana, Abigail M. Hatcher, and Sharif Sawires. 2011. "Uncovering tensions and capitalizing on synergies in HIV/AIDS and antiviolence programs." *American Journal of Public Health* 101: 995–1003; S. Krishnan, K. Subbiah, S. Khanum, P. S. Chandra,

and N. S. Padian. 2012. "An intergenerational women's empowerment intervention to mitigate domestic violence: Results of a pilot study in Bengaluru, India." *Violence Against Women*, 183: 346–370; Julia C. Kim, Charlotte H. Watts, James R. Hargreaves, Luceth X. Ndhlovu, Godfrey Phetla, and Linda A. Morison. 2007. "Understanding the impact of a microfinance-based intervention on women's empowerment and the reduction of intimate partner violence in South Africa." *American Journal of Public Health*, 97: 1794–1802; Wessel van den Berg, Lynn Hendricks, Abigail Hatcher, Patrick Godana, and Shari Dworkin. 2013. "'One man can': Shifts in fatherhood beliefs and parenting practices following a gender-transformative programme in South Africa." *Gender and Development* 21: 111–125.

35. Raewyn Connell. 1995. *Masculinities*. Berkeley: University of California Press, quote from p. 237.
36. There is some evidence, in fact, that growing global awareness of violence against women is helping to spur the growth and global connections of a renewed feminist movement. See Soraya Chemaly. 2013. "Mapping a feminist world: Violence against women activates a new global network." *Ms. Magazine* (fall), pp. 20–21.
37. Women Peacemakers Program. 2010. *Pilot training of trainers cycle 2009–2010: Final report of the first training block (2009)*. Netherlands: International Fellowship of Reconciliation, quote from p. 41.
38. Cecilia Menjivar. 2011. *Enduring violence: Ladina women's lives in Guatemala*. Berkeley: University of California Press.

REFERENCES

Ahrens, Lois. 1980. "Battered women's refuges: Feminist cooperatives vs. social service institutions." *Radical America* 14: 41–48.

Alcalde, M. Cristina. 2011. "Masculinities in motion: Latino men and violence in Kentucky." *Men and Masculinities* 14: 450–469.

Allen, Pamela. 1970. *Free space: A perspective on the small group in women's liberation.* New York: Times Change Press.

Alvarez, Lizette, and Dan Frosch. 2009. "A focus on violence by returning G.I.'s." *New York Times* (January 1).

Anderson, Eric, and Edward M. Kian. 2012. "Examining media contestation of masculinity and head trauma in the National Football League." *Men and Masculinities* 15: 152–173.

Andler, Judy, and Gail Sullivan. 1989. "The price of government funding." *Aegis: Magazine on Ending Violence Against Women* (winter/spring): 10–15.

Atherton-Zeman, Ben. 2009. "Minimizing the damage—Male accountability in stopping men's violence against women." *The Voice: The Journal of the Battered Women's Movement* (Spring): 8–13.

Baca Zinn, Maxine, Lynn Weber Cannon, Elizabeth Higgenbotham, and Bonnie Thornton Dill. 1986. "The costs of exclusionary practices in women's studies." *Signs: Journal of Women in Culture and Society* 11: 290–303.

Bagguley Paul. 2002. "Contemporary British feminism: A social movement in abeyance?" *Social Movement Studies* 1: 169–185.

Barber, Kristen, and Kelsey Kretchmer. 2013. "Walking like a man?" *Contexts* 12: 40–45.

Baumli, Francis, ed. 1985. *Men freeing men: Exploding the myth of the traditional male.* Jersey City, NJ: New Atlantis Press.

Beechy, Suzanne. 2005. "When feminism is your job: Age and power in women's policy organizations." In Jo Reger, ed. *Different wavelengths: Studies of the contemporary women's movement*, pp. 117–136. New York: Routledge.

Beneke, Timothy. 1982. *Men on rape.* New York: St. Martin's Press.

Boal, Augusto. 1993. *Theatre of the oppressed.* New York: Theatre Communications Group.

Breeze, William. 2007. "Constructing a male feminist pedagogy: Authority, practice, and authenticity in the composition classroom." *Feminist Teacher* 18: 59–73.

Bridges, Tristan S. 2010. "Men just weren't made to do this: Performances of drag at 'Walk a Mile in Her Shoes' marches." *Gender & Society* 24: 5–30.

Brod, Harry. 1983–84. "Work clothes and leisure suits: The class basis and bias of the men's movement." *M: Gentle Men for Gender Justice* 11: 10–12, 38–40.

Brod, Harry. 1987. *The making of masculinities: The new men's studies.* Boston: Allen & Unwin.

Brod, Harry. 1988. *A mensch among men: Explorations in Jewish masculinity.* Freedom, CA: Crossing Press.

Brod, Harry, and Shawn Zevit. 2010. *Brother keepers: New perspectives on Jewish masculinity.* Harriman, TN: Men's Studies Press.

Bronstein, Carolyn. 2011. *Battling pornography: The American feminist anti-pornography movement, 1976–1986.* New York: Cambridge University Press.

Brownmiller, Susan. 1975. *Against our will: Men, women and rape.* New York: Simon & Schuster.

Budig, Michelle J. 2002. "Male advantage and the gender composition of jobs: Who rides the glass escalator?" *Social Problems* 49: 258–277.

Bumiller, Kristin. 2013. "Feminist collaboration with the state in response to sexual violence: Lessons from the American experience." In Alli Mari Tripp, Myra Marx Ferree, and Christina Ewing, eds. *Gender, violence, and human security: Critical feminist perspectives,* pp. 191–213. New York: New York University Press.

Butler, Jess. 2013. "For white girls only? Postfeminism and the politics of inclusion." *Feminist Formations* 25: 35–58.

Canada, Geoffrey. 1995. *Fist, stick, knife, gun: A personal history of violence in America.* Boston: Beacon Press.

Casey, Erin. 2010. "Strategies for engaging men as anti-violence allies: Implications for ally movements." *Advances in Social Work* 11: 267–282.

Casey, Erin, and Tyler Smith. 2010. "How can I not? Men's pathways to involvement in anti-violence against women work." *Violence Against Women* 16: 953–973.

Chemaly, Soraya. 2013. "Mapping a feminist world: Violence against women activates a new global network." *Ms. Magazine* (fall): 20–21.

Chibber, K. S., and S. Krishan. 2011. "Confronting intimate partner violence: A global health priority." *Mt. Sinai Journal of Medicine* 78: 449–457.

Cho, Sumi, Kimberlé Williams Crenshaw, and Leslie McCall. 2013. "Toward a field of intersectionality studies: Theory, applications, and praxis." *Signs* 38: 785–810.

Chun, Wendy Hui Kyong. 1999. "Unbearable witness: Toward a politics of listening." *Differences: A Journal of Feminist Cultural Studies* 11: 112–149.

Collins, Patricia Hill. 1990. *Black feminist thought: Knowledge, consciousness, and the politics of empowerment.* Boston: Unwin Hyman.

Collins, Patricia Hill. 2013. "The ethos of violence." In Patricia Hill Collins, *On intellectual activism,* pp. 187–197. Philadelphia: Temple University Press.

Connell, Raewyn. 1987. *Gender & power.* Stanford, CA: Stanford University Press.

Connell, Raewyn. 1995. *Masculinities.* Berkeley: University of California Press.

Connell, Raewyn. 2010. "Lives of the businessmen: Reflections on life-history method and contemporary hegemonic masculinity." *Österreichische Zeitschrift für Soziologie* 35: 54–71.

Corrigan, Rose. 2013. *Up against the wall: Rape reform and the failure of success.* New York and London: New York University Press.

Creighton, Allan, and Paul Kivel. 2011. *Helping teens stop violence, build community and stand for justice* (Second ed.). Alameda, CA: Hunter House.

Crosset, Todd. 2000. "Athletic affiliation and violence against women: Toward a structural prevention project." In Jim McKay, Michael A. Messner, and Don

Sabo, eds. *Masculinities, gender relations, and sport*, pp. 147–161. Thousand Oaks, CA: Sage.

Crosset, Todd W., Jeffrey R. Benedict, and Mark McDonald. 1995. "Male student athletes reported for sexual assault: A survey of campus police departments and judicial affairs offices." *Journal of Sport and Social Issues* 19: 126–140.

Crosset, Todd, J. Ptacek, Jeffrey R. Benedict, and Mark McDonald. 1996. "Male student athletes and violence against women: A survey of campus judicial affairs offices." *Violence Against Women* 2: 163–179.

Curry, Timothy. 1991. "Fraternal bonding in the locker room: Pro-feminist analysis of talk about competition and women." *Sociology of Sport Journal* 8: 119–135.

Curry, Timothy. 2000. "Booze and bar fights: A journey to the dark side of college athletics." In Jim McKay, Donald F. Sabo, and Michael A. Messner, eds. *Masculinities, gender relations, and sport*, pp. 162–175. Thousand Oaks, CA: Sage.

D'Agostino, Kristin. 2009. "HAWC embraces new name, new mission." *Wicked Local Salem*, March 26. http://www.wickedlocal.com/salem/news/x1672264504/HAWC-embraces-new-name-new-mission.

Dahlberg, Linda L., and James A. Mercy. 2009. *The history of violence as a public health issue*. Atlanta: Centers for Disease Control and Prevention, Division of Violence Prevention (DVP) Annual Report.

Daniels, Jessie. 2009. "Rethinking cyberfeminism(s): Race, gender and embodiment." *Women's Studies Quarterly* 37: 101–124.

David, Deborah Sarah, and Robert Brannon. 1976. *The forty-nine percent majority: The male sex role*. New York: Addison-Wesley.

Davis, Angela. 1981. *Woman, race and class*. New York: Vintage Books.

Davis, Kathy. 1994. *Reshaping the female body: The dilemma of cosmetic surgery*. New York: Routledge.

DeGue, Sarah, Thomas R. Simon, Kathleen C. Basile, Sue Lin Yee, Karen Lang, and Howard Spivak. 2012. "Moving forward by looking back: Reflecting on a decade of CDC's work in sexual violence prevention, 2000–2010." *Journal of Women's Health* 21: 1211–1218.

Dines, Gail. 2011. *Pornland: How pornography has hijacked our sexuality*. Boston: Beacon Press.

Dragiewicz, Molly. 2008. "Patriarchy reasserted: Fathers' rights and anti-VAWA activism." *Feminist Criminology* 3: 121–144.

Dragiewicz, Molly. 2011. *Equality with a vengeance: Men's rights groups, battered women, and antifeminist backlash*. Boston: Northeastern University Press.

Dube, S. R., R. F. Anda, C. L. Whitfield, et al. 2005. "Long-term consequences of childhood sexual abuse by gender of victim." *American Journal of Preventive Medicine* 28: 430–438.

Dworkin, Andrea. 1977. *Why so-called radical men love and need pornography*. Palo Alto, CA: Frog in the Well.

Dworkin, Andrea. 1980. "Pornography and grief." In Laura Lederer, ed. *Take back the night: Women on pornography*, pp. 286–291. New York: William Morrow.

Dworkin, Andrea. (1983). 1993. "I want a 24-hour truce during which there is no rape." In *Letters from a war zone*, pp. 162–171. Chicago: Lawrence Hill Books.

Dworkin, Shari L., Megan S. Dunbar, Suneeta Krishana, Abigail M. Hatcher, and Sharif Sawires. 2011. "Uncovering tensions and capitalizing on synergies in HIV/AIDS and antiviolence programs." *American Journal of Public Health* 101: 995–1003.

Dworkin, Shari L., Christopher Colvin, Abbey Hatcher, and Dean Peacock. 2012. "Men's perceptions of women's rights and changing gender relations in South Africa: Lessons for working with men and boys in HIV and antiviolence programs." *Gender & Society* 26: 97–120.

Dworkin, Shari L., Abbey Hatcher, Chris Colvin, and Dean Peacock. 2013. "Impact of a gender-transformative HIV and antiviolence program on gender ideologies and masculinities in two rural, South African communities." *Men and Masculinities* 16: 181–202.

Echols, Alice. (1984). 2002. "The taming of the id: Feminist sexual politics, 1968–1983." In Alice Echols, *Shaky ground: The sixties and its aftershocks*, pp. 108–128. New York: Columbia University Press.

Edwards, Wade. 2008. "Teaching women with a Y-chromosome: Do men make better feminists?" *Feminist Teacher* 18: 145–159.

Eichstedt, Jennifer L. 2001. "Problematic white identities and a search for racial justice." *Sociological Forum* 16: 445–470.

Eliasoph, Nina. 2011. *Making volunteers: Civic life after welfare's end*. Princeton, NJ: Princeton University Press.

Enloe, Cynthia. 1988. *Bananas, beaches and bases: Making feminist sense of international politics*. Berkeley: University of California Press.

Enloe, Cynthia. 2000. *Maneuvers: The international politics of militarizing women's lives*. Berkeley: University of California Press.

Enloe, Cynthia. 2004. *The curious feminist: Searching for women in a new age of empire*. Berkeley: University of California Press.

Fabiano, Patricia M., H. Wesley Perkins, Alan Berkowitz, Jeff Linkenbach, and Christopher Stark. 2003. "Engaging men as social justice allies in ending violence against women: Evidence for a social norms approach." *Journal of American College Health* 52: 105–112.

Faludi, Susan. 1991. *Backlash: The undeclared war against American women*. New York: Crown.

Farrell, Warren. 1974. *The liberated man*. New York: Random House.

Farrell, Warren. 1993. *The myth of male power: Why men are the disposable sex*. New York: Simon & Schuster.

Feinglass, Robert Allen. 1981. *Male adjusted feminism: A history of an anti-sexist men's organization*. Master's thesis, San Francisco State University.

Fisher, B. S., F. T. Cullen, and M. G. Turner. 1999. "Extent and nature of the sexual victimization of college women: A national level analysis." National Institute of Justice (December) NCJ 179977: 1–2.

Flood, Michael. 2011. "Involving men in efforts to end violence against women." *Men and Masculinities* 14: 358–377.

Flood, Michael. 2011. "Men as students and teachers of feminist scholarship." *Men and masculinities* 14: 135–154.

Flood, Michael. 2003. "Men's collective struggles for gender justice: The case of anti-violence activism." In Michael Kimmel, Jeff Hearn, and R. W. Connell, eds. *The handbook of studies on men and masculinities*, pp. 458–466. Thousand Oaks, CA: Sage

Fogg, Piper. 2009. "Rape-prevention programs proliferate, but 'It's hard to know' whether they work." *Chronicle of Higher Education*. (November 15). Retrieved from http://chronicle.com/article/Rape-Prevention-Programs/49151/.

Foubert, J. D., J. T. Newberry, and J. L. Tatum. 2007. "Behavior differences seven months later: Effects of a rape prevention program on first-year men who join fraternities." *Journal of Student Affairs Research and Practice*, 44: 728–749.

Franzway, Suzanne, Dianne Court, and R. W. Connell. 1989. *Staking a claim: Feminism, bureaucracy and the state*. Sydney: Allen & Unwin.

Fregoso, Rosa-Linda, and Cynthia Bejarano, eds. 2010. *Terrorizing women: Femicide in the Americas*. Durham and London: Duke University Press.

Fried, Amy. 1994. "It's hard to change what we want to change: Rape crisis centers as organizations." *Gender & Society* 8: 562–583.

Gidycz, Christine A., Lindsay M. Orchowski, and Alan Berkowitz. 2011. "Preventing sexual aggression among college men: An evaluation of a social norms and bystander intervention program." *Violence Against Women* 17: 720–742.

Giffort, Danielle M.. 2011. "Feminist dilemmas and implicit feminism at girls' rock camp." *Gender & Society* 25: 569–588.

Gilmore, Ruth Wilson. 2007. "In the shadow of the shadow state." In INCITE! Women of Color Against Violence, ed., *The revolution will not be funded: Beyond the non-profit industrial complex*, pp. 41–52. Cambridge, MA: South End Press.

Goldberg, Herb. 1976. *The hazards of being male: Surviving the myth of masculine privilege*. New York: Signet.

Gordon, Linda. 1990. "The peaceful sex? On feminism and the peace movement." *NWSA Journal* 2: 624–634.

Greenberg, Max A., and Messner, Michael A. 2014. "Before prevention: The trajectory and tensions of feminist anti-violence." In Marcia Texler Segal and Vasilikie Demos, eds. *Gendered perspectives on conflict and violence (Part B)*, pp. 225–250. Bingley, UK: Emerald.

Griffin, Susan. 1971. "Rape: The all-American crime." *Ramparts*. September, pp. 26–35.

Heywood, Leslie, and Jennifer Drake, eds. 1997. *Third wave agenda: Being feminist, doing feminism*. Minneapolis: University of Minnesota Press.

Hoch, Paul. 1979. *White hero black beast: Racism, sexism and the mask of masculinity*. London: Pluto Press.

Hochschild, Arlie Russell (with Anne Machung). 1989. *The second shift: Working parents and the revolution at home*. New York: Viking.

Holland, Laurel L., and Sherry Cable. 2002. "Reconceptualizing social movement abeyance: The role of internal process and culture in cycles of movement abeyance and resurgence." *Sociological Focus* 35: 297–314.

Hollander, Jocelyn A. 2009. "The roots of resistance to women's self-defense." *Violence Against Women* 15: 574–594.

Hollander, Jocelyn A. 2014. "Does self-defense training prevent sexual violence against women?" *Violence Against Women*. 20: 252–269.

hooks, bell. 1984. *Feminist theory: From margin to center*. Boston: South End Press.

Hughey, Matthew W. 2012. "Stigma allure and white antiracist identity management." *Social Psychology Quarterly* 75: 219–241.

Hull, Gloria T., Patricia Bell Scott, and Barbara Smith, eds. 1993. *All the women are white, all the blacks are men, but some of us are brave*. CUNY: Feminist Press.

Jasper, James M. 2004. "A strategic approach to collective action: Looking for agency in social movement choices." *Mobilization: An International Journal* 9: 1–16.

Jasper, James M. 2011. "Emotions and social movements: Twenty years of theory and research." *Annual Review of Sociology* 37: 1–14.

Jaycox, Lisa H., Daniel McCaffrey, Beth Eiseman, Jessica Aronoff, Gene A. Shelley, Rebecca L. Collins, and Grant N. Marshall. 2006. "Impact of a school-based dating violence prevention program among Latino teens: Randomized controlled effectiveness trial." *Journal of Adolescent Health* 39: 694–704.

Jensen, Robert. 2007. *Getting off: Pornography and the end of masculinity*. Cambridge, MA: South End Press.

Johnson, John M. 1981. "Program Enterprise and official cooptation in the battered women's shelter movement." *American Behavioral Scientist* 24: 827–842.

Kandiyoti, Deniz. 1988. "Bargaining with patriarchy." *Gender & Society* 2: 274–290.

Katz, Jackson. 2006. *The Macho Paradox: Why some men hurt women and how all men can help.* Naperville, IL: Sourcebooks.

Katz, Jackson. 2010. "Not-so-nice Jewish boys: Notes on violence and the construction of Jewish-American masculinity in the late 20th and early 21st century." In Harry Brod and Shawn Zevit, eds. *Brother keepers: New perspectives on Jewish masculinity*, pp. 57–75. Harriman, TN: Men's Studies Press.

Katz, Jackson. 2013. "Violence against women: It's a men's issue." TED talk. http://www.ted.com/talks/jackson_katz_violence_against_women_it_s_a_men_s_issue.html.

Katz, Jackson, H. Alan Heisterkamp, and W. Michael Fleming. 2011. "The social justice roots of the Mentors in Violence Prevention model and its application in a high school setting." *Violence Against Women* 17: 684–702.

Kaufman, Michael. 1987. "The construction of masculinity and the triad of men's violence." In Michael Kaufman, ed. *Beyond patriarchy: Essays by men on pleasure, power and change.* Pp. 1-29. Toronto and New York: Oxford University Press.

Kim, Julia C., Charlotte H. Watts, James R. Hargreaves, Luceth X. Ndhlovu, Godfrey Phetla, and Linda A. Morison. 2007. "Understanding the impact of a microfinance-based intervention on women's empowerment and the reduction of intimate partner violence in South Africa." *American Journal of Public Health* 97: 1794–1802.

Kimmel, Michael S., ed. 1985. "Men confronting pornography." Special issue. *Changing Men: Issues in Gender, Sex and Politics* 15 (fall).

Kimmel, Michael S. 1987. "Judaism, masculinity and feminism." *Changing Men* (summer/fall).

Kimmel, Michael S., ed. 1990. *Men confront pornography.* New York: Crown.

Kimmel, Michael S., and Thomas E. Mosmiller. 1992. *Against the tide: Pro-feminist men in the United States, a documentary history.* Boston: Beacon Press.

Kivel, Paul. 2007. "Social service or social change." In INCITE! Women of Color Against Violence, ed., *The revolution will not be funded: Beyond the non-profit industrial complex*, pp. 129–149. Cambridge, MA: South End Press.

Kleinman, Arthur. 2000. "The violences of every day life." In Venna Das, Arthur Kleinman, Mamphela Ramphele, and Pamela Reynolds, eds. *Violence and subjectivity*, pp. 226–241. Berkeley: University of California Press,

Koedt, Ann. 1968. "The myth of the vaginal orgasm." In *Notes from the first year.* New York: Radical Women.

Koyama, Emi. 2013. "Silencing and intimidation of women of color at 'Men against sexism' conference." *Shakesville* (August 14). http://www.shakesville.com/2013/08/silencing-and-intimidation-of-women-of.html.

Kreager, Derek A. 2007. "Unnecessary roughness? School sports, peer networks, and male adolescent violence." *American Sociological Review* 72: 705–724.

Krebs, Christopher P., Christine H. Lindquist, Tara D. Warner, Bonnie S. Fisher, and Sandra L. Martin. 2007. *The Campus Sexual Assault (CSA) study.* National Institute of Justice (January). NIJ. 2004-WG-BX-0010.

Krishnan, S., C. H. Rocca, A. E. Hubbard, K. Subbiah, J. Edmeades, and N. S. Padian. 2010. "Do changes in spousal employment status lead to domestic violence?

Insights from a prospective study in Bangalore, India." *Social Science and Medicine*, 70(1): 136–143.

Krishnan, S., K. Subbiah, S. Khanum, P. S. Chandra, and N. S. Padian. 2012. "An intergenerational women's empowerment intervention to mitigate domestic violence: Results of a pilot study in Bengaluru, India." *Violence Against Women* 18: 346–370.

Lainer-Vos, Dan. 2014. "Masculinities in interaction: The co-production of Israeli and American Jewish men in philanthropic fundraising events." *Men and Masculinities* 17: 43–66.

Langhinrichsen-Rohling, Jennifer, John D. Foubert, Hope M. Brasfield, Brent Hill, and Shannon Shelley-Tremblay. 2011. "The men's program: Does it impact college men's self-reported bystander efficacy and willingness to intervene?" *Violence Against Women* 17: 743–759.

Lederer, Laura, ed. 1980. *Take back the night: Women on pornography.* New York: William Morrow.

Lee, David. 2011. "What are we working for? New names of sexual violence and domestic violence organizations." *PreventConnect*, April 25, 2011. http://www.preventconnect.org/2011/04/new-names-of-sexual-violence-domestic-violence-organizations/.

Lee, David. 2012. "Moving upstream 2.0." *Prevention*, May 15, 2012. http://calcasa.org/prevention/moving-upstream-2-0/.

Lichterman, Paul. 1989. "Making a politics of masculinity." *Comparative Social Research* 11: 185–208.

Lorde, Audre. 1984. "The master's tools will never dismantle the master's house." *Sister outsider: Essays and speeches.* Berkeley, CA: Crossing Press.

Magarik, Raphael. 2012. "Exile in gal-ville: How a male feminist alienated his supporters." *Atlantic* (February 13). http://www.theatlantic.com/national/archive/2012/02/exile-in-gal-ville-how-a-male-feminist-alienated-his-supporters/252915/?single_page=true.

Markowitz, Lisa, and Karen W. Tice. 2002. "Paradoxes of professionalization: Parallel dilemmas in women's organizations in the Americas." *Gender & Society* 16: 941–958.

Martin, Patricia Yancey. 1990. "Rethinking feminist organizations." *Gender & Society* 4: 182–206.

Martin, Patricia Yancey (with F. E. Schmitt). 2007. "The history of the anti-rape and rape crisis center movements." In Clarie M. Renezetti and Jeffery Edleson, eds. *Encyclopedia of interpersonal violence.* Thousand Oaks, CA: Sage;

Martin, Patricia Yancey. 2009. "Rape crisis centers: Helping victims, changing society." In Y. Hasenfeld, ed., *Human service organizations.* Second ed. Thousand Oaks, CA: Sage.

McCabe, Janice. 2005. "What's in a label? The relationship between feminist self-identification and 'feminist' attitudes among U.S. women and men." *Gender & Society* 19: 480–505.

McCarthy, John D., and Mayer N. Zald. 1977. "Resource mobilization and social movements: A partial theory." *American Journal of Sociology* 82: 1212–1241.

McClurg, Carol Mueller, and John D. McCarthy. 2003. "Cultural continuity and structural change: The logic of adaptation by radical, liberal, and socialist feminists to state reconfiguration." In Lee Ann Banaszak, Karen Beckwith, and Dieter Rucht, eds. *Women's movements facing the reconfigured state*, pp. 219–241. Cambridge: Cambridge University Press.

McGann, Patrick. 2009. "A letter to Michael Murphey in response to 'Can "men" stop rape?: Visualizing gender in the "My strength is not for hurting" rape prevention campaign'." *Men and Masculinities* 12: 131–134.

McGarry, Aidan, and James Jasper. Forthcoming. "Introduction: The identity dilemma, social movements and contested identity." In Aidan McGarry and James Jasper, eds. *The identity dilemma: Social movements and collective identity.* Philadelphia: Temple University Press.

McKinlay, John B. 1974. "A case for re-focusing upstream: The political economy of illness." In *Applying behavioral science to cardiovascular risk: Proceedings of the American Heart Association Conference*, pp. 7–17. Seattle, WA, June 17–19, American Heart Association.

Men's Consciousness-Raising Group. 1971. *Unbecoming men.* Washington, NJ: Times Change Press.

Menjívar, Cecilia. 2011. *Enduring violence: Ladina women's lives in Guatemala.* Berkeley: University of California Press.

Messerschmidt, James W. 2000. *Nine lives: Adolescent masculinities, the body, and violence.* Boulder, CO: Westview Press.

Messerschmidt, James W. 2010. "The struggle for recognition: Embodied masculinity and the victim-violence cycle of bullying in secondary schools." In Michael Kehler and Michael Atkinson, eds. *Boys' bodies: Speaking the unspoken*, pp. 113–131. New York: Peter Lang.

Messner, Michael A. 1997. *Politics of masculinities: Men in movements.* Lanham, MD: Alta Mira Press.

Messner, Michael A. 1998. "The limits of 'the male sex role': The discourse of the men's liberation and men's rights movements." *Gender & Society* 12: 255–276.

Messner, Michael A. 2005. "The triad of violence in men's sports." In E. Buchwald, P. R. Fletcher, and M. Roth, eds. *Transforming a rape culture.* Minneapolis, MN: Milkweed Editions.

Messner, Michael A. 2011. "The privilege of teaching about privilege." *Sociological Perspectives* 54: 3–13.

Messner, Michael A., and Mark A. Stevens. 2002. "Scoring without consent: Confronting male athletes' violence against women." In Margaret Gatz, Michael A. Messner, and Sandra J. Ball-Rokeach, eds. *Paradoxes of youth and sport*, pp. 225–240. Albany: State University of New York Press.

Messner, Michael A., and Nancy M. Solomon. 2007. "Social justice and men's interests: The case of Title IX." *Journal of Sport and Social Issues* 31: 162–178.

Meyer, Doug. 2012. "An intersectional analysis of lesbian, gay, bisexual and transgender (LGBT) people's evaluations of anti-queer violence." *Gender & Society* 26: 849–873.

"The military's dirty secret." 2012. Editorial. *New York Times*, December 30. http://www.nytimes.com/2012/12/31/opinion/the-militarys-dirty-secret.html?emc=eta1&_r=0.

Miller, Elizabeth, Daniel J. Tancredi, Heather L. McCauley, Michele R. Decker, Maria Catrina D. Virata, Heather A. Anderson, and Jay G. Silverman. 2011. "Coaching Boys into Men: A cluster-randomized controlled trial of a dating violence prevention program." *Journal of Adolescent Health* 48: S85–S86.

Mills, C. Wright. 1959. *The sociological imagination.* New York: Oxford University Press.

Montez de Oca, Jeffrey. 2013. *Discipline and indulgence: College football, media, and the American way of life during the Cold War.* New Brunswick, NJ: Rutgers University Press.

Morgan, Robin. 1970. "Goodbye to all that." *Rat.* (January).

Morgan, Robin. 1978. "Theory and practice: Pornography and rape." In *Going too far: The personal chronicle of a feminist* pp. 163–169. New York: Vintage.

Ms. Foundation for Women. 2010. *Efforts to address gender-based violence: A look at foundation funding.* Ms. Foundation for Women.

Murphey, Tim. 2013. "Forty years of college football's sexual assault problem." *Mother Jones* (December 5). http://www.motherjones.com/media/2013/12/college-football-sexual-assualt-jameis-winston.

Murphy, Michael J. 2009. "Can 'men' stop rape?: Visualizing gender in the 'My Strength Is Not for Hurting' rape prevention campaign." *Men and Masculinities* 12: 113–130.

Myers, Daniel J. 2008. "Ally identity: The politically gay." In Jo Reger, Daniel J. Myers, and Rachel L. Einwohner, eds. *Identity work in social movements*, pp.167–187. Minneapolis: University of Minnesota Press.

Nuñez Puente, Sonia. 2011. "Feminist cyberactivism: Violence against women, internet politics, and Spanish feminist praxis online." *Continuum: Journal of Media & Cultural Studies*, 25: 333–346.

Okun, Rob A. 2014. *Voice male: The untold story of the pro-feminist men's movement.* Northampton, MA: Interlink Publication Group.

Parrenas, Rhacel Salazar. 2011. *Illicit flirtations: Labor, migration, and sex trafficking in Tokyo.* Stanford, CA: Stanford University Press.

Pascoe, C. J. 2011. *Dude, you're a fag: Masculinity and sexuality in high school.* Berkeley: University of California Press.

Pearce, Matt. 2013. "Air Force sex-assault chief arrested on sexual battery charges." *Los Angeles Times*, May 6.

Peretz, Tal. (Under review). "Engaging diverse men: An intersectional analysis of men's pathways to antiviolence activism."

Peretz, Tal. (Under review). "Seeing the invisible knapsack: Feminist men's responses to the continuation of male privilege in feminist spaces."

Piccigallo, Jacqueline R., Terry G. Lilley, and Susan L. Miller. 2012. "It's cool to care about sexual violence: Men's experiences with sexual assault prevention." *Men and Masculinities* 15: 507–525.

Pleck, Joseph H., and Jack Sawyer, eds. 1974. *Men and masculinity.* Englewood Cliffs, NJ: Prentice-Hall.

Purkayastha, Bandana, and Kathryn Strother Ratcliff. 2014. "Routine violence: Intersectionality at the interstices." In Marcia Texler Segal and Vasilikie Demos, eds. *Gendered perspectives on conflict and violence (Part B)*, pp. 19–44. Bingley, UK: Emerald.

Rapp, Laura, Deeana M. Button, Benjamin Fleury-Steiner, and Ruth Fleury-Steiner. 2012. "The Internet as a tool for black feminist activism: Lessons from an online antirape protest." *Feminist Criminology* 5: 244–262.

Reed, Elizabeth, Anita Raj, Elizabeth Miller, and Jay G. Silverman. 2010. "Losing the 'gender' in gender-based violence: The missteps of research on dating and intimate partner violence." *Violence Against Women* 16: 348–354.

Reger, Jo. 2012. *Everywhere and nowhere: Contemporary feminism in the United States.* New York and Oxford: Oxford University Press.

Reynolds, Michael, Shobha Shagle, and Lekha Venkataraman. 2007. *A national census of women's and gender studies programs in U.S. institutions of higher education.* National Women's Studies Association (NORC Project 6433.01.62).

Rich, Marc D. 2010. "The interACT model: Considering rape prevention from a performance activism and social justice perspective." *Feminism & Psychology* 20: 511–528.

Rios, Victor. 2011. *Punished: Policing the lives of black and Latino boys*. New York: New York University Press.

Rupp, Leila J., and Verta Taylor.. 2003. *Drag queens at the 801 Cabaret*. Chicago: University of Chicago Press.

Russo, Chandra. 2014. "Allies forging collective identity: Embodiment and emotions on the migrant trail." *Mobilization: An International Quarterly*. 19: 489–505.

Sanday, Peggy. 1990. *Fraternity gang rape: Sex, brotherhood and privilege on campus*. New York: New York University Press.

Schilt, Kristen. 2011. *Just one of the guys? Transgender men and the persistence of gender inequality*. Chicago: University of Chicago Press.

Schlafly, Phyllis. 1981. "How to clean up America by stopping the Equal Rights Amendment." In Jerry Falwell, ed. 1981. *How you can help clean up America*, pp. 23–29 Washington, DC: Moral Majority.

Schrock, Douglas, and Irene Padavic. 2007. "Negotiating hegemonic masculinity in a batterer intervention program." *Gender & Society* 21: 625–649.

Sebastian, Michael. 2012. "Comedian Daniel Tosh tweets 'sincere' apology for rape joke." *Ragan's PR Daily* (July 11), http://www.prdaily.com/Main/Articles/12119.aspx.

Shepherd, Susan Elizabeth. 2013. "Man quits Internet: Goodbye, Hugo Schwyzer." *Hairpin* (August 1), http://thehairpin.com/2013/08/man-quits-internet-goodbye-hugo-schwyzer.

Snitow, Ann, Christine Stansell, and Sharon Thompson, eds. 1983. *Powers of desire: The politics of sexuality*. New York: Monthly Review Press.

Snodgrass, Jon, ed. 1977. *For men against sexism*. Albion, CA: Times Change Press.

Stacey, Judith, and Barrie Thorne. 1986. "The missing feminist revolution in sociology." *Social Problems* 32: 301–316.

Staggenborg, Suzanne. 1988. "The consequences of professionalization and formalization in the pro-choice movement." *American Sociological Review* 53: 585–605.

Staggenborg, Suzanne, and Verta Taylor. 2005. "What ever happened to the women's movement?" *Mobilization: An International Journal* 10: 37–52.

Stansell, Christine. 2010. *The feminist promise: 1792 to the present*. New York: Random House.

Staples, Robert. 1982. *Black masculinity: The black male's role in American society*. San Francisco: Black Scholar Press.

Steiner, Claude. 1977/1978. "Feminism for men, part I." *Issues in Radical Therapy*. 20 (fall); "Feminism for men, part II." *Issues in Radical Therapy* (spring).

Stoltenberg, John. 1989. *Refusing to be a man: Essays on sex and justice*. Portland, OR: Breitenbush Books.

Straton, Jack C. 1994. "The myth of the 'Battered Husband Syndrome'." *Masculinities* 2: 79–82.

Tarrant, Shira, ed. 2008. *Men speak out: Views on gender, sex, and power*. New York: Routledge.

Tarrant, Shira. 2009. *Men and feminism*. Berkeley, CA: Seal Press.

Taylor, Verta. 1989. "Social movement continuity: The women's movement in abeyance." *American Sociological Review* 54: 761–775.

Thompson, Becky. 2001. *A promise and a way of life: White antiracist activism*. Minneapolis: University of Minnesota Press.

Thompson, Cooper, Emmett Schaeffer, and Harry Brod, eds. 2003. *White men challenging racism: 35 Personal stories*. Durham, NC: Duke University Press.

Thorn, Clarisse. 2011. "Sex, drugs, theology, men and feminism: Interview with Hugo Schwyzer." *Feministe* (December 17). http://www.feministe.us/blog/archives/2011/12/17/sex-drugs-theology-men-feminism-interview-with-hugo-schwyzer/.

Thorne, Barrie, and Barbara Laslett, eds. 1997. *Feminist sociology: Life histories of a movement.* New Brunswick, NJ: Rutgers University Press.

Tierney, Kathleen J. 1982. "The battered women's movement and the creation of the wife beating problem." *Social Problems* 29: 207–220.

Tolson, Andrew. 1977 *The limits of masculinity: Male identity and women's liberation.* New York: Harper & Row.

Tripp, Aili, Myra Marx Ferree, and Christina Ewig. 2013. *Gender, violence and human security: Critical feminist perspectives.* New York: New York University Press.

U.S. Department of Defense. 2012. *Annual report on sexual harassment and violence at the military service academies: Academic program year. 2011–2012.* Department of Defense, generated on 2012 Dec 06 Ref ID: D-4399D8B.

U.S. Department of Education. 2014. "U.S. Department of Education releases list of higher education institutions with open Title IX sexual violence investigations." May 1. http://www.ed.gov/news/press-releases/us-department-education-releases-list-higher-education-institutions-open-title-i.

U.S. Department of Veterans Affairs. 2013. "Intimate partner violence." http://www.ptsd.va.gov/public/pages/domestic-violence.asp.

van den Berg, Wessel, Lynn Hendricks, Abigail Hatcher, Patrick Godana, and Shari Dworkin. 2013. "'One man can': Shifts in fatherhood beliefs and parenting practices following a gender-transformative programme in South Africa." *Gender & Development* 21: 111–125.

Vance, Carol S. 1993. *Pleasure and danger: Exploring female sexuality.* London: Pandora Press.

Walker, Lenore E. A. 1990. "A feminist therapist views the case." In Dorothy W. Cantor, ed., *Women as therapists*, pp. 78–79. New York: Spring.

Wallace, Michelle. 1979. *Black macho and the myth of the super-woman.* New York: Warner Books.

Warren, Mark R. 2010. *Fire in the heart: How white activists embrace racial justice.* New York: Oxford University Press.

Westbrook, Laurel. 2014. "Interchangeable victims? How identity-based antiviolence activism can obscure patterns of violence." *Sex and Gender News: Newsletter for the Sex and Gender Section of the American Sociological Association* (spring), pp. 2–3.

Whittier, Nancy. 1995. *Feminist generations: The persistence of the radical women's movement.* Philadelphia: Temple University Press.

Whittier, Nancy. 2014. "Rethinking coalitions: Antipornography feminists, conservatives, and relationships between collaborative adversarial movements." *Social Problems* 61: 175–193.

Williams, Christine. 1992. "The glass escalator: Hidden advantages for men in the 'female' professions." *Social Problems* 39: 253–267.

Williams, Christine. 2013. "The glass escalator, revisited: Gender inequality in neoliberal times." *Gender & Society* 27: 609–629.

Wingfield, Adia Harvey. 2009. "Racializing the glass escalator: Reconsidering men's experiences with women's work." *Gender & Society* 23: 5–26.

Wingfield, Adia Harvey. 2012. *No more invisible man: Race and gender in men's work.* Philadelphia: Temple University Press.

Wolch, Jennifer. 1990. *The shadow state: The government and the voluntary sector in transition.* New York: Foundation Center.

Women Peacemakers Program. 2010. *Pilot training of trainers cycle. 2009–2010: Final report of the first training block (2009).* Netherlands: International Fellowship of Reconciliation.

INDEX

Page number in *italics* denote illustrations.

academia: feminist professionals in, 182–183; women's studies classes as pathway to antiviolence work, 79–83, 112–113. *See also* college education

accountability: generational shifts, 164–168; MASV, 43, 54–59, 164–165; Movement Cohort, 52–53, 58–60; politics of, 160–164; RAVEN, 160, 164–165; to whom question, 160, 164–169

Act Like a Man Box, 70

Addison-Lamb, Mick, *57*

Afghanistan, 188

African American men: myth of the black rapist, 10; nurses, 228n10; working with ex-cons, 117. *See also* men of color

African American women, 219n17

Against Our Will (Brownmiller), 11, 27, 49

Ahrens, Lois, 67

Air Force violence prevention programs, 4–5, 170, 173, 175

Alcaraz, Nina, 8, 100, 153, 198

allies: accountability, 160–168; career benefits, 8–9, 15–16, 138–143; critical scrutiny of, 151–157; financial benefits, 8–9, 142, 144–146; gendered economy of gratitude toward, 141–142; genderized resentment of, 8–9, 16–17, 145–149; generational tensions, 146–147; insider/outsider status, 137; men of color, advantages to, 142–143; mentoring, 135–136; pedestal effect, 138–143, 149–151; rock stars and independent contractors, 5, 143–149, 158–160; strategies used by, 145, 147–154; upstream-downstream allegory, 189–190; women on

importance of, 7–9, 136, 140–141, 146; women's mistrust and fear of, 155. *See also* pathways to antiviolence work; violence prevention work, men in

ally, defined, 136, 227n1

Anderegg, Chris, 28, 40, 54, 56, 70, 86, 103, 130, 180, 192

Anonymous, 173

antifeminist men's rights movement, 51–53, 66–67

Anti-Sexist Men's Political Caucus (California), 40

Areán, Juan Carlos, 88, 104, 105, 144, 150, 194

Army, I.A.M. STRONG program, 170, *171–172*

Atascadero State Prison, 28, 47

Atherton-Zeman, Ben, 79, 82–83, 87, 88, 107–108, 128, 147, 150, 161, 168, 195

athletes: head injury-violence connection in, 176–177; high-school football players, 173; sexual assault by, 173, 174, 211n4; violence prevention programs for, 4, 82, 173, 174–176. *See also* organized sports

Athletes in Service to America (Northeastern University), 92

Atlantic, 158, 159

Australia, 13–14

Avakian, Seth, 121–122, 149–150, 197

Backlash (Faludi), 66

Barber, Kristen, 130

Barker, Gary, 77–78, 188–189, 194

Bay Area Women Against Rape (BAWAR), 28, 45

Beechy, Suzanne, 184

Beneke, Timothy, 32, 39–40, 53, 54, 192, 201
Benjamin, Jessica, 50
Benson-Robinson, 57
Beulow, Rob, 112–113, 163, 184, 199
Biden, Joe, 14, 93
black rapist, myth of the, 10
Blaney, Frank, 77, 96, 127, 132, 194
Botkin, Steven, 88
boy-on-boy violence as pathway to
    antiviolence work, 31–32, 77–78
boys and young men, working with:
    antipornography focus, 28, 54–55;
    antiviolence focus, 7, 71–73,
    85–88, 90–91, 95–96; beginning of
    organized attempts, 34; bystander
    approach, 4–5, 91, 121–123, 176,
    184, 211n3; creative subversion
    approach, 127–128; diversity in, 7;
    good-men approach, 121–123, 126,
    138, 179; honor, shift toward, 15, 138;
    MASV outreach in the schools, 27,
    54–55; middle-class bias affecting,
    46–47; My Strength approach, 5–6,
    15, 116–117, 123, 124–125, 126–127,
    132–133, 170, 171–172; organized
    sports for, 188; as pathway to
    antiviolence work, 115; politically
    correct approach limiting, 90, 122;
    projecting male feminist guilt onto,
    44, 55; transnational connections,
    187–189; Unlearning Everything
    summer camps for, 59. See also high
    school programs
boys and young men of color, working with:
    advantages for men of color, 60–61,
    117–118, 127; antiviolence focus,
    127; intersectional approach, 60–61;
    men's role in, 8; middle-class bias
    affecting, 46–47; understanding
    violence for, 60–61; violence
    prevention education, 6
Brannon, Bob, 166
Bridge Cohort (1980s–1990s): developing
    feminist consciousness, 76–83;
    distancing from feminism, 76;
    diversifying membership, 91–93;
    era of, 20, 109; pragmatic shaping
    of organizational structures,
    64–65; prochoice movement,
    63–64; professionalization and
    organization building, 67, 69–75, 89.
    See also transitional era feminism
    (1980s–1990s)

Bridges, Tristan, 128
Briggs, Jimmie, 122, 143, 156–157,
    188–189, 195
Brod, Harry, 22, 112
Bronstein, Carolyn, 26
Brownmiller, Susan, 26, 49, 59
Bucholtz, Jeffrey, 122–123, 128, 139,
    146–148, 154, 197
Building Movement Project, 183
bullying in schools, gender-based, 15
bystander approach to violence prevention,
    4–5, 91, 121–123, 176, 184, 211n3

California Anti-Sexist Men's Political
    Caucus (CAMP), 202
California Coalition Against Sexual Assault
    (CALCASA), xi, 97, 101, 103, 126–127
A Call to Men, 85, 161
Campos, James, 116–117, 200
Casal, Santiago, 30, 40–41, 46–48, 53, 56,
    191
Casey, Erin, 113
Cease Fire events, 163
Center for Domestic Peace (was Marin
    Abused Women's Services), 96
Center for the Study of Sport in Society
    (Northeastern University), 92
Center for Women and Men (University of
    Southern California), 118
Centers for Disease Control and Prevention
    (CDC), 98, 184
Changing Men, 73, 74
children, Unlearning Everything summer
    camps for, 59
Children's Self-Help Center, 86
Christian Right, 50, 67
Chun, Wendy, 220n1
Civil Rights Movement, 35, 75
Clark, Chris, 73
Clinton, Bill, 93
The Coalition of Free Men, 66
college athletic programs, 4, 82, 173, 174,
    175. See also organized sports
college campuses: men's antiviolence
    groups, 72, 73; sexual assault on, 1,
    173–174; training resident advisors,
    1; violence prevention programs,
    173–174
college campus organizations as pathway to
    antiviolence work, 79–83, 111
college education, 44, 79–83, 112–113, 116
Collins, Patricia Hill, 46–47, 186
Columbia Men Against Violence, 111

community-based organizations, 184
community radical therapy movement, 218n20
Connell, R. W., 14
Connell, Raewyn, 19, 32, 188
consciousness-raising groups: beginnings, 30, 34; as pathway to antiviolence work, 34, 37–38, 41, 42–43, 75; for women, 11, 37
Conway-Long, Don, 32, 38–39, 53, 57, 58, 65, 69–70, 86, 107, 108, 139, 160, 164, 192
Corben, Allen, 194
Corrigan, Rose, 94
cosmetic surgery, 105
Court, Dianne, 14
COYOTE (Call Off Your Old Tired Ethics), 50
Crawford, Eli, 197
Creighton, Allan, 1–3, 5–7, 37–38, 48, 54, 59–60, 65, 70–71, 86, 89, 106–108, 139–140, 160, 165, 191, 201–202
Crosset, Todd, 176–177, 205, 206

Daley, Nicole, 198
date rape, 49
Davis, Angela, 10
Department of Education (DOE), Office of Civil Rights investigations, 173
Department of Homeland Security (DHS), 100
Department of Justice (DOJ), 98
Department of Public Health (California), 100
Department of Public Safety (California), 100
Dias de Leon, Cindy, 115
Dias de Leon, Emiliano, 114–115, 117, 156–157, 197
domestic violence: normalization through humor, 10; as pathway to antiviolence work, 31–32, 76–77, 85, 114; reframing, 49
domestic violence prevention programs, 4, 11, 69
Domestic Violence and Sexual Assault Center, 115
Donovan, Patrick, 112, 113, 151, 154–155, 162, 198
Dworkin, Andrea, 26, 28, 49–52, 56, 59, 81

East Bay Men's Center, 38
Echols, Alice, 50
Eliasoph, Nina, 180
Ellis, Kate, 50, 73

Emerge, 30, 52, 70, 82, 86, 90
English, Deirdre, 50
Enloe, Cynthia, 187
Equal Rights Amendment (ERA), 13, 67, 104
Erickson, John, 119, 167, 199
erotica, feminist, 50
Expect Respect, 114

Faludi, Susan, 66
Falwell, Jerry, 67
Family Advocacy Program, Marine Corps, 4
Family Violence Prevention Fund (later Futures Without Violence), 96, 104
fat liberation movement, 53
fathers, violent, 32
Fear of Flying (Jong), 49
Feinglass, Robert Allen, 56
feminism: Bridge Cohort distancing from, 76; effectiveness outside U.S., 13–14; eclipsing, 106–108; generational shifts away from, 6, 67; professionally institutionalized, 14–16, 99, 180–181. *See also specific eras*
Feminist Anti-Censorship Taskforce (FACT), 73
feminist consciousness, Bridge Cohort, 76–83
feminist engagement: as pathway to antiviolence work, 34, 36–41, 77–78, 110–111; with violence against women, realms of, 11–12, *12*
feminist therapy, 183
feminist values, institutionalization of, 7, 67
Flockhart, Calista, 95
Florida State University, 231n7
fluoride feminism, 209
Ford, Harrison, 95
Frank, Phyllis B., 7, 85, 87–88, 135–138, 141, 152, 191
Franzway, Suzanne, 14
fraternities, 39–40, 121, 122–123
Freespirit, 53
Futures Without Violence (was Family Violence Prevention Fund), 9, 96, 104

gang-related violence, 5–6, 60, 185
Garcia, Cisco, 114
gay men: antipornography efforts opposed, 50; pathways to antiviolence work, 185; violence against, 15
gender-based violence: against boys and men, 66, 162; bullying in schools, 15; emergent paradigm, 15; masculinity as source of, 147; in the military, 4, 173–175; paradigm shifts, 15,

177–178; as pathway to antiviolence work, 76–77, 85, 114, 119; superficial efforts to end, 180; term use, 102; war and, 187–188; against women, 10–12, *12*, 31–32, 49, 76–77, 85, 102, 114, 212n6, 213n15. *See also* sexual violence; violence

gender-based violence prevention: domestic violence programs, 4, 11, 69; in the Global South, 187–189; intersectional strategies, 25, 182, 185–186; leaders in, 32–33, 57; legislation, 14, 93–94, 97, 98–99, 104, 180–181; male-on-male violence as route to, 166; as pathway to antiviolence work, 39; transnational connections, 25, 186–188. *See also* pathways to antiviolence work

gender oppression pathway to antiviolence work, 118–120

gender reclamation, 226n32

gendered division of labor, xi–xii

Generation Fluoride, 109

geographic pathway to antiviolence work, 85–88

Gerstel, Naomi, 206

Giffort, Danielle, 108

Giggans, Patti, 7–8, 82, 93–96, 103, 106, 146, 152, 153, 155, 186, 192

Gilmore, Ruth Wilson, 99

Gleason, Jackie, 10

Global South, 186–188

Good Men Project, 158

good-men approach to violence prevention, 121–123, 126, 138, 179. *See also* My Strength approach to violence prevention

"Goodbye to All That" (Morgan), 36

Great Peace March, 79

Greenberg, Max, 22, 202, 204–207

Greene, Trina, 102, 141, 151, 152–153, 199, 204

Greig, Alan, 165, 194

Griffin, Susan, 49

Growing American Youth, 121

Guatemala, 189

hate crimes, 119

HAVEN, 166

Hawkins, Kevin, 117–118, 120, 141, 152, 196

Healing Abuse, Working for Change (later HAWC), 96, 102

Healy, Daniel, 184, 199

hegemonic masculinity, post-WW II, 30–31

Help for Abused Women and Their Children (HAWC) (later Healing Abuse, Working for Change), 96, 102, 112

Henneman, Todd, 118, 134, 140, 144–145, 150, 196

high school campus groups, pathway to antiviolence work, 116–117

high-school football players, 173

high school programs: antipornography focus, 28, 54–55; antiviolence focus, 5, 7, 95, 116, 122, 126–127, 132; bystander approach, 91, 184; for Latino boys, 182. *See also* boys and young men, working with

Hochschild, Arlie, 141

homosocial male organizations and groups, 3. *See also specific organizations and groups*

The Honeymooners, 10

honor concept in violence prevention, 15, 138. *See also* My Strength approach to violence prevention

Houston Area Women's Center, 105

humor: Jugglers Against Rape, 128; normalizing violence, 10; rape jokes, 213n15

I.A.M. STRONG program, U. S. Army, 170, *171–172*

identity dilemma, 218n24

implicit feminism, 107–108

India, 187–188

insider/outsider status, 137, 219n17

institutional infrastructure pathway to antiviolence work, 111–112

International Fellowship of Reconciliation, Women Peacemakers Program, 189

Internet: online activism, 183; social media, 159, 182; SoJust.Org, 120, 183

Internet networking, 181

intersectional approach to violence prevention, 6, 60–61, 92, 185–186

intersectional engagements, pathway to antiviolence work, 114–121

The Invisible War, 170

Jaksch, Marla, 208

Jara, Brian, 112, 120, 128, 155, 196, 208

Jasper, James, 18, 180

Jensen, Robert, 81, 105, 108, 193

Jewish-American men, profeminist activism, 22

Jewish upbringing, pathway to antiviolence work, 33–34, 76

Jezebel, 158
Jong, Erica, 49
Jugglers Against Rape, 128

Kandiyoti, Deniz, 146
Kathanadhi, Ramesh, 105, 127, 143, 183, 197
Katz, Jackson, 3–7, 76–77, 81, 83, 90–93,
    101, 112, 118, 121–122, 145–149,
    163–166, 173–174, 184, 194, 205–206
Kaufman, Michael, 32–34, 62–65, 86,
    104–105, 132–133, 160–161, 193
Kimmel, Michael, 22
Kinnicott, Leiana, 9, 141, 145–146,
    155–156, 198
Kivel, Paul, 35, 36–37, 59–60, 65, 70–72,
    86, 103–104, 114, 121, 126, 162, 165,
    180, 191
Koedt, Ann, 49
Koyama, Emi, 166
Kretchmer, Kelsy, 130
Kusinski, Jeffrey, 170

Lancon, Danielle, 140, 197
language, gender-neutral, 102
language of rebranding, 100, 102
Latino/a population, Salinas, 5–6
Lee, David, 79, 81, 86, 89, 97, 103, 122, 126,
    131, 194
legislation, antiviolence, 14, 93–94, 97,
    98–99, 104, 180–181
lesbians: opposition to antipornography
    efforts, 50; pathways to antiviolence
    work, 185
Lichterman, Paul, 89
Lorde, Audre, 148–149
Los Angeles Commission on Assaults
    Against Women (LACAAW) (later
    Peace Over Violence), 82, 95–96,
    185–186
Los Angeles Police Department, 184
Los Angeles Unified School District, 184
Love, Timothy, 77, 78, 83–84, 150, 196

MacKinnon, Catherine, 50–51, 81
male privilege: defined, 16; genderized
    resentment of, 155; intersectional
    view of, 60, 120; persistence of, 146,
    153–154; rape culture and, 90–91;
    strategic use of, 139; working within
    systems of, 146, 151
Man Up, 122, 143, 188
Mandella, Larry, 37–39, 43–44, 55, 56, 192
March for Women's Lives, 208
Marcuse, Ricki Sherover, 59

Marin Abused Women's Services (later
    Center for Domestic Peace), 56, 70, 96
Marine Corps, violence and violence
    prevention programs, 4
Markowitz, Lisa, 67
Martin, Patricia Yancey, 67, 68, 180–181
Martin, Steve, 95
masculinity: costs and privileges of,
    42–44, 52; post-WW II hegemony,
    30–31; strategic use by antiviolence
    activists, 145, 147–149; violence
    against women defining, 11, 15
masculinized militarism, 212n5
Massacre of Montreal, 62–63
MASV (Men Against Sexist Violence):
    accountability, 43, 54–59, 164–165;
    antipornography focus, 27–28,
    53–57; beginnings, 2, 27, 29–30;
    class and race tensions, 44–48;
    demise of, 29, 42, 56–59, 61, 68–69;
    efficacy of engagement, 43–44;
    founding members, 2; goals, 43;
    member stories, 32, 37, 38–39, 43,
    86; Messner and, 201–202; minor
    reference to, 86, 130; social activism,
    36, 40–41, 43; Take Back the Night
    involvement, 28, 111
McCarthy, John D., 93
McGee, Janeen, 7, 8, 100, 141, 151, 154,
    180, 195
McPherson, Donald, 92–93, 101, 147–148,
    157, 175, 195
Men Against Domestic Violence, 86
Men Against Pornography, 52
Men Against Rape, 128
Men Against Violence, 82, 113
Men Can Stop Rape (MCSR), 110, 111, 123,
    133–134, 147
"Men Confronting Pornography" (*Changing
    Men*), 73
Men for Women's Choice, 62
men of color: advantages in working
    with boys and young men of
    color, 46–47, 60–61, 117–118, 127;
    career advantages to, 142–143;
    intersectional approach used by,
    6, 60–61; marginalizing, 44, 46;
    pathways to antiviolence work,
    84–85, 91–93, 114–121, 185; young,
    racialized scrutiny of, 156–157. *See
    also* African American men
Men of Strength campaign (CALCASA),
    126–127
Men of Strength program (POV), 96

Men Stopping Rape, 128

Men Stopping Violence, 8, 105

MenCARE, 73, 118–119, 131, 134, 140, 150

Menjivar, Cecilia, 189

Men's Awareness Sexual Health program (UMass), 3

men's liberation movement, 43, 51–52

Men's Network Against Domestic Violence (later Northwest Men's Project), 96

Men's Resource Center of Western Mass, 82, 87, 88

men's rights movement, 66–67

men's studies (the new), 225n17

men's violence, pathway to antiviolence work, 32, 77–78

Men's Work (Kivel), 114

mentoring: by feminist women, 87–88, 92, 115, 135–136, 138, 151; intergenerational, 75, 107, 150, 184; by Movement Cohort, 75, 86–88, 107; as pathway to antiviolence work, 85–88, 92, 112, 114–115; by veteran activists, 92

Mentors in Violence Prevention (MVP), 4–5, 83, 92–93, 145, 173, 184

Messerschmidt, James, 33–34

Messner, Michael, 18–23, 41, 43, 174, 201–204, 206, 208

Midwest Men's Conference, 51

military, U.S. *See specific branches*

Miller, Phyllis, 142, 193

Mills, C. Wright, 19

Molina, Brandon, 198

Monterey County Rape Crisis Center, 5, 8, 100

Montreal Massacre, 62–63

More, Charles, 195

Moreno, Claudia Garcia, 187

Morgan, Geoff, 52

Morgan, Robin, 36, 50

Mosmiller, Thomas, 17

MOVE (Men Overcoming Violence), 2, 70, 82, 86, 89–90, 160, 202–203

Movement Cohort (1970–1980s): accountability, 52–53, 58–60; antipornography focus, 53–57; class and race tensions, 44–48; college courses, 80; desire for validation from women, 53–55; era of, *20*; growing engagement, 42–43; inspiration for, 51–52; mentoring by, 87–88, 107; politics of, 41–42; role of, 27–28; shifting focus on, 73–75;

social activism, 40–41; stories of, 29–34; training of, 27

movement feminism (1970s–1980s): antifeminist backlash, 13, 66–67, 68; central tenets, 48–49; demise of, 7, 13–14, 42, 51, 65–67; forming social policy, 13–14; historic accomplishments, 10–11, 13–14, 99; institutionalization of antiviolence work, 104; institutional response to, 11; organization building, 89, 90; rise of, 10–13. *See also* women's movement, false universalization of

Moving Upstream (Virginia Department of Health Division of Injury and Violence Prevention), xi

Moving Upstream 2.0, California Coalition Against Sexual Assault (CALCASA), xi

Mueller, Carol McClurg, 93

Murphey, Cameron, 167–168, 199

Muslim Men Against Domestic Violence, 209

My Strength approach to violence prevention, 5, 15, 116–117, 126–127, 132–133

My Strength Is For Defending posters, 170, *171–172*

My Strength Is Not for Hurting posters, 123, *124–125*, 126

Myers, Daniel, 137

"The Myth of the Vaginal Orgasm" (Koedt), 49

National Abortion Rights Advocacy League (NARAL), 67

National Congress for Men, 66

National Football League (NFL), 176–177

National Organization for Changing Men (NOCM) (later NOMAS), 30, 202

National Organization for Men Against Sexism (NOMAS) (was NOCM), 59, 72–75, 120, 166, 183

National Organization for Women (NOW), 67

National Sexual Violence Resource Center, Women of Color Caucus, 168

Navy, U.S., 3, 4

networking: online, 183; pathway to antiviolence work, 110–114

New Left movement, 34–36, 41, 49

nonprofit status, shift to, 95, 98, 99–100, 185–186

Norberg-Bohm, Craig, 31–32, 38, 53, 57, 65, 69–70, 72, 86, 101, 122, 133, 160, 176, 192

Nordic nations, forming social policies beneficial to women, 13–14
Northwest Men's Project (was Men's Network Against Domestic Violence), 96
Norton, Chris, 27–28, 36, 37–38, 41, 43–44, 54–55, 56, 192, 201–202
nurses, black male, 228n10

Oakland Men's Project (OMP), 2, 60, 70–72, 82, 90, 103–104, 165
Occidental College, 173
occupational pathways to antiviolence work, 83–85, 115
Office of Civil Rights (DOE), 173
Office of Domestic Violence Prevention (New York), 152
Office on Violence Against Women, 141
Okun, Rob, 88, 183
One in Four, 113
online activism, 183
Oprah Winfrey, 70, 115
organic intersectionality, 185–186
organization building: Bridge Cohort, 67, 69–75, 89; movement feminism, 89, 90
organized sports: celebration of sexist attitudes and assaultive behaviors, 4; for violence prevention with boys and men, 188. *See also* athletes

Padavic, Irene, 131–132
parolees, working with, 117
pathways to antiviolence work: boy-on-boy violence, 31–32, 77–78; campus organizations, 79–83, 111, 116–117; college education and, 116; consciousness-raising groups, 34, 37–38, 41, 42–43, 75; dis-identification with men's violence, 77–78; domestic violence, 32, 76–77, 85, 114; feminist engagements, 34, 36–41, 77–78, 110–111; gender oppression, 118–120; geographic, 85–88; high school campus groups, 116–117; institutional infrastructure, 111–112; intersectional engagements, 114–121; Jewish upbringing, 33–34, 76; for men of color, 84–85, 91–93, 114–121; mentors, 85–88, 92, 112, 114–115; in a networked field, 110–114; nonviolent families, 33–34; occupational, 83–85, 115; racial oppression, 116; ready-made avenues, 111; sexual assault, 31; sexual oppression, 118–120; social

movement activism, 34–36, 75, 78–80; women's studies classes, 79–83, 112–113; working class background and, 116–117
patriarchy, 49–50
peace movement, 79
Peace Over Violence (POV) (was LACAAW): on involvement of men, 141, 153; leader of, 7–8; membership, 206; My Strength programs, 116, 127; name change, 95, 185–186; as pathway to antiviolence work, 116–117; shift away from feminism, 106; Start Strong program, 102
Penn State University, 173
People's Food System, 36
Peretz, Tal, 22, 113–114, 119, 138, 202, 204, 207–210
Philp, Stephen, 118–119, 126, 131, 167, 199
Pitts, Jamonte, 116–117, 127, 200
Planned Parenthood, 121
Playboy, 35–36, 49, 54
pornography: movement against, 43, 50–51, 53–57, 73, 74; reframing, 49
Pornography, Prostitution, and Trafficking task force (NOMAS), 166
Porter, Tony, 85, 87–88, 92, 100, 150, 161–162, 193, 204
postfeminism, defined, 225n16
Pretty Baby, 28
prisoners, working with, 47–48, 159
Professional Cohort (1990s–): creative subversion approach, 127–128; diversity, 110; era of, *20*, 109–110; frustrations of, 105, 127; measurement and accounting role, 130–134; mentors, 107; plug-in opportunities, 15–16; political sophistication, 180; progressive strategies, 106–107; public events to raise awareness, 128–130; racialized scrutiny of men of color, 156–157; reshaping in pragmatic directions, 14; social media use, 159, 182
professional era feminism (1990s–): costs and benefits of institutionalization, 103–108; creation of paid jobs, 101; marketization, 98–101; moments of engagement, 112–113; social changes and opportunities, 98–99; trends, 99
professional era feminism (1990s–) organizations: depoliticization of, 103–105; funding, 95, 98–101, 104, 107–108; nonprofit status, 95,

98, 99–100; rebranding of, 95–97, 100, 102; shifts in client base, 102; stakeholders, 100

professional feminists, 182–184

professionalization: paradoxes of, 67, 89, 188; transitional era, 67, 69–75, 89

professionally institutionalized feminism, 14–16, 99, 180–181

Promundo, 188

prosex feminists, 50

public health framework, 14–16, 100, 103–105, 107–108, 183–184

racial oppression pathway to antiviolence work, 116

racism, working to prevent, 59, 60–61

radical antipsychiatry movement, 218n20

rape: on college campuses, 1; date rape, 49; defining, 50; globally, 187; men's groups against, 30; naming as a social issue, 11; pornography as complicity with, 54; reframing, 49; silencing survivors of, 175; spousal, 10, 49; statistics, 1, 187. *See also* violence against women

Rape Crisis Center (Boston), 112

Rape Crisis Center (San Pablo), 56, 70

rape crisis centers/hotlines, 11

rape jokes, 213n15

rape prevention education, 5–6

rapists, 10, 49, 218n19

RAVEN (Rape and Violence Ends Now): accountability, 151, 160, 164–165; beginnings, 30–32, 38; challenges for feminist leaders, 154; changes in, 107; costs and benefits male privilege, 139, 141; education programs, 82; efficacy, 133; funding, 58, 69–70; minor reference to, 42, 120; networking contribution, 52; reasons for survival of, 57–61, 68–70, 100; working with African American ex- offenders, 117

Reagan, Ronald, administration, 71

Real Men, 4, 122

Red Cross, 121

Reger, Jo, 67, 109, 209

research interviewees, demographics, 18–23

resident advisors, training, 1

Rice, Karen, 67

Rich, Marc, 76, 81, 128, 155, 195

Ricki Lake show, 158

rock stars, 5, 158–160

Ross, Greg, 28, 35–36, 38–39, 44–46, 56, 191

Rubin, Gayle, 50, 51

Safe Horizon, 111

Safe Place, 115

Salazar, Gilbert, 5–7, 8, 115, 117, 120, 127–128, 132, 166–167, 182, 199

Salinas, CA, 5–6

Salon, 158

Samalin, Joe, 110–111, 113, 133–134, 152, 197

Samuels, Robbie, 119–120, 183, 185, 196

Sandusky Jerry, 173

Schilt, Kristen, 120

Schlafly, Phyllis, 67

Schrock, Douglas, 131–132

Schwyzer, Hugo, 158–160, 195

Serdahely, Shelley, 8–9, 141–142, 145, 155, 157, 192

sex offenders, working with, 47–48

sex wars, feminist, 13, 29, 42, 48–51, 66, 68–69, 73

sex workers, 50

Sexual Assault and Prevention Program, Air Force, 170, 175

sexual assault prevention: California Coalition Against Sexual Assault (CALCASA), xi, 97, 101, 103, 126–127; college athletic programs, 4, 82, 173, 174, 175; Domestic Violence and Sexual Assault Center, 115; Los Angeles Commission on Assaults Against Women (LACAAW) (later POV), 82, 95–96, 185–186; military, U.S., 170, 175; Moving Upstream 2.0, xi; Texas Association Against Sexual Assault (TAASA), 84, 101, 114, 115

sexual assault survivors: silencing of, 175; suicide rate by, 1

sexual harassment, reframing, 49

sexual liberation, 48–49

sexual oppression, pathway to antiviolence work, 118–120

sexual revolution, 48

sexual violence: by athletes, 173, 174, 211n4; against boys, 15, 66; on college campuses, 1, 173–174; high-school football players, 173; masculinized militarism link, 212n5; in the military, 170, 173–174; myth of the black rapist, 10; naming as a social issue, 11; as pathway to antiviolence work, 31. *See also* rape; violence against women

sexual violence prevention: consciousness-raising groups, 11; My Strength approach, 5, 15, 116–117,

123, *124–125*, 126–127, 132–133, 170, *171–172*
shelter movement, 7, 11
Simms, Abby, 206
Slutwalks, 128, 129–130, *130*
Smith, Keith, 76–77, 78, 118, 133, 154, 195
Smith, Tyler, 113
social justice paradigm, 179–180
social marketing, 123, 126
social media, use of, 159, 182
social movement activism: formalizing,
    67–68; MASV, 36, 40–41, 43; as
    pathway to antiviolence work,
    34–36, 75, 78–80
Society for the Psychological Study of Men
    and Masculinity (APA), 73
SoJust.Org, 120, 183
Some Men, interviewees: life trajectories,
    18–23; list with demographic
    descriptors, 191–200
South Africa, 187–188
spousal rape, 10, 49
Staggenborg, Suzanne, 68
Stanton, Therese, 73
Start Strong program (POV), 102
Stevens, Mark, 33–34, 38, 54, 57–59, 72–75,
    82, 90–91, 121, 132, 140, 174, 193
St. Louis Men's Project (SLUMP), 31
Stoltenberg, John, 15, 73, 123
stranger rape, 10
suicide by sexual assault victims, 1
Sweet Tea Southern Queer Men's
    Collective, 209

Tailhook scandal, 4
Take Back the Night, 26–28, 50, 82–83,
    110–112, 113, 134, 205, 208
Tarrant, Shira, 140, 149, 159, 195
Tate, Sean, 115–116, 117–118, 142–143, 198
Taylor, Verta, 13
Texas Association Against Sexual Assault
    (TAASA), 84, 101, 114, 115
Texas Council on Family Violence (TCFV), 143
Texas Council on Violence Prevention, 115
third wave feminists, 228n15
Thomson, Dillon, 167–168, 200
Tosh, Daniel, 213n15
Tough Guise (Katz), 145, 212n6
transitional era feminism (1980s–1990s):
    focus of, 72; funding, 82;
    institutionalization of, 104;
    professionalization, 67, 89;
    reframing men's involvement, 82. *See
    also* Bridge Cohort (1980s–1990s)

United Nations Declaration on the
    Elimination of Violence against
    Women, 189
University of Southern California, 173
upstream-downstream allegory, xi, 189–190
Urban Justice Center, Abusive Partners
    Intervention Program, 85

The Vagina Monologues, 168, 208
Vietnam veterans, 38–39, 44–46, 230n4
Vietnam Veterans Against the War, 35, 56
Vietnam war protests, 34–36, 41, 75
violence: celebratory, 177; defined, 186, 189,
    232n25; as pathway to antiviolence
    work, 31–32. *See also* gender-based
    violence
violence against women: 1950s–1960s, 10;
    feminist engagements with, 11–12,
    12; historic shifts in view of, 9–10;
    normalization through humor, 10,
    212n6, 213n15; term use, 102. *See
    also* gender-based violence; rape
Violence Against Women Act (VAWA), 14,
    93–94, 97, 98–99, 104, 180–181
violence prevention organizations: Air
    Force violence prevention programs,
    4–5, 170, 173, 175; Family Violence
    Prevention Fund (later Futures
    Without Violence), 96; funding, 186;
    funding for men, 2; Futures Without
    Violence (was Family Violence
    Prevention Fund), 9, 96, 104; need
    for measurement and accounting,
    130–133; rebranding, 186; shifts to
    nonprofit status, 185–186; strategies
    to adapt and compete, 95–97
violence prevention programs: for athletes,
    4, 82, 173, 174–176; demand for, 98;
    depoliticizing, 15; diversity in, 7;
    efficacy, 173–176; funding, 98–99;
    military, U.S., 4, 4–5, 170, *171–172*,
    173, 175. *See also* boys and young
    men, working with
violence prevention work: broadening base,
    6; depoliticizing, 6, 103–105, 162;
    funding, 6, 14, 188; gendered division
    of labor, xi–xii; institutionalization
    of, 93–94, 106–108, 180–181;
    intersectional approach to, 60–61,
    92, 185–186; paradigmatic shifts
    in, 177–179, *178*; public health
    framework, 14–16, 100, 103–105,
    107–108, 183–184; social justice
    paradigm, 179–180; as a system

of tributaries, 190; transnational connections, 186–189. *See also* boys and young men, working with violence prevention work, men in: beginnings, 2–3; in the context of professionally institutionalized feminism, 15–16; former perpetrators, 155–156; growth in, 136–137; historical moments of engagement, 17, 18–23, *20*; income, 2; interviewees demographic descriptors, 191–200; life trajectories, 18–23; research questions, 17–18; strategic use of masculinity, 145, 147–149; sustaining motivation, 131–134. *See also* pathways to antiviolence work; *specific cohorts*

Virginia Department of Health Division of Injury and Violence Prevention, xi

Voice Male, 183

"Voices of Men" (Atherton-Zeman), 128

volunteerism, limits of, 231n14

Walcott, Quentin, 76, 78, 152, 157, 162, 196

Walk a Mile in Her Shoes, 128–129, *129*

war, 188

We End Violence, 146

Western Europe, forming social policies beneficial to women, 13–14

Western Men against Violence, 128

White, Aaronette, 208–209

White Ribbon Campaign, 62–65, 70, 90, 104–105, 133, 160–161

"Why So-Called Radical Men Love and Need Pornography" (Dworkin), 56

Wild Intrepid Men Protesting Sexism (WIMPS), 82

Williams, Christine, 142

Willis, Ellen, 50

Wingfield, Adia Harvey, 116, 142

Wives of the Houston Astros, 105

Wolch, Jennifer, 99

women: sexual objectification and bodily domination of, 49–50; shelter movement, 7, 11; violence against, 10–12, *12*, 102, 212n6, 213n15

Women Against Violence in Pornography and Media (WAVPM), 27–28, 50, 54

Women of Color Caucus, National Sexual Violence Resource Center, 168

Women Peacemakers Program, International Fellowship of Reconciliation, 189

women's movement, false universalization of, 44, 66. *See also* movement feminism (1970s–1980s)

Women's Self Help Center, 38

women's studies classes, 79–83, 112–113

working-class: background as pathway to antiviolence work, 116–117; boys, working with, 127; MASV bias and, 44–48; middle-class bias affecting, 46–47; pathways to antiviolence work, 84–85

World Health Organization (WHO), 187, 188

Wright, Gwen, 142, 152, 161, 168–169, 193

young men. *See* athletes; boys and young men, working with; high school programs

Youth Alternatives to Violence program (Sunrise House), 5

YWCA, 112

Zinn, Maxine Baca, 44, 66